First World War
and Army of Occupation
War Diary
France, Belgium and Germany

3 CAVALRY DIVISION
6 Cavalry Brigade
Headquarters
19 September 1914 - 27 February 1919

WO95/1152/1

The Naval & Military Press Ltd
www.nmarchive.com
Published in association with The National Archives

Published by

The Naval & Military Press Ltd

Unit 10 Ridgewood Industrial Park,

Uckfield, East Sussex,

TN22 5QE England

Tel: +44 (0) 1825 749494

www.naval-military-press.com

www.nmarchive.com

This diary has been reprinted in facsimile from the original. Any imperfections are inevitably reproduced and the quality may fall short of modern type and cartographic standards.

© **Crown Copyright**
Images reproduced by permission of The National Archives, London, England, 2015.

Contents

Document type	Place/Title	Date From	Date To
Heading	WO95/1152/1 3 Cavalry Division 6 Cavalry Brigade Headquarters Sept 1914-Feb 1919.		
Heading	1914-1919 3rd Cavalry Division 6th Cavalry Brigade Headquarters Sep 1914-Feb 1919		
War Diary	Ludgershall	19/09/1914	06/10/1914
War Diary	Southampton	06/10/1914	06/10/1914
War Diary	At Sea	07/10/1914	07/10/1914
War Diary	Ostend	08/10/1914	08/10/1914
War Diary	Bruges	09/10/1914	09/10/1914
War Diary	Thourout	10/10/1914	11/10/1914
War Diary	Roulers	12/10/1914	12/10/1914
War Diary	Ledeghem	13/10/1914	13/10/1914
War Diary	Wytschaete	14/10/1914	15/10/1914
War Diary	Zonnebeke	16/10/1914	17/10/1914
War Diary	Passchendaele	18/10/1914	18/10/1914
War Diary	Poelcappelle	19/10/1914	19/10/1914
War Diary	Pilkem	20/10/1914	20/10/1914
War Diary	Zandvoorde.	21/10/1914	22/10/1914
War Diary	Kleinzillebeke	23/10/1914	24/10/1914
War Diary	Zandvoorde	25/10/1914	26/10/1914
War Diary	Zillebeke	30/10/1914	30/10/1914
War Diary	Hooge	31/10/1914	02/11/1914
War Diary	Farm N E of Ypres	03/11/1914	04/11/1914
War Diary	Wood S of Veldhoek	05/11/1914	05/11/1914
War Diary	Farm N.E. of Ypres	06/11/1914	06/11/1914
War Diary	Farm N E of Halte	07/11/1914	13/11/1914
War Diary	Farm S. of Vlamertinghe.	14/11/1914	14/11/1914
War Diary	Trenches S and S.E. of Zillebeke.	15/11/1914	17/11/1914
War Diary	Farm S. of Vlamertinghe.	17/11/1914	19/11/1914
War Diary	Les Lauriers 7 miles S.E. Hazebrouck	20/11/1914	30/11/1914
Miscellaneous	Report on Operations 15th. 16th and 17th. November.	18/11/1914	18/11/1914
Miscellaneous	1B G.O.C. 6th. Cavalry Brigade,		
Miscellaneous	Report on part taken by the 6th. Cavalry Brigade in the operations of November 16th. and 17th.	16/11/1914	16/11/1914
Miscellaneous	G.O.C. 1st. A.C.,	20/11/1914	20/11/1914
War Diary	Les Lauriers	01/12/1900	13/12/1900
War Diary	Bailleul	14/12/1900	15/12/1900
War Diary	Les Lauriers	16/12/1900	31/12/1900
Heading	6th Cavalry Brigade Vol III 1.1.-28.2.15		
War Diary	Les Lauriers	01/01/1915	27/01/1915
War Diary	Thiennes	28/01/1915	28/01/1915
War Diary	Thiennes and Steenbecque	29/01/1915	02/02/1915
War Diary	Ypres.	03/02/1915	07/02/1915
War Diary	Trenches 1 mile S.E. of Zillebeke.	08/02/1915	12/02/1915
War Diary	Relieved in Trenches, and Bde returned to Steenbecque Bilects Area.	13/02/1915	13/02/1915
War Diary	Steenbecque	14/02/1915	28/02/1915
Heading	6th Cavalry Brigade Vol IV 1-31.3.15		
War Diary	Steenbecque	01/03/1915	10/03/1915
War Diary	Merville.	11/03/1915	12/03/1915

War Diary	Steenbecque	13/03/1915	13/03/1915
War Diary	Steenbecque Bilecting Area.	14/03/1915	31/03/1915
Heading	6th Cavalry Brigade Vol V 1.4-1.5.15		
War Diary	Steenbecque	01/04/1915	23/04/1915
War Diary	Eecke	24/04/1915	24/04/1915
War Diary	Boescheppe	25/04/1915	25/04/1915
War Diary	Houtkerque	26/04/1915	26/04/1915
War Diary	Vlamertinghe	27/04/1915	28/04/1915
War Diary	Forge	29/04/1915	01/05/1915
Heading	3rd Cavalry Division 6th Cavalry Brigade Vol VI 1-31.5.15		
War Diary	Forge	02/05/1915	02/05/1915
War Diary	Farm 1/2 mile S. W. of Proven	03/05/1915	07/05/1915
War Diary	Steenbecque	08/05/1915	09/05/1915
War Diary	Huts in H 5 a, N of 3 kils show on Ypres-Vlamertinghe road	10/05/1915	12/05/1915
War Diary	Railway Crossing in I 11 b	13/05/1915	14/05/1915
War Diary	Potizje Chateau	14/05/1915	14/05/1915
War Diary	Vlamertinghe	15/05/1915	21/05/1915
War Diary	Steenbecque	21/05/1915	31/05/1915
Miscellaneous	A Form. Messages And Signals.		
Miscellaneous	C Form (Duplicate). Messages And Signals.		
Miscellaneous	A Form. Messages And Signals.		
Miscellaneous			
Miscellaneous	A Form. Messages And Signals.		
Miscellaneous	B Form. Messages & Signals.		
Miscellaneous	A Form. Messages And Signals.		
Miscellaneous	6th Cavalry Bde 12.45		
Miscellaneous	6th Cavalry Order.	18/05/1915	18/05/1915
Heading	3rd Cavalry Division 6th Cavalry Brigade Vol VII 1-30.6.15		
War Diary	Ypres.	01/06/1915	06/06/1915
War Diary	Steenbecque	05/06/1915	30/06/1915
Heading	3rd Cavalry Division 6th Cavalry Brigade Vol VIII 29-6-31-7-15		
War Diary	Steenbecque	29/06/1915	31/07/1915
Heading	3rd Cavalry Division 6th Cavalry Brigade Vol IX From 3-30.8.15		
War Diary	Steenbecque.	03/08/1915	06/08/1915
War Diary	Febvin Palfart	13/08/1915	30/08/1915
Heading	War Diary Headquarters, 6th Cavalry Brigade. (3rd Cavalry Division) September 1915		
Miscellaneous	Report on Movements and Action of the 6th Cavalry Brigade between 12.30 p.m. on September 26th and 2 a.m. on September 27th, 1915.		
Miscellaneous	Reference Map 36c (N.W.1) 1/10,000.	18/11/1915	18/11/1915
Miscellaneous	Reference Map 36c. (N.W.1) 1/10,000. Report on Movements and Action of the 6th Cavalry Brigade Between 12. 30 p.m. on September 26th and 2 a.m. on September 27th, 1915.	18/11/1915	18/11/1915
Miscellaneous	6 Cavalry Bde 3 Cavalry Div		
Miscellaneous	Copy of letter from O.C. 6th Cavalry Bde.		
Heading	War Diary.		
War Diary		20/09/1915	29/09/1915
Heading	3 Cavalry Division 6th Cavalry Brigade Vol XI Oct 15		
War Diary		01/10/1915	31/10/1915

Type	Description	Start	End
Heading	3rd Cavalry Division 6th Cav. Bde. Nov. 1915 Vol XII		
War Diary		01/11/1915	30/11/1915
Heading	3rd C D 6 Cavalry Bde. Dec 1915 Vol. XIII		
War Diary		01/12/1915	30/09/1916
Heading	War Diary. 6th Cavalry Brigade. 1st to 31st October, 1916.		
War Diary		01/10/1916	27/03/1917
Heading	War Diary of 6th Cavalry Brigade. April 1917.		
War Diary		01/04/1917	11/04/1917
War Diary	N 4. C.	01/04/1917	11/04/1917
War Diary	South of Louez L 17 d.	12/04/1917	12/04/1917
War Diary	Fosseux	13/04/1917	16/04/1917
War Diary	Le Boisle	19/04/1917	19/04/1917
War Diary	Maintenay	21/04/1917	30/04/1917
War Diary	Arras	25/03/1917	18/04/1917
War Diary	Frevent.	21/04/1917	21/04/1917
Miscellaneous	6th Cavalry Brigade Concentration Order No. 1	09/04/1917	09/04/1917
Operation(al) Order(s)	3rd Cavalry Division Concentration Order No. 2.	08/04/1917	08/04/1917
Map	App B		
Operation(al) Order(s)	Appendix "C". 6th Cavalry Brigade Operation Order No. 1.	08/04/1917	08/04/1917
War Diary		05/04/1917	19/04/1917
War Diary	Maintenay.	01/05/1917	13/05/1917
War Diary	Tortefontaine.	13/05/1917	13/05/1917
War Diary	Frohen Le Grand	14/05/1917	14/05/1917
War Diary	Havernas	15/05/1917	15/05/1917
War Diary	Bussy Les Daours	16/05/1917	17/05/1917
War Diary	Bayonvillers	18/05/1917	18/05/1917
War Diary	Buire	19/05/1917	24/05/1917
War Diary	Field.	23/05/1917	31/05/1917
Miscellaneous	3rd D.Gds. Royals. N.S.Y. 6th M.Gun Sqn. App A	22/05/1917	22/05/1917
Miscellaneous	Bell-Smyth's Brigade D. Sector. Appendix B.		
Miscellaneous	3rd Cavalry Division Defence Scheme.	21/05/1917	21/05/1917
Miscellaneous	Appendix "A".		
War Diary	Field.	23/05/1917	31/05/1917
Miscellaneous	Establishment for Brigade H.Q. "D" Sector. App C		
Miscellaneous	War Establishment for Dismounted Regiment A Regiment of H.Q., and 3 Squadrons.		
Miscellaneous	(A) Headquarters details found by each Regiment not finding Sub-sector H.Q.		
Miscellaneous	Proposed War Establishment for a Dismounted Squadron. Appendix A.		
Miscellaneous	War Establishment of a Dismounted Machine Gun Squadron- (12 Guns.)		
War Diary	D Sector	01/06/1917	03/06/1917
War Diary	Buire	04/06/1917	11/06/1917
War Diary	Field	14/06/1917	30/06/1917
Miscellaneous	6th Cavalry Bridade Order for Concentration and move to First position of readiness.		
Miscellaneous	3rd D.G's. Royals, N.S.Y. "C" Battery. 6th M.G. Sqn. 6th C.F.A. 13th M.V.S. Supply Officer Transport Officer 6th Signal Troop. Camp Commandant. 2/Lt. J.P. Brill	05/06/1917	05/06/1917

Miscellaneous	3rd Dragoon Gds. Royals. Royals. N.S.Y. 6th M. Gun Sqn. 6th C.F.A. "D" Sector (2 Copies) 7th Cav. Bde. Details. Supply Officer Ref.Map. 1/20.000 62c.NE., 62B N.W. 57C. S.E. App B	09/06/1917	09/06/1917
Miscellaneous	Appendix "A"		
Miscellaneous	Movement Table For Reliefs in "D" 2 Sun-Sector.		
War Diary	Field.	01/06/1917	28/06/1917
War Diary	Buire	01/07/1917	03/07/1917
War Diary	Suzanne	04/07/1917	04/07/1917
War Diary	Heilly	05/07/1917	05/07/1917
War Diary	Orville	06/07/1917	06/07/1917
War Diary	Rebreuviette	07/07/1917	07/07/1917
War Diary	Auchel	07/07/1917	15/07/1917
War Diary	Les Lauriers	23/07/1917	31/08/1917
War Diary	Les Lauriers Ref Map 36 A 1/40,000 K 14 d.	01/09/1917	27/09/1917
War Diary	Les Lauriers	29/09/1917	19/10/1917
War Diary	Tangry	22/10/1917	22/10/1917
War Diary	Rebreuve	23/10/1917	23/10/1917
War Diary	Gorenflos	24/10/1917	24/10/1917
War Diary	Longuet	27/10/1917	17/11/1917
War Diary	Beaucourt	18/11/1917	18/11/1917
War Diary	Suzanne	20/11/1917	23/11/1917
War Diary	Talmas	23/11/1917	02/12/1917
War Diary	Molliens Au Bois.	10/12/1917	21/12/1917
War Diary	Longuet	21/12/1917	29/01/1918
War Diary	Marcelcave	30/01/1918	30/01/1918
War Diary	Tertry	01/02/1918	13/03/1918
War Diary	Devise	14/03/1918	21/03/1918
War Diary	Beaumont	22/03/1918	22/03/1918
War Diary	Pontoise	23/03/1918	23/03/1918
War Diary	Carlepont	25/03/1918	26/03/1918
War Diary	Choisy Au Bac	27/03/1918	27/03/1918
War Diary	Choisy	28/03/1918	29/03/1918
War Diary	Airion	30/03/1918	30/03/1918
War Diary	Sains.	31/03/1918	31/03/1918
Miscellaneous	Special Order by Brigadier General A.E.W. Harman. D.S.O. Commanding 6th Cavalry Brigade.	12/03/1918	12/03/1918
War Diary	Appendix C.	21/03/1918	26/03/1918
Heading	3rd Cav. Div. War Diary Headquarters, 6th Cavalry Brigade. April 1918		
War Diary	Sains-En-Amienois.	01/04/1918	01/04/1918
War Diary	N.34.c.	02/04/1918	02/04/1918
War Diary	N.28.d.1.5.	03/04/1918	03/04/1918
War Diary	Fouilloy.	03/04/1918	04/04/1918
War Diary	O.23.d.	04/04/1918	05/04/1918
War Diary	O.17.C.4.9.	05/04/1918	05/04/1918
War Diary	N.34.c. Camon	06/04/1918	06/04/1918
War Diary	Camon.	06/04/1918	10/04/1918
War Diary	Buire-Au-Bois.	11/04/1918	11/04/1918
War Diary	Conteville.	12/04/1918	12/04/1918
War Diary	Ferfay.	13/04/1918	23/04/1918
War Diary	Fontaine-Lez-Hermans.	24/04/1918	30/04/1918
Miscellaneous	Appendices "A" and "B".		
Miscellaneous	Casualties. April, 1918 Officers. Killed.		
Miscellaneous	Honours And Rewards. (Immediate rewards)		
War Diary	Fontaine-Lez-Herman.	01/05/1918	01/05/1918

Type	Location/Description	From	To
War Diary	Vacquerie-Le Boucq	04/05/1918	04/05/1918
War Diary	Frohen-Le-Grand.	05/05/1918	05/05/1918
War Diary	Contay	06/05/1918	17/05/1918
War Diary	Belloy.	19/05/1918	30/05/1918
War Diary	Behencourt	31/05/1918	12/06/1918
War Diary	Belloy-Sur-Somme.	14/06/1918	25/06/1918
War Diary	Le Mesge.	25/06/1918	06/08/1918
War Diary	Renancourt N.31.D.	07/08/1918	08/08/1918
War Diary	D.16.A.	08/08/1918	08/08/1918
War Diary	D.16.B.	08/08/1918	08/08/1918
War Diary	E 7.A.0.8.	08/08/1918	08/08/1918
War Diary	E.14.d.8.7.	08/08/1918	09/08/1918
War Diary	W.26.c.	09/08/1918	10/08/1918
War Diary	E.30.a.	10/08/1918	10/08/1918
War Diary	K.11.c.8.5.	10/08/1918	10/08/1918
War Diary	K.12.c.5.0.	10/08/1918	10/08/1918
War Diary	L.25.b.5.0.	10/08/1918	11/08/1918
War Diary	Fouencamp	13/08/1918	15/08/1918
War Diary	Le Mesge	16/08/1918	21/08/1918
War Diary	Fieffes	22/08/1918	25/08/1918
War Diary	Gueschart.	26/08/1918	26/08/1918
War Diary	Nuncq.	26/08/1918	31/08/1918
Miscellaneous	Appendix A Casualties. Officers. Cas. Other Ranks. K. W. M.		
Operation(al) Order(s)	6th Cavalry Brigade Order No.11	04/08/1918	04/08/1918
Miscellaneous	March Table 5/8/1918.		
Operation(al) Order(s)	6th Cavalry Brigade Order No.12. Ref.Map 1/40,000 Sheet 62E.	06/08/1918	06/08/1918
Miscellaneous	March Table "A"-Night 6th/7th August. Issued with 6th Cavalry Brigade Order No. 12.		
Operation(al) Order(s)	6th Cavalry Brigade Order No.14	06/08/1918	06/08/1918
Miscellaneous	Appendix "A" (Issued with 6th Cavalry Brigade Order No. 14). Detail of Detached Parties.		
Operation(al) Order(s)	6th Cavalry Brigade Order No.16	15/08/1918	15/08/1918
Miscellaneous	March Table-Night 15/16th August. Issued with 6th Cavalry Brigade Order No. 16. dated 15/8/18.		
Miscellaneous	A Form. Messages And Signals.		
Operation(al) Order(s)	6th Cavalry Brigade Order No.17	16/08/1918	16/08/1918
War Diary	E.15.B.1.9.	08/08/1918	08/08/1918
War Diary	E.14.D.8.7	08/08/1918	08/08/1918
War Diary	E.14.d.8.7.	08/08/1918	09/08/1918
War Diary	W.26.c.	09/08/1918	10/08/1918
War Diary	E.30.a.	10/08/1918	10/08/1918
War Diary	E.30.a.1.9.	10/08/1918	10/08/1918
War Diary	K.11.c.8.5.	10/08/1918	10/08/1918
War Diary	K.12.c.5.0.	10/08/1918	10/08/1918
War Diary	L.25.b.5.0.	10/08/1918	11/08/1918
War Diary	Nuncq	01/09/1918	05/09/1918
War Diary	Le Placiton	06/09/1918	16/09/1918
War Diary	Hesdin	16/09/1918	17/09/1918
War Diary	Le Placiton.	18/09/1918	18/09/1918
War Diary	Rebreuve	19/09/1918	25/09/1918
War Diary	Bus-Les-Artois	26/09/1918	26/09/1918
War Diary	Meaulte	27/09/1918	27/09/1918
War Diary	Hem	28/09/1918	29/09/1918
War Diary	Vermand	30/09/1918	03/10/1918

War Diary	S.W. of Bellenglise.	03/10/1918	03/10/1918
War Diary	S.W. of Joncourt.	03/10/1918	03/10/1918
War Diary	H.17.b.6.2	03/10/1918	05/10/1918
War Diary	Trefcon.	05/10/1918	08/10/1918
War Diary	Sheet 62B G.35.b.2.2. H.19.b.	09/10/1918	09/10/1918
War Diary	C.12.d.1.1.	09/10/1918	09/10/1918
War Diary	C.2.cent.	09/10/1918	09/10/1918
War Diary	S. of Maretz	09/10/1918	09/10/1918
War Diary	Sheet 57C. V.1.b.	09/10/1918	09/10/1918
War Diary	Sheet 57B. V.1.b.	09/10/1918	09/10/1918
War Diary	P.28.cent. Honnechy	09/10/1918	09/10/1918
War Diary	P.18.c.	09/10/1918	09/10/1918
War Diary	P.17.c.7.8.	09/10/1918	10/10/1918
War Diary	P.5.cent.	10/10/1918	10/10/1918
War Diary	J.30.c.Cent.	10/10/1918	10/10/1918
War Diary	P.5.c.9.5.	10/10/1918	10/10/1918
War Diary	O.6.c.7.3.	10/10/1918	11/10/1918
War Diary	Elincourt	11/10/1918	13/10/1918
War Diary	Banteux	13/10/1918	14/10/1918
War Diary	Hennois Wood.	15/10/1918	31/10/1918
Miscellaneous	6th Cavalry Brigade. Narrative of Operations, October 9th, 1918.	11/10/1918	11/10/1918
War Diary	Hennois Wood.	01/11/1918	05/11/1918
War Diary	Marquion	06/11/1918	06/11/1918
War Diary	Esquerchin.	07/11/1918	07/11/1918
War Diary	Peronne	08/11/1918	09/11/1918
War Diary	Rumes & Ramecroix	10/11/1918	11/11/1918
War Diary	Pontenche	12/11/1918	16/11/1918
War Diary	37 mile stone on Ath-Enghien Road.	17/11/1918	17/11/1918
War Diary	Saintes	18/11/1918	20/11/1918
War Diary	Ottignies.	21/11/1918	21/11/1918
War Diary	Eghezee	22/11/1918	22/11/1918
War Diary	Upigny	24/11/1918	10/12/1918
War Diary	Vinalmont.	09/12/1918	10/12/1918
War Diary	Chateau De Warfusee.	12/12/1918	28/12/1918
War Diary	Stockay.	01/01/1919	27/02/1919

(1)

WO 95/1152.

8 Cavalry Division
6 Cavalry Brigade

Headquarters

Sept 1914 — Feb 1919.

1914-1919
3RD. CAVALRY DIVISION
6TH CAVALRY BRIGADE.

BRIGADE HEADQUARTERS.

SEP 1914-FEB 1919

WAR DIARY or INTELLIGENCE SUMMARY.

(Erase heading not required.)

Army Form C. 2118.

Sept 1914 – Feb 1919

Hour, Date, Place	Summary of Events and Information	Remarks and references to Appendices
19.IX LODGERSHALL	The Royal Dragoons arrived from SOUTHAMPTON. Strength – Officers 20, NCOs and Men 558, Horses 47. "Reserve Regiment" at YORK arrived with 4 Officers and 8 men from the Royal Dragoons to form the Royal Dragoons.	
20.IX	G.O.C. Bde arrived. Brigade Staff completed. Eleven Horses from MELTON MOWBRAY Remount Depot arrived on posting to Bde H.Qurtrs.	
21.IX	3 Officers and 102 NCOs and men, the advance party of the 10th Hussars, arrived from SOUTHAMPTON. Inspection of the Horses of the Royal Dragoons by the P.V.O. Southern Command.	
22.IX	Verbal Orders received from Major Gen the Administrator Southern Command, to prepare billeting scheme of the Brigade in the event of bad weather.	
23.IX	Forty in-broken South African Remounts Royal Dragoons. Left for ARBORFIELD CROSS Remount Depot. Eighty-six Horses arrived from South Wales Mounted Brigade. The 10th Hussars – Strength 15 Officers and 437 other Ranks – arrived from SOUTHAMPTON.	
24.IX	One Rd. Section from the South Midland Mtd. Bde. and 40 horses from the Notts and Derby Mtd Bde arrived to Report to the Regt.	
26.IX	Sixty-one horses of the Royal Dragoons transferred to Remount Cavalry Regt at TIDWORTH.	

Army Form C. 2118.

WAR DIARY
or
INTELLIGENCE SUMMARY.
(Erase heading not required.)

Instructions regarding War Diaries and Intelligence Summaries are contained in F. S. Regs., Part II. and the Staff Manual respectively. Title pages will be prepared in manuscript.

Hour, Date, Place	Summary of Events and Information	Remarks and references to Appendices
26. 1x LUDGERSHALL	Orders arrived for the formation of No 6 Sqn & Troop - Capt W. H. Atken, Royal Dragoons, to command.	
28. 1x	Inspection of the Brigade on TIDWORTH DOWN by H.M. the King. Royal Dragoons mounted and to be dismounted. Two N.C.O.s and 10 men of the 3rd Dragoon Guards arrived for 3rd Reserve Cavalry Regiment, CANTERBURY, as an Advance party.	
29. 1x	410 Horses (10 Troopers & S.S. Dragoons) arrived in Camp. 100 Horses from S.W. Mtd Bde arrived. 60 Transport Horses from WOOLWICH arrived. Led on to Bde Staff and O.C. Units by Capt D. Campbell 9th Lancers. 100 Horses from Welsh Border Bde arrived from BURGAX, were officers instruments received to be ready to move at 48 hours notice. G.O.C. Division arrived in Camp.	
1 x	1st Royal Dragoons are awaiting for services except for within Twenty-four R.H.A. horses arrived for Machine Gun Section. A Brigade Bomb maker of 37 privates from Infantry of Officers of the Brigade. Orders to be ready to move at 48 hours notice.	
2 x	G.O.C's Inspection of the Royal Dragoons in marching order. Orders to Officers to exchange 300 South African horses for others from Aldershot at Tidworth Races Cl. Rfle. Twelve horses from R.H.A. Cookrich arrived to replace Cl. Rfles. 10 Horses have been allowed to return home. Capt Cojole A.S.C. Bde Supply Officer and Capt Putter A.P.C. Registerg Officer joined Bde A.G. but have been nominated to War Office.	
3 x		
4 x	6 Signal Troop orders to proceed marching camp of the 3rd Dragoon Guards.	

WAR DIARY or INTELLIGENCE SUMMARY

Army Form C. 2118.

(Erase heading not required.)

Instructions regarding War Diaries and Intelligence Summaries are contained in F. S. Regs., Part II. and the Staff Manual respectively. Title pages will be prepared in manuscript.

Hour, Date, Place		Summary of Events and Information	Remarks and references to Appendices
4.	LUDGERSHALL	36 Horses arrived for Reserve Cavalry Regiment, Tidworth. 9 horses arrived for Wessex Div. Arty T.F. Pte C. Rendes "D" Squadron committed suicide. Orders issued as to crew of members and Drivers of Transport. Probably all the Transport vehicles for No. 10 note Regt. and	
5.	×	Orders received to embark tonight - subsequently countermanded. No. 10 ure complete in New Forces agreement. Capt Towson 9" Lancers arrived as Brigade Transport Officer. Orders received at 9.30 p.m. to entrain tomorrow morning.	
6.	×	The Regt. entrained at AMESBURY at 4.30 A.M. for SOUTHAMPTON. No. 10 entrained at TIDWORTH at 6.40 A.M. for SOUTHAMPTON	
×	SOUTHAMPTON	Embarked immediately on arrival and sailed 3 pm. the night. Bde. Headquarters and 6th Signal Troop sailed in "Armenian" 73 men and 61 horses embarked on S.S. Algeria, one of the whole line.	Message altered.
7.	×	At sea	Message received from Bde. 2nd july the "Armenian" is present standing in convoy to DOVER, which orders were received to proceed to the DOWNS, which lies close to the bank, and then steered under escort of 12 destroyers to OSTEND (10 transports) and ZEEBRUGGER (4 transports)	
8.	×	OSTEND	Arrived 1 A.M. and lay in La Rade off OSTEND. Disembarked at noon. Encamped at the Races Course. The whole Brigade less Bde. H.Q. and one Squadron 10" Hussars, and one Squadron Royals. 1 Tst and 1st yet disembarked. H.Q. and 2 Squadrons Reg. That had disembarked at ZEEBRUGGER marched to OSTEND. arriving about 10 p.m. The 7" Division entrailed their way from BRUGES to OSTEND.	

Forms/C. 2118/10.

Army Form C. 2118.

WAR DIARY
or
INTELLIGENCE SUMMARY.
(Erase heading not required.)

Instructions regarding War Diaries and Intelligence Summaries are contained in F. S. Regs., Part II. and the Staff Manual respectively. Title pages will be prepared in manuscript.

Hour, Date, Place	Summary of Events and Information	Remarks and references to Appendices
9. × BRUGES	Orders received for the Brigade to what for ECCLOO and take up a defensive line between ST GEORGES and GHENT. These orders subsequently cancelled. Marched at 1.30 from BRUGES. The Brigade being ordered to what in the villages S.W. of BRUGES. Position at night fall, each unit responsible for its own protection. 10th — JABBEKE, ZERKEGHEM, BEKEGHEM. 1st R.Dn — ST MICHEL, VARSSENAERE, SNELLEGHEM. Bde H.Q. — ST ANDRE (9O.C. of BRUGES) Weather — fine. Roads — mostly pavé but flat.	
10. × THOUROUT	The Brigade concentrated at LOPHEM (5 miles S.S.W. BRUGES) at 2 p.m. and marched to THOUROUT (9 miles) went into billets. Two advanced troops sent on to CORTEMARCK and LICHTERVELDE. The 3rd Cavalry Division has now come under the orders of Sir J. French. Weather — fine. Roads — crowded with civilians and Belgian soldiery, pavé and flat. No enemy reported North of a line LENDELEDES - ZONNEBEKE.	
11. × THOUROUT	Halted for the day. Weather fine. Arrived note an reconnaissance — 2 armoured cars and one armoured attached reporting to the Brigade, and manned by a church of Marines — improved a German Cavalry patrol S. of YPRES, wounding three and capturing two men. All belongs to the 7th Jaegers.	
12. × ROULERS.	Marched at 9 A.M. to ROULERS (9 miles).	

WAR DIARY or INTELLIGENCE SUMMARY.

Army Form C. 2118.

(Erase heading not required.)

Instructions regarding War Diaries and Intelligence Summaries are contained in F. S. Regs., Part II. and the Staff Manual respectively. Title pages will be prepared in manuscript.

Hour, Date, Place	Summary of Events and Information	Remarks and references to Appendices
12. × ROULERS	Occupied & picketed line ZONNEBEKE – MOORSLEDE – to Kt ROULERS – MOORSLEDE Road enclosive. Detachments at WESTROOSEBEKE and OOSTNIEUWKERKE. Property line not determined, provided by Royal Dragoons. 10th Hussars in billets at ROULERS.	
13. × LEDEGHEM	Marched at 7.15 AM to YPRES (14 miles) arriving by Royal Dragoons to halt. Arrived YPRES 11.35 AM for 1½ hours then marched to GHELUVELT (6 miles). Offensive patrol to Hussars sent out to watch post on the outskirts of COMINES and the one man captured took up in his motor. K.R. Bn's going into billets – DADIZEELE – 2 Squadrons Royal Dragoons LEDEGHEM – B.H.Q. H.Q. – one Squadron Royal Dragoons H.Q. and 2 Squadrons 10th Hussars. ROLLEGHEMCAPPELLE – one squadron 10th Hussars.	
14. × WYTSCHAETE	Wakin – fine till midday Continuous rain from 3 P.M. Marched en route to YPRES (11 miles) followed by Lt 7th Brigade. Marched 1½ miles S. of YPRES. Fired at a German TAUBE flying at about 1800 feet and brought it down about 2 miles N of YPRES – machine slightly damaged. (No pros were left pilot captured on nightboy made). A Belist patrols the point towards 11.30 AM marched to KEMMEL (7 miles) Commander returns at LA CLYTTE with the 2nd Cav. Div (3rd – 5th Bns). Advanced to NEUVE EGLISE (3 miles) not drawn into billets at WYTSCHAETE (4 miles). Canteens – one man of the Royal injury and also 10 billets accounted for a wounded dragon.	

Army Form C. 2118.

WAR DIARY
or
INTELLIGENCE SUMMARY.
(Erase heading not required.)

Instructions regarding War Diaries and Intelligence Summaries are contained in F. S. Regs., Part II. and the Staff Manual respectively. Title pages will be prepared in manuscript.

Hour, Date, Place		Summary of Events and Information	Remarks and references to Appendices
15	x. WYTSCHAETE	Halted for the day. 10th Hussars patrols to HOLLEBEKE and ZANDVOORDE. Supporting squadron made a reconnaissance on MENIN. 18th Hussars held the line HOLLEBEKE - HOUTHEM for the night with two squadrons.	
16	x. ZONNEBEKE	Invested at 8 A.M. through YPRES to WYDJE (7½ miles) Remained between WYDJE and ST JULIAN in support of the 7th Cavalry Brigade. At 5 p.m. ordered to billet on the ZONNEBEKE - PASSCHENDAELE Road. ZONNEBEKE occupied by the 22nd Infantry Brigade: the Royals occupied outside the town, and the 10th Hussars made the line of Infantry outposts.	
17	x. ZONNEBEKE	Halted for the day. 10th Hussars ordered to send two squadrons to observe the MENIN - ROULERS Road. 3 men of the 10th wounded. The Royals moved where the line of Infantry trenches. The 2nd Inf. Bde. marched out at daybreak.	
18	x. PASSCHENDAELE	One squadron Royals to observe the MENIN - ROULERS Road. One troop Royals to support an armoured car reconnaissance towards DADIZEELE. Invested at 3.45 p.m. 10th to PASSCHENDAELE (2 miles) and Royals to MOORSLEDE (3 miles)	
19	x. POELCAPPELLE	C Battery R.H.A. temporarily attached to the Brigade. Marched at 7 a.m. with 10th and C Battery to MOORSLEDE (2 miles) Royals to ST PIETER where reconnaissance towards LEDEGHEM and ROLLEGHEMCAPPELLE encountered strong opposition at former village.	

(9 29 6) W 3332—1107 100,000 10/13 H W V Forms/C. 2118/10.

WAR DIARY or INTELLIGENCE SUMMARY

Army Form C. 2118.

Hour, Date, Place	Summary of Events and Information	Remarks and references to Appendices
19 POELCAPPELLE	Two Squadrons 10th Hussars sent recce E of LEDEGHEM to ascertain the enemy's position. At 12 noon 2 Bn Kings Royal Rifles reported advancing on ROLLEGHEMCAPPELLE from the NE. At 1 pm Bde intdr to SNOESKOT (S.E. of MOORSLEDE) and thence to PASSCHENDAELE to cover retirement of 7th Cav Bde. Bde went to WALK at POELCAPPELLE via 2 Sqdns 10th Hussars at SPRIET and PASSCHENDAELE respectively. Casualties — 1 Officer (Lt Luke Ryan) and 7 men wounded. 1 Officer (Lt de Trafford Royds) and 1 man injured. 1 man killed. 9 men missing.	
20 PILKEM	Marched at 4.30 AM to WESTROOSEBEKE (3 miles) and took up a defensive position W. of the WESTROOSEBEKE-PASSCHENDAELE Road. Entrenched a portion not commanded. Enemy attacked at 8 AM. Capt Chenevix Royds RHA HQ at CP position thus 12 noon and then withdrew to 1 mile S. of POELCAPPELLE. At 2.30 pm received orders to go into billets at LANGEMARCK. At 3.25 pm fighting began, probably enemy deploying infantry column on POELCAPPELLE. Rifle attack took up a line which NE of PILKEM on LANGEMARCK Road. Not attacked, LANGEMARCK, but was heavily supplied. Brigade stood to arms — 1 Officer wounded, 1 man killed. 4 men wounded.	
21 ZANDVOORDE	Marched at 5 AM to YPRES (4 miles) met place of debt report with Railway Station. At 9 am sent into Bde Transport Officer Marched to HOOGE (3 miles) At 1 pm ordered to say to cover bridge N of HOLLEBEKE. Mr 4th Hussars in support of HOLLEBEKE. Orders received at 6.30 pm to march to ZANDVOORDE (3 miles) and take over the trenches at the South Guards Relieved by South Gaarda at 11 pm. 660 men of 1/2 Brigade to trenches	

WAR DIARY or INTELLIGENCE SUMMARY

Army Form C. 2118.

Hour, Date, Place	Summary of Events and Information	Remarks and references to Appendices
22 x ZANDVOORDE	Enemy commenced shelling the town about 7 A.M. - moved the Horses to the outside and outskirts of the town. Extended the line by occupying the CHATEAU with one squadron of the Royals. German wireless messages intercepted ordering an attack on ZANDVOORDE. Reinforced by 2 squadrons 7th Cavalry Brigade and a Maxim company of the Rangers. Heavy firing during the night but attack apparently without difficulty.	
23 x KLEINZILLEBEKE	Royals relieved at 9 A.M. by a Regiment of the 7th Cav. Bde. but firing too heavy to enable the 10th Hrs. to go in. The enemy bombarded ZANDVOORDE, their ranging being exceptionally accurate. 7th Brigade trenches at KLEINZILLEBEKE less C Battery, who were left in reserve at ZANDVOORDE. Casualties – 4 Officers (Lt. Col Barne, Major Ton, C. Kippford and Capt Stuart 10th Hussars and Lieut Tebutt C Batty) wounded.	
24 x KLEINZILLEBEKE	Halted for the day. 3 men killed and 10 wounded.	
25 x ZANDVOORDE	Took over the trenches of the 7th Cavalry Bde at 5.30 p.m. Enemy attacked at 5 P.M. attacks lasted half an hour and many succumbed at over 500. Casualties – 1 man C Battery wounded.	
26 x ZANDVOORDE	Heavy shelling all day. Orders came for a general advance of the Cavalry Corps, but subsequently countermanded on account of retreat of 20th Inf. Bde. Casualties – Capt S.F. Rose and Lieut Turner, 10th Hussars killed. 5 men killed and 9 men wounded.	

WAR DIARY
or
INTELLIGENCE SUMMARY.
(Erase heading not required.)

Army Form C. 2118.

Instructions regarding War Diaries and Intelligence Summaries are contained in F. S. Regs., Part II. and the Staff Manual respectively. Title pages will be prepared in manuscript.

Hour, Date, Place	Summary of Events and Information	Remarks and References to Appendices
27. x KLEINZILLEBEKE.	Relieved at 5 p.m. by the 7th Cavalry Brigade. Left one Squadron and M.G. Section Regt. to hold the CHATEAU. Casualties 5 men wounded.	
28. x KLEINZILLEBEKE	Remainder of Brigade returned to bivouac at KLEINZILLEBEKE. Halted for the day.	
29. x KLEINZILLEBEKE	A draft of one Officer and 20 n.c. owners to join Royal Dragoons. Hostile (?) at 12.30 p.m. when orders received to support the right of 22nd Infantry Brigade in counter attack on line Cross Roads S.E. GHELUVELT (Kilo 9.) - KRUISEIK. Marched towards ZANDVOORDE 10th Hussars advanced dismounted through woods on CHATEAU. to N.E. ZANDVOOR. Royal Horse Guards Touch gained with 22nd Brigade. Slight opposition and enemy withdrew to the East. Returned to Bivouac at KLEINZILLEBEKE. Casualties 5 men wounded of whom 2 are missing.	
30. x ZILLEBEKE.	7th Cavalry Brigade heavily shelled at dawn some trenches being blown in and retired from ZANDVOORDE RIDGE back towards KLEINZILLEBEKE	

WAR DIARY or INTELLIGENCE SUMMARY.

Army Form C. 2118.

Hour, Date, Place	Summary of Events and Information	Remarks and References to Appendices
30. x. ZILLEBEKE (continued)	Brigade ordered at 7 a.m. to cover retreat of 7th Brigade and to occupy second line of trenches E. of KLEINZILLEBEKE. Heavy shelling and strong infantry attack developing along whole front. Squadron Royal Dragoons driven out of HOLLEBEKE CHATEAU, and retired N. with their right on the Railway and left connecting with remainder of Brigade the line thus being retained. Enemy shelled the trenches and ZANDVOORDE - ZILLEBEKE Road. Two Battalions 4th Guards Brigade arrived in support at 7 p.m. and took over the line of trenches, relief concluded at 2.30 A.M. Brigade withdrew to bivouac on S. outskirts of ZILLEBEKE. Casualties — Officers 3 killed (Major Lord C. Nairne Royal Dragoons, J. Lisputa Huntgarth Staff Capt. Kincaid R.A.M.C. attached Royal Dragoons, and 2nd Lieut. BURN. Royal Dragoons). Officers 8 wounded (Lieut. PEYTON, A.D.C. Lyon LEIGHTON, Lieut. SWIRE and HEWETT Royal Dragoons, Lieut CRICHTON Capt. Hon. H. BARING, M. FIELDEN, and Q.C. STEWART, 10th Hussars). Officers 1 wounded missing (Capt. H. JUMP, Royal Dragoons)	

Army Form C. 2118.

WAR DIARY
or
INTELLIGENCE SUMMARY.
(Erase heading not required.)

Instructions regarding War Diaries and Intelligence Summaries are contained in F. S. Regs., Part II. and the Staff Manual respectively. Title pages will be prepared in manuscript.

Hour, Date, Place	Summary of Events and Information	Remarks and References to Appendices
30 x ZILLEBEKE (continued)	Casualties. Men - Killed 12.	
	Wounded 37.	
	Unaccounted and Missing 3.	
	Missing 4	
	Congratulatory Message from C-in-C attached.	Appendix.
31 x HOOGE	ZILLEBEKE VILLAGE heavily shelled at dawn. Marched at 7.30 A.M. to a hedge row on the road ½ mile S. of HOOGE, and came under the orders of G.O.C. 7th Army Corps. At 1 p.m. attacked in position E. of HOOGE, in support, reinforced that infantry in front were retiring. At 3 p.m. ordered to support the left of the 2nd Inf. Bde. in woods S.E. HOOGE. The Royals and 2 Squadrons 10th Hussars advanced through the woods dismounted, met fallen the enemy retiring. Bivouac withdrawn at dusk. Bivouacked at HOOGE.	
1 x HOOGE.	Halted all the morning, the Brigade is now being used as a Mobile Mounted Reserve. At 1 p.m. ordered to march to the Road Junction on the HOOGE - KLEINZILLEBEKE Road, and support the 2nd Inf. Bde. who were being hard pressed. Supported the left of the line with one dismounted Squadron 10th Hussars and filled a gap on the	

Form/C. 2118/11.

(9 20 6) W 2794 100,000 8/11 H W V

Army Form C. 2118.

WAR DIARY
or
INTELLIGENCE SUMMARY. 6th Cav Bde HQ
(Erase heading not required.)

November 1914.

Instructions regarding War Diaries and Intelligence Summaries are contained in F. S. Regs., Part II. and the Staff Manual respectively. Title pages will be prepared in manuscript.

Hour, Date, Place	Summary of Events and Information	Remarks and References to Appendices
1. XI. HOOGE	Copied from preceding diary. Halted all the morning; the Brigade is now being used as a mobile mounted reserve. At 1 p.m. ordered to march to the road junction on the HOOGE — KLEINZILLEBEKE Road, and support the 2nd Inf. Bde who were being hard pressed. Supported the left of the line with one dismounted squadron 10th Hussars, and filled a gap on the	

WAR DIARY
or
INTELLIGENCE SUMMARY.
(Erase heading not required.)

Army Form C. 2118.

Instructions regarding War Diaries and Intelligence Summaries are contained in F. S. Regs., Part II. and the Staff Manual respectively. Title pages will be prepared in manuscript.

Hour, Date, Place	Summary of Events and Information	Remarks and References to Appendices
1. N. HOOGE (continued)	night caused by retirement of the Irish Guards into 2 squadrons Royal Dragoons dismounted. Position shelled by the enemy. Relieved by the Infantry of 6th Cavalry Brigade who drew to trenches near Hooge on N. of HOOGE-MENIN Road. Casualties. Officers wounded 2 (Capt. G. Kelly, 10th Hussars, and Lieut. Pitt-Rivers, Royal Dragoons). Men killed 2. wounded 9.	G.A. Kel
2. XI. HOOGE	Ready to move at 5.45 A.M. in support S.E. of HOOGE in rear of 4th Cavalry Bde. and remained as Corps Reserve the night of the Brunnels near HOOGE on N. of HOOGE-MENIN Road. Casualties. Officers wounded 1 (Lt. Col. R. BARNES, D.S.O., 10th Hussars). Men wounded 1.	
3. XI. Farm N.E of YPRES	Ready to move at 6.30 a.m. in trenches N.W. of HOOGE and remained as Corps Reserve the night of the. The enemy shelled YPRES badly and along the major Brigade bivouacked in farm N.E of YPRES.	

Army Form C. 2118.

WAR DIARY
or
INTELLIGENCE SUMMARY.
(Erase heading not required.)

Instructions regarding War Diaries and Intelligence Summaries are contained in F. S. Regs., Part II. and the Staff Manual respectively. Title pages will be prepared in manuscript.

Hour, Date, Place	Summary of Events and Information	Remarks and References to Appendices
4. X1 Farm N.E. of YPRES	Halted all day	
	3rd D.G.'s marched in from CASSEL arriving 6.30 p.m. Strength	6 Officers
	Officers — 28	
	N.C.O.'s and men — 530	
	Horses — 597	
	A draft of one Officer and up to men 10 Horses and 95 Remounts arrived last night. Casualty 1 man (A.S.C.) wounded.	
5. X1 Wood S. of VELDHOEK	Marched at 5 p.m., 1200 Rifles and 5 machine guns to the our trenches of the 3rd Inf. Bde. in wood ½ mile S. of VELDHOEK. Paraded dismounted. Relief commenced at 8 p.m. and completed in 1½ hours. 3rd D.G.'s and 10th Hussars from Royals in Reserve. C Battery R.H.A. and Reg. Transport with all Red Horses remained at Farm N.E. of YPRES. A line broke out in a barn close to Bde. H.Q.d The whole building was burnt to the ground. Fire started about 10.30 p.m. Casualties (in fire) 5 killed and 8 wounded	
6. X1 Farm N.E. of YPRES	Trenches all day. attacks in the afternoon, chiefly shell fire	

WAR DIARY or INTELLIGENCE SUMMARY

Army Form C. 2118.

Hour, Date, Place	Summary of Events and Information	Remarks and References to Appendices
6. XI. Farm N E of YPRES (continued)	Reinforced by 3rd D.G's. and 2 troops Royal Dragoons and one M.G. Relieved at 11 p.m. by Gren Batralion 9th Inf Bde. and returned to bivouac at Farm N E of YPRES. Casualties – Killed 20 men (inc. clerks) 4 Officers (Major SHEARMAN, 10 Hussars, Capt G HODGKINSON, Kevin DAVIES. Lieut TALBOT 3rd D.G's) and 45 men. One man missing.	E. Hbar
7. XI. Farm N E of HALTE	Marched at 12 noon to support Lord CAVAN's Inf Bde and to relieve Gen 7th Cav Bde. Moved forward for remainder of day. Marched at 4 p.m. to a bivouac on the N.W. edge of ETANG DE ZILLEBEKE, but found it unsuitable, bivouacked near a Farm N E of HALTE. Two fires never ceasing the night. Cav Bgde being harassed at 12 midnight, and the 10th Hussars at 3 A.M. G.O.C. sick and proceeded to BOULOGNE. Col. SMITH-BINGHAM 3rd Dragoon Guards taking over temporary command of the Brigade. Casualties: 3 men wounded and one missing.	
8. XI. Farm N E of HALTE	Halted for the day. Relieved the 3rd Inf Bde. in the trenches between ZILLEBEKE and KLEINZILLEBEKE and to the east of the ZILLEBEKE – KLEINZILLEBEKE Road. Reached Chateau at 5.20	

WAR DIARY
or
INTELLIGENCE SUMMARY.
(Erase heading not required.)

Army Form C. 2118.

Hour, Date, Place	Summary of Events and Information	Remarks and References to Appendices
8. X1 Jan N.E of HALTE (completed)	rifles (300 Royals and 220 3rd D.G's) and 2 Maxim guns under Col STEEL, Royal Dragoons. Relief completed 10 p.m.	
9. X1 Jan N E of HALTE	Detachment returned in trenches 7 pm by 7th Cavalry Brigade. and returned to bivouac. No attack on the trenches. Col D CAMPBELL took over command of the Brigade. Casualties – Six men wounded.	6.65/a/
10. X1 Jan N.E. of HALTE	Brigade turned out at 1 pm to support Lord CAVAN's line, and formed up in support of the centre of his line. The 3rd D.G's remained out till after dark. Relieved the 7th Cav Bde in the trenches on the ZILLEBEKE - KLEINZILLEBEKE Road with 520 rifles (300 to "Hussars and 220 Royals) under Major SITWELLMAN. 10 "Hussars. Relief completed 11 pm. Cold wintry weather. Commdres Letters 3rd Dgs and 2mm commanded.	
11. X1 Jan N.E of HALTE	The 3rd Dragoon Guards went up in support of Lord CAVAN's line and remained out till dark. No relief possible in the trenches but changed the two from the firing line to the support trenches and vice versa. Tonretable keeps in the arming. Casualties included with those on 12th	

WAR DIARY
or
INTELLIGENCE SUMMARY.
(Erase heading not required.)

Army Form C. 2118.

Hour, Date, Place	Summary of Events and Information	Remarks and References to Appendices
12. XI. Farm N.E. of HALTE	Men 3rd D.G's turned out at 1.30 pm to support Lord CAVAN's Bde were relieved at 4.30 pm by a Regiment of the 7th Cavalry Brigade, and proceeded to take trenches on the ZILLEBEKE - KLEINZILLEBEKE Road. Staying at the trenches had to drop Lon Packers right of Captain SHEARMAN's detachment returned by 300 3rd D.G's and 100 Royals under Col. O. SMITH-BINGHAM, 3rd D.G's. Casualties were 2 Officers (Major the Hon W. CADOGAN, to Hospital and Capt. T. BARINGTON now missing.) Regt Dragoons) and 7 men killed; 1 Officer (Capt. PALMES to Hospital and 16 men wounded. One man missing.	6/6/bl
13 XI. Farm N.E. of HALTE	The North Somersetshire Yeomanry arrived 2 pm from DRANOUTRE and joined the Brigade. Meeting on staff. Officers — 26. N.C.O's and Men 467. Horses — 498. Brigade (less detachment in the trenches) turned out at 3.30 pm to support Lord CAVAN's Bde and returned to Farm at 6 pm	

WAR DIARY or INTELLIGENCE SUMMARY.

Army Form C. 2118.

(Erase heading not required.)

Hour, Date, Place	Summary of Events and Information	Remarks and References to Appendices
13. X1. 10am N.E. of HALTE (continued)	Col. SMITH BINGHAM'S detachment in the trenches relieved by 7" Cavalry Brigade at 5.30 p.m. Enemy shelled to houses during the day. Casualties. 1. In trenches. One Officer Lieut. H TALBOT, 3rd Dragoon Guards and 5 men killed, and 20 men wounded. (b) in houses 2 men killed and 6 wounded; 30 horses killed and 70 horses wounded.	6 F 60
14. X1. 2am S. of VLAMERTINGHE	Bivouac. Halted again. Orders received for Ca. Brigade (less C Battery) to rendezvous to bivouac in farms S. of VLAMERTINGHE. Roads had previously been reconnoitred. 3rd D.G's unnamed out to support Lord CAVAN and reached bivouac at 8.30 p.m. H. Brigade in turn in Reserve for 48 hours at the end of which will relieve Ca. 7th C. Bde. providing 200 rifles for the trenches. Lord CAVAN'S support and Corps Reserve. Casualties. N.L.	
15. X1. Trenches S. and S.E. of ZILLEBEKE	The 10" Hussars paraded at 4.30 A.M. and marched to BELLEWAARDE in support to 3rd Dragoon Gds. returned to bivouac at 2 p.m. Fall of snow in the morning	

WAR DIARY
or
INTELLIGENCE SUMMARY.
(Erase heading not required.)

Army Form C. 2118.

Hour, Date, Place	Summary of Events and Information	Remarks and References to Appendices
15. Trenches S. and SE of ZILLEBEKE. (Continued)	K1. Brigade paraded 3.30 p.m. and marched to YPRES Railway Station, where the horses were sent back to bivouac. Brigade paraded 1200 rifles (300 per unit) for the trenches as under:—	6 Nov
	I. 500 Rifles (300 3rd D.G's and 200 Somerset Yeo.) under Lt. Col. O. SMITH-BINGHAM DSO to relieve the 7th Cav. Bde in the trenches on the ZILLEBEKE — KLEINZILLEBEKE Road.	
	II. 500 Rifles (300 Royal Dragoons and 200 10th Hussars) under Lt. Col. Q. STEELE to relieve the 2nd Cav. Bde in the trenches on the left of Lord CAVAN's Line and EAST of ZILLEBEKE.	
	III. 200 Rifles (100 10th Hussars and 100 Somerset Yeo) under Major SHEARMAN in Charge as reserve in trenches of Lord CAVAN's Headquarters.	
	Relief owing to various encumbrances not carried out till 4 p.m. Bde H.Q. in Cottage on road leading from ZILLEBEKE to Lord CAVAN's Headquarters.	

WAR DIARY
or
INTELLIGENCE SUMMARY.
(Erase heading not required.)

Army Form C. 2118.

Hour, Date, Place	Summary of Events and Information	Remarks and References to Appendices
16. XI. Trenches S and S.E. of ZILLEBEKE.	Desultory sniping during the day but a practical cessation of shell fire. The Reserve under Major SHEARMAN moved back from the woods to a farm midway between ZILLEBEKE and HOOGE. Dug-outs constructed there. Casualties - Capt. Hon. A ANNESLEY, 1st Hussars, Killed and two men wounded.	a M 601
17. XI. Trenches S. and S.E. of ZILLEBEKE.	At 9 A.M. a heavy and continuous shell fire was directed against the trenches held by Colonel SMITH BINGHAM's detachment. At 1 p.m. an infantry attack was developed against his right and centre of Colonel SMITH BINGHAM's line; the enemy advanced with gallantry, coming on to within 20 yards of the trenches, but the attack was repulsed with heavy loss to the enemy, our shrapnel being very effective when the enemy retired. The enemy subsequently subjected these trenches to a severe bombardment. About 3.45 p.m. another infantry attack was developed, chiefly against the trenches on the left of Col. SMITH-BINGHAM's line, held by "C" Squadron 3rd Dragoon Guards.	

WAR DIARY
or
INTELLIGENCE SUMMARY.
(Erase heading not required.)

Army Form C. 2118.

Hour, Date, Place	Summary of Events and Information	Remarks and References to Appendices
17. Trenches S. and SE of ZILLEBEKE. (Continued)	who suffered heavily in Officers and men the five trenches were reinforced by B. Squadron 3rd Dragoon Guards and A Squadron North Somersetshire Yeomanry from the support line when they were replaced by two companies of the Coldstream Guards who came up by Lord CAVAN's orders. This second attack the more determined of the two, was repulsed with heavy loss to the enemy. In the transit of the trenches held by "C" Squadron 3rd Dragoon Guards was a farm building that the enemy succeeded in occupying three times it was attacked by "C" Squadron, at the third attempt which was led by Captain WRIGHT, possession was gained Captain WRIGHT himself shooting four Germans with his revolver. Colonel SMITH-BINGHAM's detachment relieved by the 7th Cavalry Brigade. An attack was delivered about 12 noon against the line	6 C.O. End

WAR DIARY
or
INTELLIGENCE SUMMARY.
(Erase heading not required.)

Army Form C. 2118.

Hour, Date, Place	Summary of Events and Information	Remarks and References to Appendices
17.xi. Trenches S. and S.E. of ZILLEBEKE (continued)	of trenches, held by Colonel STEELE'S detachment, on the left of Lord CAVAN's line. The enemy massed under cover of a farm in front of the trenches occupied by the 10" Hussars. The movement was reported by Lieut Hon J GRENFELL, Royal Dragoons, who had been reconnoitring in front of the trenches. The Germans attacked with great bravery, some being shot within 10 yards of the trenches. The attack was repulsed about 4.40 pm, the enemy losing heavily. Colonel STEELE's detachment was relieved by the 1st Bn. Hertfordshire Regiment T.F. Casualties. 6 Officers killed (Capt PETO, Lieut DRAKE 10" Hussars, Capt WRIGHT, Lieut CHAPMAN, 3rd Dragoon Guards, Capt LIEBERT and Lieut DAVEY, North Somersetshire Yeomanry) 4 Officers wounded (2nd Lieut BURN, Royal Dragoons, Capt STEWART 3rd Dragoon Guards, 2nd Lieut BARNARD, North Somersetshire Yeomanry and Capt. SG BATES 7th Hussars Attd North Somersetshire Yeomanry)	6 A Coy

WAR DIARY or INTELLIGENCE SUMMARY.

Army Form C. 2118.

Hour, Date, Place	Summary of Events and Information	Remarks and References to Appendices
17.XI. Trenches S. and S.E. of ZILLEBEKE (Continued)	Casualties (continued) - R.S.M STEWART, 3rd Dragoon Guards and two N.C.O's and men killed, 85 N.C.O's and men wounded, and 3 men missing. The Brigade returned to bivouac at the farms S. of VLAMERTINGE, several squadrons not arriving till 3 A.M. the following morning.	6°d/gen
17.XI. farms S. of VLAMERTINGHE	Lieut BECKETT, 9th Lancers, joined as Bde Hqt Officer vice Capt. GLYN appointed temporary A.D.C. to G.O.C. Bde. A draft of one Officer and 52 N.C.O's and men arrived and joined the Royal Dragoons. A draft of three Officers and 78 N.C.O's and men arrived and joined the 10th Hussars.	

Army Form C. 2118.

WAR DIARY
or
INTELLIGENCE SUMMARY.
(Erase heading not required.)

Instructions regarding War Diaries and Intelligence Summaries are contained in F. S. Regs., Part II. and the Staff Manual respectively. Title pages will be prepared in manuscript.

Hour, Date, Place	Summary of Events and Information	Remarks and References to Appendices
18. XI. Farm S. of VLAMERTINGHE.	Brigade rested, one Regiment being saddled up at a time. Congratulatory telegram received from G.O.C. 1st Army Corps on the behaviour of the Brigade yesterday. Staff Captain proceeded to HAZEBROUCK to arrange billets in the Concentration Area.	6/6/61
19. XI. ditto	Brigade Lalted. Fall of snow in the afternoon.	
20. XI. LES LAURIERS 7 miles S.E. HAZEBROUCK	Billeting parties and Transport marched at 7.30 A.M. A fresh fall of snow during the night. The Brigade marched at 3.30 p.m. via OUDERDOM, RENINGHELST, WESTOUTRE, LA MANCHE, METEREN, STRAZEELE, VIEUX BERQUIN, LA COURONNE (18 miles) to the Concentration Area S.E. of HAZEBROUCK. Brigade billetted as under:- H.Q. - LES LAURIERS. Royal Dragoons - CHAP le BONNE. 3rd Dragoon Guards - L'EPINETTE. N. Somerset Yeo - Chateau 100 yds W. of TISSAGE.	

WAR DIARY
or
INTELLIGENCE SUMMARY.
(*Erase heading not required.*)

Army Form C. 2118.

Instructions regarding War Diaries and Intelligence Summaries are contained in F. S. Regs., Part II. and the Staff Manual respectively. Title pages will be prepared in manuscript.

Hour, Date, Place	Summary of Events and Information	Remarks and References to Appendices
20. XI. LES LAURIERS	Roads very slippery and freezing hard; marched on foot	
7 h.b. S.E. HAZEBROUCK (continued)	most of the way. H.Q. arrived 10.30 p.m. but 3rd D.G's and N Somerset Yeomanry came in considerably later and some transport never arrived at all.	6 O.R (e.p)
	10:15 Horses left the Brigade & arrived in Coincentration Area on transfer to the 8th Cav Bde.	
21. XI. ditto	Hetrich all men and horses are now under cover. Remainder of Transport arrived during the day. Froze again.	
22. XI. ditto	Halted still freezing. A draft of 1 Officer, 3 N.C.O.s and 40 men joined the 3rd D.G's Lt. Col. D CAMPBELL 9th Sister Bde. General from 8th November.	
XI ditto	Marched still freezing Line to England sanctioned for 72 hours for 25 p.c. out of Officers.	
24 to 30. XI ditto	Brigade remained in Billets.	

Report on operations 15th, 16th and 17th November.

On Sunday November 15th. the 3rd. Dragoon Guards and two Squadrons of the North Somerset Yeomanry were ordered to take over the trenches situated directly on the eastern side of the ZILLEBEKE - KLEINZELLEBEKE road. The trenches were taken over from the 1st. Life Guards 7.30 p.m.

B Squadron 3rd. Dragoon Guards on the right.
A   ,,   North Somerset Yeo. centre.
C   ,,   3rd. Dragoon Guards on the left.
A   ,,   ,,   ,,   ,,   were in support.
B   ,,   North Somerset Yeo. in reserve.

The night of the 15th.—16th November passed quietly only a certain amount of sniping being noticeable.

On the morning of the 16th. shortly after daybreak the trenches were heavily shelled and shelling continued more or less severely practically the whole day, but there was very little rifle fire during the day.

At 8 p.m. having previously received instructions that we were to remain on duty in the same trenches for another 24 hours, I effected the following reliefs:-

A Squadron 3rd. Dragoon Guards moved up into the fore trenches on the right of my line in relief of B. Squadron 3rd. D.G. who fell back to the support trench.

B. Squadron North. Somerset Yeo. took over the fire trenches of their A. Squadron who retired to the reserve trenches.

C Squadron 3rd. D.G. remaining in their fire trenches on the left of the line.

At 8.30 p.m. and 11.45 p.m. there was some heavy rifle fire chiefly on the left of the line. The remainder of the night passed quietly except for a considerable amount of sniping.

At 8 a.m. very heavy and continuous gun fire was brought to bear on all the trenches and the whole area was subject to a terrific shelling. Shortly after the commencement of this heavy fire my Regt. Sergt. Major (Mr. Stewart) was killed by a shell.

At 1 p.m. the Germans attacked my line on the right and centre (A Squadron 3rd. D.G. and B. Squad. N.Somerset Yeo.) coming on to to within 20 yards or so of the trenches. This attack was repulsed with heavy loss to the enemy, our shrapnel being very effective when the enemy retired. Shelling from the enemy's guns naturally slackening for the time being. After the repulse of this attack gun fire again broke out in great intensity and about 3.45 p.m. another attack developed, this chiefly against the left of the line defended by C. Squad. 3rd. D.G. who suffered heavily in the loss of Officers and men. I was able to move up two troops of B. Squad. 3rd. D.G. to reinforce C. Squad., 3rd. D.G. and I also moved up two troops of A. Squad. N. Somerset Yeomanry into the support trenches and shortly afterwards moved the remaining two troops of B. Squad. 3rd. D.G. into the fire trenches and brought the other two troops of A. Squad. N. Somerset Yeo. up to the support trenches, having under Lord Cavan's orders sent for the Coldstream Guards to come up to form the reserve. On arrival of the Coldstream I reinforced the firing line with 30 men of A. Squad. N.Somerset Yeo. The attack which was very determined was repulsed. The loss to the enemy cannot be estimated as dusk was coming on but it must have been heavy.

Situated in the vicinity of Capt. Wright's trenches (C.Squad. 3rd. D.G. left of line) was a farm building. Some Germans got possession of it. Three times it was attacked by C. Squad. at the third attempt, which was led by Capt. Wright, possession of it was gained, Capt Wright himself shooting 4 Germans with his revolver.

The trenches were taken over about 7.30 p.m. by the 7th. Cavalry Brigade.

The casualties of the force under my command for the 48 hours consisted of:-

```
Capt. Wright, 3rd. D.G.,    Killed.                 ) C. Squad.
  ,,  Stewart  ,,     ,,    Wounded                 ) 3rd. D.G.
Lieut. Chapman,,     ,,     Wounded (since dead).)
Capt. F.Liebert, B. Squad. N.Som. Yeo.    Killed.
Lieut. J.Davey.   ,,   ,,      ,,         Killed
  ,,   J.Bailward ,,   ,,      ,,         Wounded.
Capt. & Adjt. S.G.Bates. (7th. Hussars)   Wounded
N.C.Os and men 3rd. D.G. Killed. 11.  Wounded 41.
  ,,     ,,   N. Som.Yeo. Killed 21.  ,,      27
                                              Total
```

Total 32 killed, 68 wounded.

Where all did so well it is hard to particularise and the N. Som. Yeo. were very steady under fire and behaved gallantly. I should however like to mention that:-

Colonel Glynn D.S.O., N.Som. Yeo. was of the greatest possible assistance to me, cool, and determined and had his men well under control.

Major Browne 14th. Hussars, was most useful and continually carried messages under heavy fire.

Lieut. Coles 3rd. D.G. was also most useful in the same way.

Capt. Wright was conspicuously gallant in attacking the farm, himself killing four Germans.

Capt. Stewart and Lieut. Chapman behaved bravely throughout the 48 hours.

Lieut. Holroyd Smyth (att. 3rd. D.G.) led up the support into the firing line under heavy fire.

Lieut. Grimshaw 3rd. D.G. behaved in a most cool and determined manner during the attack on his trenches (A Squad.)

DEN GROENEN JAGE   Sd. C.B.Bingham, Lt. Col.
18/11/14.   3rd. D.G.

1B

G.O.C. 6th. Cavalry Brigade,

Nov. 18th. 1914.

At about 12.30 p.m. 17th. November the Germans attacked the outposts held by the 10th. Hussars near the cross roads just north of the N. in ZWARTLEEN (K.23). They advanced with the utmost bravery, some being shot within 10 yards of our trenches. The attack was repulsed by 1.45 p.m. Capt. Peto was killed and Lieut. Wilson took command of the squadron at a critical period. I should like to bring this officer to your notice for the initiative he displayed.

I would also bring to your notice Lieut. the Hon. J. Grenfell Royal Dragoons. On the 16th. he crawled up to the German trenches and shot a German through the loophole, and on the 17th. he crawled back behind the German trenches and shot two more Germans. It was from him that we first heard that the Germans were massing towards our right.

5241 Sergt Mac Lellan and 231 Corpl. Kelman, Royal Dragoons, also crawled out and killed 2 Germans out of a party of 30 whom they came across. Cpl. Kelman was wounded.

I gather that the Germans must have lost nearly 100 men during the attack. Our casualties were slight.

Sd. G.F.Steele, Lt. Col.
The Royal Dragoons.

Report on part taken by the 6th. Cavalry Brigade in the
operations of November 16th. and 17th.

On the evening of November 16th. I was ordered to find the following detachments for outpost duty.

(a) 500 men to take over the trenches on the right of Lord Cavan's Brigade.
(b) 500 men to take over the trenches on the left of Lord Cavan's brigade.
(c) 200 men as a central support to the above line.

I ordered the 3rd. Dragoon Guards and two Squadrons North Somerset Yeomanry to take over (a) under the command of Lieut Colonel Smith Bingham.

The 1st. Royal Dragoons and two Squadrons 10th. Hussars to take over (b) under the command of Lieut. Col. Steele.

One Squadron 10th. Hussars and one Squadron North Somerset Yeomanry to form the central support under Major Shearman.

I attach reports from Lt. Col. Smith Bingham and Lt. Col. Steele dealing with the operations which took place in the sections of the outpost line of which they were in command.

I wish especially to bring to your notice the way in which the North Somerset Yeomanry behaved under circumstances of a most trying nature more especially to a yeomanry regt. lately arrived from Home.

I especially wish to bring to your notice the names of the following Officers N.C.Os and men:-

1st. Royal Dragoons.
Lieut. the Hon. J.Grenfell.
No. 5241, Sergt. Mac Lellan.
No. 231 Corpl. Kelman.

3rd. Dragoon Guards.
Major J.G.Browne (14th. Hussars attached).
Lieut. E.R.Coles.
Captain E.Wright (killed).
2/Lieut. H.A.Grimshaw.

10th. Royal Hussars.
Lieut. C.Wilson.

North Somerset Yeomanry.
Lieut. Col. Glyn.
Major Geoffery Lubbock.
Lieut. Guy Gibbs.
Lieut. Ralph Gibbs.
Lieut. Lionel Gibbs.
R.S.M. W.Shakespeare.

Sd. David M.Campbell, Lt. Col.
Commanding 6th. Cav

3

G.O.C. 1st. A.C.,

I attach the reports of the Brigadier and the two commanders of sections of trenches on the attack on the 6th. Cavalry Brigade on November 17th.

My reason for doing so is to draw attention to the conduct of the North Somerset Yeomanry. This Regt. has only been in the area of operations three days and it was its first experience in the trenches.

I consider that the return of their casualties viz:- 21 killed and 27 wounded is a clear proof of staunch behaviour in action.

I would also draw attention to the plucky and valuable reconnaisssance of Lieut. Hon. J.Grenfell, No. 5241 Sergt. MacLellan and No. 231 Corpl. Kelman, all of the Royal Dragoons on the 16th. and 17th. November. I would also mention the gallant conduct of Capt. Wright and Lieut. Chapman (both killed) 3rd. Dragoon Guards, in the recapture of some farm buildings in the possession of the Germans.

         Sd. J.Byng, Major General,

20/11/14.   Commanding 3rd. Cavalry Div.

4

A.G. G.H.Q.

This was a brilliant affair & I wish to bring to the immediate notice of the C in C the splendid behaviour of the North Somerset Yeomanry.

I quite agree with the remarks of Major General Byng and I confidently recommend the officers & men mentioned above for reward.

      (sd) D. Haig
      General
      Comdg 1st Army Corps.

Headquarters
1st Army Corps
21.11.14.

Army Form C. 2118.

WAR DIARY
INTELLIGENCE SUMMARY.
(Erase heading not required.)

Instructions regarding War Diaries and Intelligence Summaries are contained in F. S. Regs., Part II. and the Staff Manual respectively. Title pages will be prepared in manuscript.

Hour, Date, Place	Summary of Events and Information	Remarks and References to Appendices
1 to 13. XII LES LAURIERS	Brigade in Billets.	
14. XII BAILLEUL	Brigade Sunday roused at LA COURONNE at 7.15 A.M. and marched through BAILLEUL to a position about 1½ miles beyond BAILLEUL on the LOCRE Road (9 miles) Halted tea 2 p.m. and then received orders to go into billets at BAILLEUL, the men in glass houses and the horses in the open.	
15. XII ditto	Brigade remained in billets under orders to be ready to turn out at ½ an hours notice.	
16. XII LES LAURIERS	Brigade marched at 9.30 A.M. and returned to billets in the area S.E. of HAZEBROUCK. Brigade billeted as on November 20.	
17 to 31. XII LES LAURIERS	Brigade in Billets.	

121/4559

6th Cavalry Brigade.

Vol III 1.1. — 28.2.15

Army Form C. 21

WAR DIARY
or
INTELLIGENCE SUMMARY.
(Erase heading not required.)

Instructions regarding War Diaries and Intelligence Summaries are contained in F. S. Regs, Part II. and the Staff Manual respectively. Title pages will be prepared in manuscript.

Hour, Date, Place	Summary of Events and Information	Remarks and References to Appendices
1915		
1 to 27. I. LES LAURIERS	Brigade in billets. The same as on November 20th 1914.	
28. I. THIENNES	Brigade marched at 9 a.m. to new billeting area.	
	Bde H.Q. - THIENNES	
	H.Q. 3rd Dragoon Gds. - BOESEGHEM	
	H.Q. Royal Dragoons - BLARINGHEM	
	H.Q. North Somersets - STEENBECQUE	
29 I to 2 II THIENNES and STEENBECQUE	Brigade in Billets. Bde H.Q. moved on 1/2 to a house on the STEENBECQUE - STEENBECQUE STATION Road.	
3. II. YPRES	Brigade strength in officers, embarked at 2 p.m. at STEENVOORDE, and moved via STEENVOORDE POPERINGHE WOESTINGHE, to YPRES. Jonny delayed considerably by transport of 16th French Corps who were moving south. Buses arrived at 9 p.m. at YPRES [the men were off-loaded in the GRAND PLACE and were billeted in houses of Rue Shoti, south of the GRAND PLACE.] Bde H.Q. and Signal Troop - 4 Officers and 9 men.	

WAR DIARY or INTELLIGENCE SUMMARY.

(Erase heading not required.)

Army Form C. 21

Instructions regarding War Diaries and Intelligence Summaries are contained in F. S. Regs., Part II. and the Staff Manual respectively. Title pages will be prepared in manuscript.

Hour, Date, Place	Summary of Events and Information	Remarks and References to Appendices
3. II. YPRES (Continued)	3rd Dragoon Guards — 250 rifles and 2 machine guns. Royal Dragoons — 250 rifles and 4 machine guns. North Somersetshire Yeo — 200 rifles and 2 machine guns. Escort A Transport and machine gun limbers and teams sent back to POPERINGHE under the Bde Transport Officer. Brigade billetted in houses in YPRES. [The town was shelled about 10 p.m. on the 4th and on the morning of the 6th but no damage was done.]	
4. II. to 7. II. YPRES	All C.O's. Squadron and Troop Leaders and instructors. Officers spent 24 hours in the trenches which the Brigade has been ordered to take over on Feb 8th.	
8. II. Trenches 1 mile S.E. of ZILLEBEKE	Relieved the 7th Cav. Bde in about 850 yards of trenches situated 1 mile S.E. of ZILLEBEKE. [Regiments bivouac in YPRES at ¾ hour interval and marched via ZILLEBEKE to the trenches.] Relief commenced 12 midnight and was concluded by 4 A.M. on the 9th. Led horses, G.S. ammunition wagon fm guns and pack mules in bivouac.	

Forms/C. 2118/11.

Army Form C. 2118

WAR DIARY
or
INTELLIGENCE SUMMARY
(Erase heading not required.)

Instructions regarding War Diaries and Intelligence Summaries are contained in F. S. Regs., Part II. and the Staff Manual respectively. Title pages will be prepared in manuscript.

Hour, Date, Place	Summary of Events and Information	Remarks and references to Appendices
8. II. Trenches 1 mile SE of ZILLEBEKE (entries contd)	Regiment were brought up to Lord CAVANS Dg. ent. The Transport and Machine Gun Team subsequently returned to POPERINGHE under Bde. Transport Officer. On the left of the Brigade in the trenches were the 10th Hussars of the 6th Cavalry Brigade, and on the right the 28th Divion of the 5th Corps. There were no casualties during the relief. Seven squadrons occupied the line trenches — one from left to right, 3 squadron Royal Dragoons, 2 North Somerset Yeomanry and 2 3rd Dragoons Guards. Two squadrons, one of the North Somerset Yeomanry and one of the 3rd Dragoon Guards occupied the support trenches about 150 yards in rear of the right of the line. Bde. H.Q. were with Horse supports. The reserves were provided by a Battalion of a Lancer Infantry Regiment (71st) and the supports of Artillery was French. Some machine guns were placed in the fire trenches other machine guns were kept south of the supports.	

WAR DIARY
or
INTELLIGENCE SUMMARY

(Erase heading not required.)

Army Form C. 211

Instructions regarding War Diaries and Intelligence Summaries are contained in F. S. Regs., Part II. and the Staff Manual respectively. Title pages will be prepared in manuscript.

Hour, Date, Place	Summary of Events and Information	Remarks and references to Appendices
9. II. Trenches 1 mile S.E. of ZILLEBEKE.	The trenches were wet in places. The Royal Dragoons prepared to resist the German counter attack from 20 to 250 yards distant. Six men 6th Signal Troop and 20 men North Somerset Yeomanry arrived as reinforcements. Supplies which occupied four hours, below from Regiment was brought up at 9 p.m. to Lord CAVAN's Dug-out. Casualties — one man wounded.	
10. II. ditto	Support dug-outs shelled during line of trenches, and a bit north brought into action against the ruin of Lt. Bryan's troop. Some bombs were thrown at the Royal Dragoon trenches & the enemy, and signs of enemy sapping were noticed opposite the Royal Dragoons and North Somerset Yeomanry. Casualties — one man wounded.	
11. II. ditto	A few enemy bombs thrown about noon, but silenced by our trench mortars met four of French 75's. Casualties — (Capt. E.L. GIBBS North Somerset Yeomanry and one man killed, and 2 men wounded.)	

Army Form C. 2118.

WAR DIARY
or
INTELLIGENCE SUMMARY
(Erase heading not required.)

Instructions regarding War Diaries and Intelligence Summaries are contained in F. S. Regs., Part II. and the Staff Manual respectively. Title pages will be prepared in manuscript.

Hour, Date, Place	Summary of Events and Information	Remarks and references to Appendices
12. Trenches 1 mile S.E. of ZILLEBEKE	II. Snow and rain in the morning; the trenches being wet. A new "Sap" was dug opposite the Machine gun of the North Somersetshire Yeomanry, but was noticed and several men were hit. Enemy trench Squadron R.E. had very near the fire of French 75's. Casualties - one man killed.	
13. Relief in trenches and Billets to STEENBECQUE Rail Stn.	13. Heavy rain in the morning. Relieved in the trenches by 4th Cav. Bde; relief commenced at 10 p.m. and concluded soon after midnight. Troops marched via [in Regimental arrangement to YPRES] where motor buses were waiting to [GRAND PLACE]. The Brigade returned in buses to [STEENBECQUE billeting area] the buses proceeding direct to Regt. Headquarters. Men they marched between 6.30 and 7.30 a.m. and there the men debussed on the 14th Feb. Casualties (one man killed and six wounded) The Machine Gun Section and Echelon A Transport remain for the night at POPERINGHE.	

WAR DIARY or INTELLIGENCE SUMMARY

Army Form C. 2118

Hour, Date, Place	Summary of Events and Information	Remarks and references to Appendices
13. II Relieved in trenches, and Bde returned to STEENBECQUE Billeting Area (cavalry)	All picks and shovels, bivouacs, periscopes, periscope guns, knife rests and Bde return etc were left in the trenches for the use of the 4th Cav. Bde. The night was stormy and windy, which assisted the conduct of the relief. The relief was carried out without incident. The 3rd Dragoon Guards were relieved by the Carabineers, the Royal Dragoons by the 3rd Hussars, the North Somerset Yeo. by the Oxfordshire Yeo.	
14. II. STEENBECQUE	"A" Echelon Transport and Machine Gun Brigade Section returned from POPERINGHE. Brigade in Billets.	
15 II to 28 II. STEENBECQUE	Brigade in Billets. Parties of 3 Officers and 100 Men each of the 3rd Dragoon Guards and Royal Dragoons proceeded on the 23rd and 25th respectively, the former to FONTAINE HOUCK and the latter to FLETRE - to groom the horses of the 4th Dragoon Guards and 11th Hussars respectively whilst the 1st Cavalry Division was occupying the trenches at YPRES.	

Army Form C. 2118

WAR DIARY
or
INTELLIGENCE SUMMARY
(Erase heading not required.)

Instructions regarding War Diaries and Intelligence Summaries are contained in F.S. Regs., Part II. and the Staff Manual respectively. Title pages will be prepared in manuscript.

Hour, Date, Place	Summary of Events and Information	Remarks and references to Appendices
15 II L 28 E STEENBECQUE	Two machine guns 3rd Dragoon Guards proceeded on Feb 23rd to YPRES, on attachment to 1st Cavalry Divn. No let the latter were in the trenches.	

121/4871

6th Cavalry Brigade

Vol IV 1-31.3.15

Army Form C. 2118.

WAR DIARY
or
INTELLIGENCE SUMMARY.
(Erase heading not required.)

Instructions regarding War Diaries and Intelligence Summaries are contained in F. S. Regs., Part II. and the Staff Manual respectively. Title pages will be prepared in manuscript.

Hour, Date, Place	Summary of Events and Information	Remarks and References to Appendices
1.III to 10.III STEENBECQUE	Brigade in Billets.	
11.III MERVILLE	Brigade (less Echelon B) paraded at 5.30 A.M. at STEENBECQUE and marched via LE PARC to the junction of the RUE DES MORTS and the main HAZEBROUCK - MERVILLE Road. 5 miles. The whole of the 3rd Cavalry Division concentrated in the vicinity of LA MOTTE. Orders received at 3 p.m. to move into billets in the LE SART - VIEUXHOUCK - L of LA GORGUE (excluding MERVILLE) area. Headquarters on the northern outskirt of MERVILLE. Echelon B concentrated and billeted at STEENBECQUE. The Division has moved into position as Mobile Reserve to the 1st Army during the Eastern attack on NEUVE CHAPELLE.	
12.III MERVILLE	The Brigade stood to at 5.30 A.M. and remained saddled up during the day	

Army Form C. 2118.

WAR DIARY
or
INTELLIGENCE SUMMARY

(Erase heading not required.)

Instructions regarding War Diaries and Intelligence Summaries are contained in F.S. Regs., Part II. and the Staff Manual respectively. Title pages will be prepared in manuscript.

Hour, Date, Place	Summary of Events and Information	Remarks and references to Appendices
12. III. MERVILLE (continued)	Echelon B Transport under the Brigade Transport Officer arrived in the evening from STEENBECQUE	
13. III. STEENBECQUE	Brigade stood to at 6 A.M. Brigade received orders to be ready to move at two hours notice. Orders received at 2.30 p.m. for Brigade to inform its decks to billets at STEENBECQUE. Paraded at 6.30 p.m. on N.W. outskirt of MERVILLE, and marched via HAVERSKERQUE to be some billets as evacuated by the Brigade on leaving it. Brigade in Billets.	
14. III. to 31. III. STEENBECQUE Billeting Area		

1247 W 3299 200,000 (E) 8/14 J.B.C. & A. Forms/C. 2118/11.

121/2321

6th Cavalry Brigade

Vol II 1.4. — 1.5.15.

Army Form C. 2118.

WAR DIARY
INTELLIGENCE SUMMARY

(Erase heading not required.)

6th Cav. Brigade

Instructions regarding War Diaries and Intelligence Summaries are contained in F.S. Regs, Part II. and the Staff Manual respectively. Title pages will be prepared in manuscript.

Hour, Date, Place		Summary of Events and Information	Remarks and references to Appendices
April 1st & 22nd STEENBECQUE	—	The Brigade remained in billets in the STEENBECQUE area.	
Apr 23rd	5.30 a.m.	Information received that the Germans during previous evening delivered a strong attack between LANGEMARCK and BIKSCHOOTE, & drove the French back 3 kilometres.	
	2 p.m.	Brigade marched via HAZEBROUCK, LE GREARDE, CAESTRE, GODEWAERSVELDE & ABEELE. Division concentrated, delayed en route by motor transport bringing up French troops from ST. POL. Halted in a field near ABEELE Sta. watered fed. Marched on GOSEWERSVELDE via Etches road.	
	6.30 p.m.	EECKE 6 miles. The Brigadier in temporary command of the Division. Lt. Col. Smith Bingham DSO 3rd Dragoon Guards commanded the Brigade. Echelon "B" remained in STEENBECQUE billeting area under command of Brigade transport officer.	
24th EECKE	10.30 p.m.	Marched via MONT DES CATS – BOESCHEPPE WESTOUTRE to grouped 1½ mile SW of VLAMERTINGHE – 13½ miles) whole Div concentrated.	

1247 W 3290 200,000 (E) 8/14 J.B.C. & A. Forms/C. 2118/11.

Army Form C. 2118.

WAR DIARY
or
INTELLIGENCE SUMMARY
(Erase heading not required.)

Instructions regarding War Diaries and Intelligence Summaries are contained in F.S. Regs, Part II. and the Staff Manual respectively. Title pages will be prepared in manuscript.

Hour, Date, Place		Summary of Events and Information	Remarks and references to Appendices
April 24th	7 p.m.	Off-saddled till 7 p.m. when Brigade marched via Billets road BOESCHEPPE – 6 miles	
" 25th BOESCHEPPE	9.30 a.m.	Saddled up and "stood to" at 6 a.m. Marched to Invgs 1½ miles N.W. of RENINGHELST, 3 miles – and off saddled.	
"	1.45 p.m.	Marched keeping ⅔ mile W. of POPERINGHE, to a point about ½ mile N.W. of POPERINGHE on POPERINGHE – CROMBEKE road – 7 miles.	
"	3.45 p.m.	Marched via Billets road HOUTKERQUE – 6 miles.	
" 26th HOUTKERQUE	8.30 a.m.	Brigade rendezvoused at rendezvous ½ mile E. of HOUTKERQUE, and off-saddled. Marched at 11 a.m. to cross roads 1½ mile W. of ST. JANS-TER-BIEZEN, 3 miles, and off saddled.	
"	9 p.m.	Marched to turnip fields near INN at crossroads on POPERINGHE – PROVEN road, about 2 miles W. of POPERINGHE, off-saddled + picqueted horses.	
"	11.15 p.m.	Paraded dismounted at 11.15 p.m. strength of	

WAR DIARY or INTELLIGENCE SUMMARY

Army Form C. 2118.

Hour, Date, Place	Summary of Events and Information	Remarks and references to Appendices
	Strength of units	

	Offrs.	O.R.	In.g.det.
H.Q.	6	19	—
3rd Sqn.	15	278	20
Hands	14	244	36
N.S.Y.	14	290	22
Totals	49	831	78

Echelon "A" machine guns with detachments for accompanying the Brigade, marched via POPERINGHE to billets at VLAMERTINGHE 7 miles away with Capt. Reid Dopson, 2nd in charge of horse transport men.

Apr 27. VLAMERTINGHE 1.45 a.m.
Brigade reaches VLAMERTINGHE
Brigade arranged in billets all day, VLAMERTINGHE
9 p.m. Enemy shells in the afternoon.
Brigade paraded at 9 p.m. with orders to march to BRIELEN on report that the German were advancing through BRIELEN on the YPERS canal & no Canadians left before the Brigade turned off.

" 28.   "   11.30 a.m.
Casualties – 2 men Rangers wounded.
Brigade marched & bivouacked at Point 35 on the POPERINGHE-OUVERSTA Road 1 – POPERINGHE — 2 miles W. POPERINGHE where horses had been left – 7 miles. Arrived at 3.30 p.m.

Army Form C. 2118.

WAR DIARY
or
INTELLIGENCE SUMMARY

(Erase heading not required.)

Instructions regarding War Diaries and Intelligence Summaries are contained in F. S. Regs., Part II. and the Staff Manual respectively. Title pages will be prepared in manuscript.

Hour, Date, Place	Summary of Events and Information	Remarks and references to Appendices
April 28th 7pm	Branches followed in area ST JANS-TER-BIEZEN — FORCE RATTEKOT. Bde HQ at FORCE	
April 29th FORCE 8.30am	Rendezvous at a point 2 mile W. of POPERINGHE. Offs. saddled, ready to move at 1/2 hour notice.	
6.30pm	Brigade returned to previous night's billets.	
April 30th	Same as 29th inst.	
May 1st	do. do.	

W. C. Howard Vyse
Bde. to Cav. Bde.

151/5609

3rd Cavalry Division

8th Cavalry Brigade

Vol VI 1 — 31.5.15.

Army Form C. 2118.

WAR DIARY
or
INTELLIGENCE SUMMARY
(Erase heading not required.)

6th Cavalry Brigade

Hour, Date, Place	Summary of Events and Information	Remarks and references to Appendices
May 2nd FORCE 8.30a.m	Rendezvous at a point 2 miles W. of POPERINGHE Off-saddled ready for a move at 1/2 hours notice	
4 p.m.	Marched to billets in the area PROVEN - WATOU ST JANS-TER-BIEZEN. Bgde H.Q. at a farm 1/2 m. SW of PROVEN N.51. Provided a detachment of 2 officers & 30 other ranks to hold road between VLAMERTINGHE and YPRES, West of Rd 2 Can Div came out of the line E. of YPRES.	
3rd From H.Q. S.W. of PROVEN	Brigade alerted & issuing arms, in readiness to march on. The days of rest when everyone is to be at the ready & under orders to move at any time. Received orders 12 noon to move at once and march on YPRES.	
4.45p.m.	Rendezvoused and marched on POPERINGHE from 3.5. 2 m.l.s. S.E. of POPERINGHE - Bn le, where horses were bivouacked and left under command of Lt Col Steele Royal Dragoons. Dismounted men marched and numbers of VLAMERTINGHE but a full 1 mile W of YPRES arrived here 2 am.	
5 am	Returned to billets in PROVEN - WATOU area	

Army Form C. 2118.

WAR DIARY
or
INTELLIGENCE SUMMARY
(Erase heading not required.)

Instructions regarding War Diaries and Intelligence Summaries are contained in F. S. Regs., Part II. and the Staff Manual respectively. Title pages will be prepared in manuscript.

Hour, Date, Place	Summary of Events and Information	Remarks and references to Appendices
May 4th Farm 1 m SW of PLOEGS	Brigade remains in billets. Capt HC Howard 16th Lancers assumed duties of Brigade Major vice Major B S Fisher DSO 17 Lancers, appointed G.S.O. 2 1st Cav Div	
May 5th	The Brigade were ordered to send a party of 300 rifles under Major GM Cope in taking up defensive and marched at 3 p.m. for a point 2½ miles N of YPRES. On arriving there first the horses were left & the 300 rifles marched to the S end of YPRES on the EKE road where reinforcements were detailed and went up over on return composed of R.S. from 3pm 5th—to dawn of 6th. Evening this — Lieut Gartside N.S.Y. wounded	
6th	OR the Bay 1, wounded 4 12.15am. The Brigade returned to its Farms, marched back 1 to billets v. the WATOU-PROVEN are, where it remained in billets for the rest of the day	
7th 2.30pm	Brigade embussed and marched via LA FORGE — BEAUVOORDE — STEENVOORDE — ST SYLVESTRE CAPPEL — to billets in the vicinity of STEENBECQUE, arriving there after 7.30pm. 20 miles	
8th STEENBECQUE	Brigade remained in billets. Degree of wakefulness 3 hrs. 40 min. after reveille.	A.R.H
	Veg. Brigade arrived at Bde HQrs	

WAR DIARY or INTELLIGENCE SUMMARY

Army Form C. 2118.

(3)

Instructions regarding War Diaries and Intelligence Summaries are contained in F. S. Regs., Part II. and the Staff Manual respectively. Title pages will be prepared in manuscript.

Hour, Date, Place	Summary of Events and Information	Remarks and references to Appendices
May 9th STEENBECQUE 5.30am	Everyone anxiously that 3rd Cav Div had been placed at disposal of 2nd Army, and that the Bde was to be ready to entrain within 1 hour from receipt of orders. Bivouac of Bde HQ~	
9am	Staff officer was sent for from Dn HQ and ordered Bde to move to the vicinity of YPRES - 37 trains available for the Bde	
10am X 10.30am	First orders came & Regts to march dismounted with machine guns & ambulances, via routes known to Brigadiers to provide. Echelon A to proceed to Pont INN just N of POPERINGHE on PROVEN road, & march hence off Bde to vicinity of Pt 33 - SW of POPERINGHE Of Pt 33 - SW of POPERINGHE By Bde strength 500 all ranks & horses with 3 officers, moved from Bde Hndyms via MAZEBROUCKE SYLVESTRE CAPPEL- STEENVOORDE- POPERINGHE. Point between 7 & 8 kilos shown POPERINGHE- VLAMER- TINGHE road, reaching there about 7pm Bde	
12 pm		
5pm	Men were rejoined to hut & H.5.a & remained there through the night. Phillips & machineguns were sent up earlier to route to left of shelters	
	Returned to bivouac about 4.7c. The 37 trains ordered were not sent, this being 30 German but 2 in emergency through the day his Bde got through all right	

WAR DIARY
or
INTELLIGENCE SUMMARY

Army Form C. 2118.

Hour, Date, Place	Summary of Events and Information	Remarks and references to Appendices
May 16. trenches in N side N of 3 Kilo Stone on YPRES - VLAMERTINGHE road.	Bde remained in huts.	
May 11.	Bde remained in huts. Q staff officer from Bde provided to add 80 Eng Bde and native Brig's XII/IX N road & then wind forward in line of Arties between bivouac & rail N of PERUWELMAERDE. Every I escorts to meet then with a stores to taking our the Bde down to first trench YPRES to anything crossing in I.b. & then on line of bridge from N end of BRIELEMAERDE Farm to railway line I.b.c. to channel. On right the N somewhat up with 300 rifles, occupied the line so far as the front of BELLEWAARDE Farm. 2nd + 3rd Bde continued the left with 311 rifles. The Royals were in support & dug outs behind Railway wood in I.7.d. Bde HQ at same place	
	Strength	

	Offrs	Rifles	M. g. H.G	
3rd Dgds	14	311	2	
Royals	19	230	2	
N.S.G.	16	300	2	
Bde HQrs + troops	5	45	12	

Totals
Offrs 49
Rifles 841
M.g.H.G. 798 $\underline{}$ 920

AG

Army Form C. 2118.

WAR DIARY
or
INTELLIGENCE SUMMARY

(Erase heading not required.)

Instructions regarding War Diaries and Intelligence Summaries are contained in F.S. Regs., Part II. and the Staff Manual respectively. Title pages will be prepared in manuscript.

Hour, Date, Place	Summary of Events and Information	Remarks and references to Appendices
13th Aug Railway Crossing Sw I.11.c.8		
1 am	Message received from 3rd Cav Div that Sqn V.C.O.'s Horse op the railway viaduct, that line was held by 1st Cav Div & was not to be manned. Further case of the railway working a important outpost in the line. A counter-attack must at all times be made to keep the line intact.	
2 am	Relief completed	
4 am	A very heavy bombardment started	
4.15 am	80th Bde informed by telephone and artillery support asked for. 99th Battery also informed by telephone	
4.45 am	All telephone communication cut off. Except to 99th Battery & to possibility of communicating with 3rd Cav Div	
5.15 to 5.45 am	Bombardment ceased & an enemy aeroplane flew over west, after which the bombardment recommenced	
5 am	Message urgently sent by despatch to 3rd Cav Div but it did not get through.	
7 am	A verbal report was received from O.C. 3rd Sqn that the line had been broken & was through. The advance was coming through from this information, G.O.C. ordered the troop to retire forward & re-establish the line, and despatches	CH 30 – M 77 I

WAR DIARY
or
INTELLIGENCE SUMMARY

(Erase heading not required.)

Army Form C. 2118.

Hour, Date, Place	Summary of Events and Information	Remarks and references to Appendices
Aug 13th Railway cutting 7.15 a.m. in I.11.b.0	A Staff Officer was sent to inform O.C. Inf. Bde & 3rd Can. Div. of the situation. At the same time the Lincolns' Bearers, who were occupying trenches in continuation of left of the Bn. were seen retiring.	
	Got orders for Bn. to push two troops forward towards high ground between Railway wood & advanced line with a view to going to a point of reunion. Remainder of Bn to look up reserve.	
	Bn. on with two troops detached to watch by the flank all those movements took place under a heavy fire.	
8 a.m.	Report received from left that the 3rd ... that attached Yeomanry infantry had been driven on the right.	
8.35 a.m.	Report from N. announced that after very heavy shelling a hostile attack had been delivered against left wing of the line in N.14 in consequence of which, although the front line trench was entirely repulsed, also that trenches occupied by 2 troops of right guard was being gradually driven in, also that in the event of a counter attack the 3rd K.R.R. has arranged to deliver a counter attack.	

Army Form C. 2118.

WAR DIARY
or
INTELLIGENCE SUMMARY
(Erase heading not required.)

Hour, Date, Place	Summary of Events and Information	Remarks and references to Appendices
13th Hvy Arty Group HQ in I.11.b 8.15a	Message to 3rd Cav Div that 15th Bde Artillery reported him that Grenadier Posts outside Klein Mendes & noting that Klein stands to be taken, cavalry has been ordered to that that attack has been repulsed for the present. Communication very difficult. Re-inforcements required. The message was ended "3rd Guards never replaced to a better moment" at 11 am	
9.30 a	Message to 3rd L.D. (CM 32)	App 2
10.30 a	Heavy arty fire on 3 Cav [day?] was asked to report App 3	App 3
11 am	Bombardment which had continued without cessation be came less, rifle fire opened again Message to 3rd Guards Div. (CM 33)	App 4
noon	Artillery along railway informed that enemy was collecting in farm I.5 & I.9, a battery of howitzers officers cars be sent to Bde HQ N/26 by present tour but battery by I.5 was shelled. Then requested Battery cavalry to fire as usual, En.[?] and Dead main Bethune Wood shell	
12.30 p.m	Further message from I5 & I.9, also heavy German artillery in I.6 to report, they appear to be concentrating about troops & are ordered under covering to the artillery from I.6 a I.5 &	

Army Form C. 2118.

WAR DIARY
or
INTELLIGENCE SUMMARY
(Erase heading not required.)

Hour, Date, Place	Summary of Events and Information	Remarks and references to Appendices
May 13th Railway crossing in I.11.B	orders re counter attack received C 54 M	
12.39pm		
1.10pm	Royal Irish Fus. heads arriving & reconnoitred ground + consulted with O.C. as to direction of this counter-attack.	App. 5
1.20pm	C 57 M and C 58 M received	
	Royals sent to re-inforce N Somerset Yeo	App. 6 & 7
1.30pm	R Inniskilling Fus. replaced by G.S. O.3. 3rd Cav Div who furnished 1 & 2 platoons moved forward to re-inforce 3rd S Gds on walking ground, a heavy fire	
2 pm		
2.30pm	Counter attack by R.I.F. Gds commence	App. 8
4.15pm	message to 3rd Cav. Div Out 37	
4.25pm	message from N Somerset Yeo that re-inforcements of Royals (R.I. Fus. had arrived) that of 2 platoons replied two other 2 platoons had gone to him. This was done at once. Two of R.I. Fus. was asked if he would send up another Co. to A Coy R.I.F.	
5 pm	message from Royals that had taken over the lines of N Somerset Yeo repair to every ready condition in front & Two kept	

WAR DIARY
or
INTELLIGENCE SUMMARY

Army Form C. 2118

Hour, Date, Place	Summary of Events and Information	Remarks and references to Appendices
Aug 13th Railway crossing on I.11.b 6.20pm	About 6.22 pm Infantrymen arrived for Rgts. all 3 officers with this party had been Casualties coming up.	App. 9
7.25pm	Message to 3rd Cav Div CM 38	App. 10
8 pm	Ca 39	App. 11
8.50pm	Recd G 66	
8.45pm	from —	
	Staff officer went round trenches for a Bttn to right treated our trenches verbally & 3rd Bde to close up about 40 yds to their left, for other units to line up accordingly. The line was formed & held as follows :— 3rd D Gds - 50 N S1 - 60 R J F to - 40 N S1 - Royals, by Rail with 3 rd KRR on arrival at N.Q. of 3 L KRR. It was found that orders had been given by OC 3rd Bde to take numbers from line left R Blues - orders from ? Brgt R JFs. was to take our Blues on the left, that on the knt of railway. Arrangements were accordingly made by officer in relay of Royals & Gunners of Blues, completed by possible by 1 am.	
11 pm		

WAR DIARY
or
INTELLIGENCE SUMMARY
(Erase heading not required.)

Army Form C. 2118.

Instructions regarding War Diaries and Intelligence Summaries are contained in F. S. Regs., Part II. and the Staff Manual respectively. Title pages will be prepared in manuscript.

Hour, Date, Place	Summary of Events and Information	Remarks and references to Appendices
14th Aug. Railway Crossing in I.11.b. 12.30 a.m.	Orders to relief received C.75.M.G. arrangements made by GOC North of R.S. Field & later over.	App. 12
1.30 a.m.	Staff of 3rd Cav Byde to reconnoitre new line of trenches.	
2.30 a.m.	Relief of Brigade by Cav Bde completed.	
3.15 a.m.	New line of trenches occupies on following orders.	
	3rd D. Gds. 160 rifles.	
	Royals 180 "	
	10th Hrs. 60 " – (Upland under orders of GOC)	
	N.S. Dragoons moves GHQ line reserve under orders of Officer Bde.	
	The new line, marked darker L.9 Zwistvale had only been able to work on during report about sent 150 yds in front of railway crossing in I.11.b. thence N to about 100 150 yds in front of the road prior about 400 yds SE of road junction in I.S(c)37. Where it was continued by officer Bde. Bde HQ. moves hedge out at Chaleron at P.O.T. 2.16	

Army Form C. 2118.

WAR DIARY
or
INTELLIGENCE SUMMARY
(Erase heading not required.)

Instructions regarding War Diaries and Intelligence Summaries are contained in F. S. Regs., Part II. and the Staff Manual respectively. Title pages will be prepared in manuscript.

Hour, Date, Place	Summary of Events and Information	Remarks and references to Appendices
14th Aug POTIZJE chateau 7 pm	The day passed quietly with little shelling. Staff Officer came forward from 3rd Bgde & made him party forward with a view to seeing if it would be possible to pepper a line about 400 yards further forward during the night. Bulk of 3rd Bgde got orders 6 o'clock forward, that were passed to Gren. Shel. Recede patrol about somewhere but not met company.	
9.30 pm	Relief by 5th Cav Bde commenced. Royds reinforcements were relieved by 10 pm, but any fielding the 3rd Bgde. were not relieved till 11.15 pm. (approximately) Regt marched out to VLAMERTINGHE [where they reported to this Bivouac, arriving thereat intervals between 1 & 3 am.	
15/16 VLAMERTINGHE	Bde remained in refuge at this comfortable were first up, hundred from presented to My C. 12 offrs & 194 other ranks - (a certain number of offrs & 194 other ranks were inducted back to fine area in this during the afternoon.)	
11 am	The Brigade attended church parade.	
17	Nothing remarkable to announce - somewhere	

WAR DIARY
or
INTELLIGENCE SUMMARY
(Erase heading not required.)

Army Form C. 2118.

Instructions regarding War Diaries and Intelligence Summaries are contained in F. S. Regs., Part II. and the Staff Manual respectively. Title pages will be prepared in manuscript.

Hour, Date, Place	Summary of Events and Information	Remarks and references to Appendices

17th Aug. VI AMERTINGHE   Casualties Ribbon Aug Bde 13/14th Aug

Officers

	Killed	Wounded	Missing	Total	
Bde HQ	1	3	–	4	**Bde HQ** — Brig Gen D Campbell, Capt R Fisher & J Glyn ADC (Killed)
3=DGds	2	5	–	7	17 TT m Kaye TT (Black Yr)
Royals	4	7	–	11	**3=D Gds** — Lt Col OB Smith Bingham dso, Major, Capt L V Newton, Lt E J Leslie, Lt Ard Greenshaw, — J S Stewart
NSY	3	8	–	11	
					Royals — Lt Col of E Meade Cay, Brig Gen T Spenser dso, Capt Hon T Fitzgerald dso Lt T Phelan, — A W Sydenham, Lt G Williams Wynn, — A W Arkwright

Other ranks

	Killed	Wounded	Missing	Total
Bde HQ	1	8	–	9
3=D Gds	32	37	–	69
Royals	22	93	2	117
NSY	23	79	3	105
Totals Offrs 10.	78	217	–	300 (?)
OR				
Total	88	240	5	333

Officers killed

Bde HQ Capt Lord Athumer (Royal troops)
3=D Gds { Capt T V T Neville N S Y { Brig LR Langfield dso
         { — B K Fisher   { Capt Help S J Baker
Royals { Lt A Humphries   { — R J English
       { Lt J M Leslie
       { — C K Bingham
       { N F Briston

WAR DIARY or INTELLIGENCE SUMMARY

Army Form C. 2118

Instructions regarding War Diaries and Intelligence Summaries are contained in F. S. Regs., Part II. and the Staff Manual respectively. Title pages will be prepared in manuscript.

(Erase heading not required.)

Hour, Date, Place	Summary of Events and Information	Remarks and references to Appendices
18th July VLAMERTINGHE	The Bde remained in same place.	
	Bde order established fixing list of N.C.O.s & men whose services have been brought to notice of GOC 6th Cav Bde	App. 13
8 pm	Good work 12th to 17th May. Bde ordered to be ready to rendezvous at 1½ hrs notice either from time of receipt of orders at Bde HQ found as on 2., until the Reserve with 1 Bn 1st Life Bde	
	Working party of 100 under Capt Kennedy Dawson 3rd Dgds provided to POTIJZE & bonds return to bivouac at ½ hour Lt.Col	
8 pm	Bde ordered to be ready to rendezvous at ½ hour N.S.Y. wounded from time of receipt of orders at Bde HQ formed as No.1 but to Reserve with 1 Bn 1st Life Bde.	
8 pm	Bde became No 3 mob'le reserve	
	Working party of 100 under Capt Arnander, Royal Dragoons, proceed to EDGE DE BIENFAISANCE on MENIN road.	
9 pm	Composition mil. 1st Brigade entrained & returned to billets in VLSTEENSTRAATE & returned between 12 & 1 am	
21st	12 men 3rd Dgds & 5 Royal Dragoons arrived as reinforcements.	
20/15		
21st STEENBECQUE	7 officers & 80 other ranks 3rd D Gds arrived as reinforcements for accidents	

WAR DIARY
or
INTELLIGENCE SUMMARY
(Erase heading not required.)

Army Form C. 2118

Instructions regarding War Diaries and Intelligence Summaries are contained in F.S. Regs., Part II. and the Staff Manual respectively. Title pages will be prepared in manuscript.

Hour, Date, Place	Summary of Events and Information	Remarks and references to Appendices
Aug 22nd STEENBECQUE	The Brigade remained at St Lieuk. A Brigade roadhouse pass idea was started for numbers of personnel.	
Aug 23rd "		
Aug 25th "	7 offrs + 54 men arrived as reinforcement to Royal Dragoons	
26th "	A staff officer proceeded to YPRES to reconnoitre line to be taken up from 3rd Cav Bde.	
	Conference at Div. H.Q. at 2.30 pm. Staff Officers proceeded to YPRES in the evening	
	Return to be in unloaded at 6 am at VLAMERTINGHE.	
29th "	First line transport preceded the Bde.	
	Strength 1 offr. 125 or. 213 horses	
	The Bde. m 3b horses used off from Brigade rendezvous	
" 1pm	& proceeded to VLAMERTINGHE Bde H moved to a farm in the area north of YPRES + took over the line 3 Cav Bde.	
	3rd Sqn. at house, Bde kent with 8 Hus Bde on right N.S.Y. in support	
	Strength 7 offrs. 3 G offrs SSS 0177 ifles + 7 machine guns	
30th 2 am	Major Sir Berkeley Sulman (8 Hus Bde) only was seriously	
	wounded in centre of country. Lieut Major Rait Ket officiating in command of 5th Bk. East. Cavalry	
" 6 Car Bde with 5th Bk. York Regt.		
Aug 29-31st St GEORGE(AUS)	The weather - heavy rain. Reinforced ends joined Regt at Pulivendle. 2nd Lieu. 3rd Dgh 7 or.d Royals. 18 o.r N.S.Y 60 o.r.	

"A" Form. Army Form C. 2121.

MESSAGES AND SIGNALS.

TO 3rd Cav Div.

Sender's Number: CH 30 Day of Month: twelfth AAA

The night has been quiet but about 4 am the enemy opened a heavy bombardment which is still going on with shrapnel and high explosive AAA It is difficult to get communication with anyone except 99 Battery RFA as all wires appear to be cut AAA

App I

Unable to get through will verbal report at 7.15 a

From 6 Cav Bde.
Place
Time 5 am

Priority

"A" Form.   Army Form C. 2121.

MESSAGES AND SIGNALS.   No. of Message

Prefix	Code	m.	Words	Charge	This message is on a/c of:	Recd. at	m.
Office of Origin and Service Instructions.			Sent			Date	
			At	m.	Service.	From	
			To				
			By		(Signature of "Franking Officer.")	By	

TO   3rd Cav. Div through
      8 Cav Bde.

Sender's Number: CH 32   Day of Month: Twelfth   In reply to Number: AAA

Can only find one Squadron Leicestershire Yeomanry on my left AAA they are across railway crossing in H11 b, in line with my support which now consist of about one hundred men AAA we are on side at level crossing in H11b AAA It is essential that steps shortly be taken to protect my left as Squadron of Leicester Yeomanry appears to have lost touch with anybody on their left.

App 2.

From: 6 CB
Place:
Time: 6.30 a.m.

The above may be forwarded as now corrected. (Z)

"C" Form (Duplicate).　　Army Form C. 2123.
MESSAGES AND SIGNALS.　No. of Message

Service Instructions.
Priority

Handed in at _____ Office 7.38 m. Received 7.53 m.

TO　6th Cav Bde

Sender's Number	Day of Month	In reply to Number	AAA
	13		

Can you report situation on your front

App 3.

FROM PLACE & TIME　3rd Cav Div 7.35 am

"A" Form. Army Form C. 2121.

MESSAGES AND SIGNALS.

No. of Message

Prefix ___ Code ___ m.	Words / Charge	This message is on a/c of:	Recd. at ___ m.
Office of Origin and Service Instructions.	Sent At ___ m. To ___ By ___	___ Service. (Signature of "Franking Officer.")	Date ___ From ___ By ___

TO 8th Cav. Bde. App. 4

Sender's Number	Day of Month	In reply to Number	AAA
[illegible] 33	[illegible]		

[illegible] AAA [illegible] AAA [illegible] AAA [illegible] Casualties AAA [illegible] AAA [illegible] AAA [illegible] AAA [illegible] AAA [illegible] AAA [illegible] AAA [illegible]

From 6 [illegible]

Place [illegible]

Time 11 am

The above may be forwarded as now corrected. (Z) [illegible signature]

Censor. Signature of Addressor or person authorized to telegraph in his name

* This line should be erased if not required.

158 S. B. Ltd. Wt. W5673/619—50,000. 10/14. Forms C2121/10.

"A" Form. Army Form C. 2121.
MESSAGES AND SIGNALS.

TO 6' Cavalry Bde App. 5.

Sender's Number: C.54.M
Day of Month: 13
AAA

I am anxious to be informed more fully as to true situation aaa where are your regiments and what line are they holding aaa are you in touch with left of 8o' Infantry Brigade aaa R.H.G. are now being sent to gain touch with you and to reconnoitre with a view to counter-attack ~~which~~ on your left flank aaa until this attack is ordered they will be under your command for purpose of protecting your left and connecting up with G.H.G. line aaa unless otherwise ordered R.H.G. and 10' Hussars and about C.29.B will counter-attack at 2.30 p.m. to regain the lost trenches aaa.

From 3 Cav. Div.
11.15 a.m.
12.54 p.m.

The above may be forwarded as now corrected. (Z)
M H Gage Lt

P.T.O.

You will co-operate with the counter attack if you have lost any trenches. aaa.

JMcy.

"A" Form.
MESSAGES AND SIGNALS

TO:
{ Addressed 8th Cavalry Bde, repeated
6th, 7th Cavalry Bde — C.R.A. 28th Division —
O.C. Armoured motors — G.O.C. Cav. Force }

Sender's Number: 6.57.M.   Day of Month: 13   AAA

The Division has been ordered to retake the trenches lost this morning at all costs aaa The lost line extends from road I.6.a. to the railway I.6.c. aaa The attack will be undertaken by the 8th Cavalry Bde under General Bulkeley Johnson at 2.30 p.m. assisted by some machine guns aaa All guns in support of the cavalry line will bombard the line behind the lost trenches from 2 to 2.30 p.m. after which they will extend their range to prevent hostile support being brought up aaa The farm buildings at I.5.D.7.9 and I.5.B.7.8 will be bombarded with high explosive from 2 p.m. until 2.30 p.m. aaa

App b

"A" Form.   Army Form C. 2121.

MESSAGES AND SIGNALS.   No. of Message _____

Code	Words.	Charge.	This message is on a/c of:	Recd. at ___ m.
of Origin and Service Instructions.	Sent			Date ___
	At ___ m.		Service.	From ___
	To ___			
	By ___		(Signature of "Franking Officer.")	By ___

G.O.C. 6th Cavalry B'de

Sender's Number	Day of Month	In reply to Number	AAA
G 58 M	13		

Re G.57.M and counter attack. Since the R.H.G. will be attacking with their right on your left will you please assist O/C with your advice as to the manner in which his attack should be carried out aaa 18th Hussars are attacking from POTIJZE–VERLORENHOEK road aaa

App. 7

From   8 Cav Div
Place
Time   1 pm

The above may be forwarded as now corrected.   (Z)

Censor.   Signature of Addressor or person authorised to telegraph in his name

"A" Form. — MESSAGES AND SIGNALS. — Army Form C. 2121.

Shadws to consolidate the line
parties will be carried up in
rear of the attack by a detachment
of the Royals which has been
ordered to report to 8th Cav. Bde aaa.
Shadws for 10th Hussars on the left if
the attack will be carried to men
of 7th Cav. Bde. aaa. O/C Armoured
Motors will report to G.O.C. 8th Cavalry
Bde for orders aaa 1 regiment
of 7th Cavalry Brigade will be prepared
to support the counter-attack aaa.

From: 3rd Cav. Div.
Place:
Time: 12.45 p.m.

J. H. Gage, Lt.-Col.

B Form.   MESSAGES & SIGNALS.   Army Form C 2122.

No. of Message _____

Prefix _____ Code _____ m.   Received At _____ m.   Sent At _____ m.   Office Stamp.

Office of Origin and Service Instructions.   Words.   From _____   To _____

By _____   By _____

TO   3rd Cav Div   App 8

*Sender's Number	Day of Month	In reply to Number	A. A. A.
CM 37	Twelfth		

Lord Alastair Innes Ker reports that the Blues advanced some distance and were then held up by machine gun fire and that Lord Tweedmouth ordered the Regt to retire AAA I have sent word to Lord Tweedmouth that he must hold on in as advanced position as possible AAA I believe my Blues are still intact but have had to send up my platoon of Irish Fusiliers to reinforce them being now casualties AAA OC Irish Fusiliers has sent another

FROM 2 platoons to my HQ to be at my disposal AAA
PLACE our casualties so far as can be judged
TIME have been very heavy

App

B Form.		MESSAGES & SIGNALS.		Army Form C 2122.

TO

| | | 2 | | |

| Sender's Number | Day of Month | In reply to Number | A. A. A. |

	writing	the attacked been	an
from	R H Q to	reports that small	parties
are	still holding	on sharp face	J 5499
and	open	ridge to S of to but unable
to	move aaa	This appears no reply to fire
a	certain a	previous wire report from
would	me	that the show of Rifles
	got them		forced
them	back	aaa I have had to send
up	two more	platoons for 2nd Twos
to reinforce my	right and	then asked
for	another	company to	

FROM	6 C B			
PLACE				
TIME	9.15 am			

(5824) Wt. W 7504-1562. 10,000 Pads. Wy. & S., LTD. Sch. 13.   Army Form C 2122.

B Form.   MESSAGES & SIGNALS.   No. of Message _____

Prefix _____ Code _____ m.	Received	Sent	Office Stamp.
Office of Origin and Service Instructions. Words.	At _____ m. From _____ By _____	At _____ m. To _____ By _____	

TO 20th Brigade   App 9

*Sender's Number	Day of Month	In reply to Number	A. A. A.
CH 38	Twelfth		

There	was	no	counterattack	on
the	right	of	Railway	as
my	Brigade	did	not	lose
any	trenches	AAA	The	counterattack
on	the	left	of	Railway
failed	AAA	Situation	now	is
E Cav Bde	with	assistance	of	one
Company	R I F	is	holding	their
original	line	with	one	company
R I F	in	support	AAA	My
Support	is	at	Canal	crossing
I 11 6	AAA	The	7th Cav	Brigade
on	my	left	has	_____
from	_____	_____	_____	_____

FROM				
PLACE				
TIME				

* This line should be erased if not required.

MESSAGES & SIGNALS.

B Form.   Army Form C 2122.

Prefix	Code	m.	Received	Sent	Office Stamp.
			At .... m.	At .... m.	
Office of Origin and Service Instructions.	Words.		From	To	
			By	By	

TO

* Sender's Number	Day of Month	In reply to Number	A. A. A.

no troops further forward than
in line with my supports
at any rate on right
of 7th Bde AAA In consequence
situation is most unsatisfactory as
my left flank on Railway
is completely in l'air AAA
Casualties on my Brigade have
have very heavy and for
been reason it was necessary
this ? ? ask for
for my to the
the assistance of this
reinforcement of Infantry and it
will be impossible to withdraw

FROM
PLACE
TIME

* This line should be erased if not required.

(5824) Wt. W 7504-1562. 10,000 Pads. Wy. & S., Ltd. Sch. 13.   Army Form C 2122.

B Form.   **MESSAGES & SIGNALS.**   No. of Message _____

Prefix _____ Code _____ .m.	Received	Sent	Office Stamp.
Office of Origin and Service Instructions. Words.	At _____ .m. From _____ By _____	At _____ .m. To _____ By _____	

TO

* Sender's Number	Day of Month	In reply to Number	**A. A. A.**

Then	~~without~~	unless	replaced	with
other	troops	AAA		

FROM	GOC	ER	Cavalry Brigade	
PLACE				
TIME	7.25PM			

* This line should be erased if not required.

(5824) Wt. W 7504-1562. 10,000 Pads. Wy. & S., Ltd. Sch. 13.　　　　　　　　　　　　　　　Army Form C 2122.

B Form.　　　　　　　MESSAGES & SIGNALS.　　　　　No. of Message _____

Prefix●	Code	.m.	Received	Sent	Office Stamp.
Office of Origin and Service Instructions.		Words.	At ____.m. From ____ By ____	At ____.m. To ____ By ____	

TO　　3rd Cav Div

App 19

Sender's Number	Day of Month	In reply to Number	A. A. A.
Ct 39	Thirteenth		

The Germans now appear to be working round against my left flank AAA The Blues are back on the N of the railway in line with my supports AAA What arrangements will be made for covering my left flank AAA The Blues consist of about 60 men AAA the remainder of Inf I am at present employing to assist in protecting my left and this will leave me with no reserve of any sort AAA In addition I am doubtful if I shall have sufficient men for properly holding the advanced trenches (if this) I cannot tell till I have more detailed list of casualties

FROM　6 CB
PLACE
TIME　　　　(see next page)

* This line should be erased if not required.

B Form. MESSAGES & SIGNALS. Army Form C 2122.

and any determined attack on my left could not be held up by the troops at my disposal.

FROM
PLACE
TIME 8pm

"A" Form.   Army Form C. 2121.
                    MESSAGES AND SIGNALS.   No. of Message _____

Prefix ____ Code ____ m   Words. Charge.   This message is on a/c of: Recd. at _____ m.
Office of Or... and Service Instructions.   Date _____
                                    Sent   From _____
                           At _____ m.   _____ Service.
                           To _____
                           By _____   (Signature of "Franking Officer,")   By _____

TO { _____   App.11
     _____
     _____

Sender's Number | Day of Month | In reply to Number | AAA
    G.66. | 13 | |

Dear General,
            General Briggs wishes me to say,
in reply to your note that he thoroughly
realises your situation and has strongly
represented it both to Cavalry and Army
Headquarters. His present orders are to
hold on at all costs; he is sending
some shattered remains of the
7th Brigade to try and protect your
left, and to dig a fresh line
connecting your present line out
with the POTIJZE - VERLORENHOEK
road. Both the other Brigades have
had terrible losses. Will you please
let me know as soon as you can
where you would like your supplies
sent and also anything we can
do in which we can help. Wishing you
the best of luck and many congratulations
on your splendid fight, yours

From
Place
Time
                                                    M. Kaye
6.35p.
                    Censor.   Signature of Addressee or person authorised to telegraph in his name

* This line should be erased if not required.
(24473). M.R.Co.,Ltd. Wt.W4843/541. 50,000. 9/14. Forms C2121/10.

"A" Form. Army Form C. 2?

MESSAGES AND SIGNALS.

No. of Message _____

Prefix _____ Code _____ m | Words. | Charge. | This message is on a/c of: | Recd. at _____ m.
Office of Origin and Service Instructions. | Sent At _____ m. To _____ By _____ | | Service. (Signature of "Franking Officer.") | Date _____ From _____ By _____

TO { 6ᵈ Cavalry Brigade   App 12.
    (Repeated) 8ᵗʰ Cavalry Brigade

Sender's Number: G.75.M. Day of Month: 13   In reply to Number: AAA

80ᵗʰ Infantry Brigade has been ordered to relieve your line to-night aaa A new line is being dug to-night connecting your left with 1ˢᵗ Cavalry Division the troops of which will extend some 600 yard South of POTIJZE – VERLORENHOEK road aaa. You will command this new line and will hold it with 3ʳᵈ Dragoon Guards and Royal Dragoons aaa a Regiment (10ᵗʰ Hʳˢ - 100 strong) from the 8ᵗʰ Cavalry Bᵈᵉ will be placed at your disposal and will move to your present H.Q. via the railway at once aaa The North Somerset Yeomanry will move to the G.H.Q. line and come under the orders of 8ᵗʰ Cavalry Brigade aaa

From _____
Place _____
Time _____

The above may be forwarded as now corrected. (Z)

Censor. Signature of Addressee or person authorised to telegraph in his name
* This line should be erased if not required.

"A" Form. Army Form C. 2121.
MESSAGES AND SIGNALS.   No. of Message _____

| Prefix ___ Code ___ m. | Words. | Charge. | This message is on a/c of: | Recd. at ___ m. |
| Office of Origin and Service Instructions. | Sent At ___ m. To ___ By ___ | | _____ Service. (Signature of "Franking Officer.") | Date ___ From ___ By ___ |

TO {

Sender's Number	Day of Month	In reply to Number	**A A A**
You	will	make	your	H.Q.
at	POTJZE	in the	dug out	near
the	chateau	aaa		

From: 8 Cav Div.
Place:
Time: 12 midnight

The above may be forwarded as now corrected. (Z)

6th Cavalry Bde

12.40?

6th (Cavalry) Order

The following names of N.C.O.'s and men have been brought to the notice of the G.O.C. for good work during the operations about 12th – 14th May, 1915.

App. 13.

3rd DRAGOON GUARDS

- 2450 Pte. Norris J. ✓
- 5805 L/cpl. Flecknell J. ✓
- 5169 Pte. Jones J. ✓
- 2314 Pte. Jackson R. ✓
- 7409 Pte. Stewart G.P. ✓
- 5419 L/cpl. Moulton D. ✓
- 4457 L/cpl. McCullock R. ✓
- 8015 Pte. Cornish S.G. ✓
- 5359 Cpl. Cooley W. ✓
- 1870 L/cpl. Grant R.G. (Late)
- 6350 L/cpl. C. Van Schaick (Late) ✓
- 2589 Pte. Buck J. A.W. ✓ (Buck)
- 1262 L/sgt. Sutton H. ✓
- 6268 Pte. Tedder A.G. ✓
- 4295 Pte. Lorimer W. ✓
- 5578 Pte. Macmillan V. ✓

1st ROYAL DRAGOONS

- ✓ 4274 Sgt. Mortimer J.
- ✓ 7110 Cpl. Proctor B.
- ✓ 752 Pte. McCann P.
- ✓ 108 L/cpl. Fox R.J.D. (Late)
- ✓ 5500 Cpl. Talbot J.J.
- ✓ 6254 L/cpl. Allsebrook J.J.
- ✓ 3604 Pte. Shaw R.
- ✓ 7995 L/cpl. Dickenson E. (Late)

14/5/1915

NORTH SOMERSET YEOMANRY

- 389 L/Sgt. Chard A.J. ✓
- 1368 Pte. Harding S.L. ✓
- 309 Sgt. Cross W.A. ✓
- 4164 S.S.M. Blyth J.W. [P. Staff]
- 355 L/cpl. Salridge E.W. ✓
- 647 Sgt. Absdell A.J. (Late)
- 1595 Cpl. Francis H. /WILTS RAMC(T)
- 189 Cpl. Henderson W.W. ✓
- ✓ 801 Pte. Grant M. ✓
- 91 Sgt. Goodman J.A. ✓
- 622 Sgt. Jenkins N.T. ✓
- 774 Pte. Higgins J.R. ✓
- 250 L/cpl. Harris C. ✓
- 1276 Pte. Ham W. ✓

6th SIGNAL TROOP

- 2872 L/cpl. Bernard D. 1st Royal Dragoons
- 4459 Pte. Jackson J. 3rd Dragoon Gds.
- 5651 Pte. Naylor A.P. 3rd Dragoon Gds.

6th CAVALRY FIELD AMBULANCE

- 790 A/Sgt. Watchorn Rich. RAMC(T.F)
- 1143 Pte. Gurnee J. RAMC(T.F)
- 1521 A/cpl. Barton J.S. RAMC.T.F.
- M/T 08135 Dr. Horsfall G.P. ASC.
- M/T 08894 Dr. Bell H.S. ASC.
- M/T 08463 Dr. Hayes ASC.
- M/T 018715 Dr. Stones W.E. ASC.

G./. H.C. Howard (Captain)
Bgde. Major 6th (Cav) Bde.

187/5991

3rd Cavalry Division

8th Cavalry Brigade

Vol VII 1 — 30.6.15.

Army Form C. 2118.

6th Cavalry Brigade
JUNE (1)

WAR DIARY
or
INTELLIGENCE SUMMARY
(Erase heading not required.)

Hour, Date, Place	Summary of Events and Information	Remarks and references to Appendices
June 1st, YPRES.	Col. Bell Smyth K.D.G.s took on command of the 6th Cav. Bde. as the finer day. But during the afternoon Brig. Genl. Campbell took over from Brig. Genl. Bulkeley Johnson. The 3rd D. Gds. trenches were very heavily shelled during the day. They were relieved during the night by 1st Household Cavalry from the ramparts.	
2nd "		
5th " 10 p.m.	The 3rd D. Gds. were relieved by the 10th Hussars at VLAMERTINGHE. The N.S.Y. also marched there on relief.	
6th " 1.30 a.m.	The Royals were relieved & marched to VLAMERTINGHE reaching there about 4 a.m.	
" " 12 noon.	The Brigade entrained & returned to the STEENBECQUE area.	
	(For full particulars of the trenches see war diary of 8th Cavalry Brigade.)	

Casualties.

	Officers			Other ranks			
	K.	W.	M.	K.	W.	M.	
6th Royal Troop	–	–	–	1	1	–	
3rd D. Guards	1 ✕	4 ✱	–	34	87	4 Bellowed	
Royals	–	1 ⊙	–	4	13	–	4 R.
N.S.Y.	–	1 ✕	–	3	20	–	
Totals	1	6	–	42	115	4	

✕ 2nd Lt. A. C. Clifford
✱ Capt. G. R. Kersh. Davis
   & D. Stewart
   Lt. W. Black
   H. H. Dodere
⊙ 2/Lt. A. Hopkinson
✕ W. R. O'Kelly (Recvd. atts.)

Total casualties 7 offs. 161 o.r.

WAR DIARY or INTELLIGENCE SUMMARY

Army Form C. 2118.

(2)

Hour, Date, Place	Summary of Events and Information	Remarks and references to Appendices
June 5th to June 30. STEENBECQUE. 5th 6th 7th to 12th 11th to 18th 19th to 30th	In addition to these casualties the following across this period the Regt was attached to R.D Gds during the following casualties:— Officers K. 1 x O.R K. 22 W. 6 x Died of wounds 4 W. 44 M. 7 Totals. 7. 77. Reinforcements received by units as under:— 3rd S.Gds. 4 o.r. Royals 5 officers 75 o.r. N.S.Y. 5 officers 5 o.r. 3rd S.Gds 9 officers 44 o.r. Royals 1 officer N.S.Y. 10 o.r. 3rd D.Gds 69 o.r. N.S.Y. 2 offrs. 8 o.r. Royals. 5 offrs. 10 o.r.	x Capt W.G.F. Reader x Major R.L. Hurst Capt W.R.F. Cooper Lt Alexander Lt D.L.J. Corbett-Smith 2-Lt F.K. Murray-Threipland Capt R.W. Dickson Poole(a.V.C.) These reinforcements brought all Regts up to establishment in Officers & to 350 sts. Royal Dragoons in other ranks. The N.S.Y at Rebedel & the Royals were till over 80 under establishment.

Army Form C. 2118.

WAR DIARY
or
INTELLIGENCE SUMMARY
(Erase heading not required.)

(3)

Hour, Date, Place	Summary of Events and Information	Remarks and references to Appendices
June 24th STEENBECQUE	The G.O.C. inspected the 3rd D.G.s. in marching order	
" 25th "	" " " " Royal Dragoons " "	
June 6th h June 30th STEENBECQUE	The Brigade remained in permanent billets in the BOESEGHEM, THIENNES, STEENBECQUE area.	

3rd Cavalry Division

131/6341

6th Cavalry Brigade
Vol VIII
29-6-31-7-15
Nil

Army Form C. 2118.

6th Cav Bde

WAR DIARY
or
INTELLIGENCE SUMMARY
(Erase heading not required.)

for July

Instructions regarding War Diaries and Intelligence Summaries are contained in F. S. Regs., Part II. and the Staff Manual respectively. Title pages will be prepared in manuscript.

Hour, Date, Place	Summary of Events and Information	Remarks and references to Appendices
June 29th STEENVOORDE	A digging party - 1 Off 66 or 3rd D.Gds, 2 - 66 - Royal Dragoons) proceeded by motor lorries to NEUVE EGLISE for work under III Corps.	
	The above party was relieved by another of equal strength.	
July 6th		
July 11th	A digging party of 1 Off 44 or from all 3 Regts proceeded by Motor lorries to the vicinity of SAILLY for work under 8th Hussars Major Burn. N.S.F. Commanded this party.	
July 20th	The party at NEUVE EGLISE was relieved by another of equal strength.	
23rd	The party at SAILLY returned to their Regts.	
29th	The NEUVE EGLISE party returned to their Regts. 3rd D.Gds 2 Off 59 or) proceeded KEMMELSHOEK Regts 1 - 58 -) for work under VI Corps 1 - 25 -)	

Army Form C. 2118.

WAR DIARY
or
INTELLIGENCE SUMMARY
(Erase heading not required.)

Instructions regarding War Diaries and Intelligence Summaries are contained in F. S. Regs., Part II. and the Staff Manual respectively. Title pages will be prepared in manuscript.

Hour, Date, Place	Summary of Events and Information	Remarks and references to Appendices
July 26. STEENBECQUE	The parties at ELVERDINGHE of Royal Dragoons & N.S.Y. returned to the 6. The remainder of 3 sqds. 10 offrs & 270 or. proceeded to ELVERDINGHE by motor transport. The party already there. The Brigade remained in the billeting area.	
July 1st to 31st		A.H.Adams Capt. for Lt Col Blackbrook

3rd Cavy Brown

121/1099

1 Cavalry Brigade
Ord IX
from 3 – 30. 6. 15

Army Form C. 2118.

WAR DIARY
or
INTELLIGENCE SUMMARY
(Erase heading not required.)

6 Cav Bde for Aug 1915

Instructions regarding War Diaries and Intelligence Summaries are contained in F. S. Regs., Part II. and the Staff Manual respectively. Title pages will be prepared in manuscript.

Hour, Date, Place	Summary of Events and Information	Remarks and references to Appendices
Aug. 3rd STEENBECQUE	The Royal Dragoons marched by a bus Battery area with Hdqrs at FONTAINE-LES-HERMANS, Squadrons at AMETTES(2), NEDONCHELLES.	
" 5.	3rd D.Gs dropping party returned to billets by sections two.	
" 6.	The Brigade (less Royals) dragoons moved to a new Billeting area as follows:- Bde HQ FEBVIN PALFART 3rd D/Gs WITTERNESSE, QUERNES-LIETTRES, LINCHEM, ESTREES BLANCHE, FLECHINELLE N.S.Y. "C"Battery 6 Courlands } FLECHIN 13 units total. LIGNY-LES-AIRE Parties were to continued work on a line of defence from Es des JARDINS to K of L/S at HOUPLINES k ARMENTIERES. The following Ranges were provided 3rd D/Gs 7 offrs. 200 or E. Battery 10 offr. 31 or. Royals 6 " 200 " N.S.Y. 7 " 200 "	
"13." FEBVIN PALFART.		

Forms/C. 2118/11.

Army Form C. 2118.

(2)

WAR DIARY
or
INTELLIGENCE SUMMARY

(Erase heading not required.)

Instructions regarding War Diaries and Intelligence Summaries are contained in F. S. Regs., Part II. and the Staff Manual respectively. Title pages will be prepared in manuscript.

Hour, Date, Place	Summary of Events and Information	Remarks and references to Appendices
24 Aug.	1 Lt. 31 C. "C" Battery ordered from ARMENTIERES by motor bus to permanent billet	
26. "	1 man 3rd D/S. killed by a shell in ARMENTIERES	
30. "	2/Lt. Smith 3rd Field Ops. R.E. killed by a shell whilst performing round the different lines at ARMENTIERES. This officer was attached to 6th Cav. Bde. during staffing operations.	

A.C. Brown Capt.
Bde 6 C.B.

Headquarters,

6th CAVALRY BRIGADE.

(3rd Cavalry Division)

S E P T E M B E R

1 9 1 5

Attached:

Report of Operations
26th/27th Sept.

REPORT ON MOVEMENTS AND ACTION OF THE
6TH CAVALRY BRIGADE BETWEEN 12.30 P.M.
ON SEPTEMBER 26TH AND 2 A.M. ON SEPTEM-
BER 27th, 1915.

REFERENCE Map 36c N.W.1 1:10.000

Report on movements and actions of the 6th Cavalry Brigade between 12.30 p.m. on Sept. 26th and 2 A.M. on September 27th. 1915.

At about 12 noon on September 26th General Briggs informed me that two regiments of my Brigade were under the orders of the G.O.C. 15th Division. Soon afterwards General McCracken informed me that he was afraid his troops were retiring from Hill 70 and Loos, that he had no reserves in hand, that he did not know whether or not he still had troops in Loos or whether even the front line of the German trenches were in our hands or not. He ordered me to move up two regiments to the British old front line and then to work forward and occupy the German front line between the LENS ROAD REDOUBT and the LOOS ROAD REDOUBT.

At about 12.30 p.m. the 3rd Dragoon Guards under Lt. Colonel Smith Bingham and 1st Royal Dragoons under Lieut. Colonel McNeile moved forward and occupied this line without difficulty, and commenced to consolidate the position. The 3rd Dragoon Guards were on the right and the 1st Royals on the left.

At this time the old British front line was occupied by men of the 15th Division who had been collected there after retiring from Loos.

2

There were also considerable bodies of the 21st Division retiring up the hill. They were in disorder and without officers. They said they had an order to retire.

As soon as we had taken over our line I went to Quality Street, in accordance with my orders and telephoned the information to the 15th Division.

At Quality Street I saw Generals Wilkinson Wallenstein and Matheson. They informed me that so far as they knew there were no British Troops in LOOS but whether the Germans were in it or not no one seemed to know. I now received orders to push my two Regiments into LOOS and to hold it (G.164 from IV Corps). I returned to the front line where I met General Matheson and informed him what my orders were. He said he was sure his men were E of LOOS and he could see the flags. This however was incorrect as the flags had been left when the men retired.

I ordered the 3rd Dragoon Guards and Royals to advance and occupy LOOS. Taking the Pylons and Crassier as the dividing line - the 3rd Dragoon Gds to occupy the right half of the town including the Crassier and the Royals the left half.

3.

I had no information at all that the 47th Division were forming a defensive flank and so made arrangements to occupy the whole town. The Royals and 3rd Dragoon Guards advanced under considerable shell fire in the steadiest possible manner.

On arrival at LOOS the OC Royals found some infantry west of the town and some more including 9th Gordons, Camerons and Argyle and Sutherland Highlanders retiring through the town. These latter regiments numbered about 400 men and they returned with him and re-occupied trenches S.E. and N.E. of the town.

The 3rd Dragoon Guards connected up with the 141st Brigade on the right and with the Argyle and Sutherland Highlanders on the left.

The line then held by the troops under my command was from CHALK PIT M6 a 8.8 - across the CRASSIER - G 36 c. - round the S.E and N.E outskirts of the village to about point 58 - G.29 d 58.

Having visited General Thwaites and ascertained his dispositions and having received a report from Major Campbell - Argyle and Sutherland Highlanders that his men were completely done up, I relieved them by one Squadron 3rd Dragoon Guards

4.

who now came under the command of Colonel McNeile, commanding the left Sector.

A Staff Officer of the 3rd Cavalry Division visited me between 6 and 7 p.m. I explained the situation and told him that although I should be alright during the night I thought more troops ought certainly to be sent up as the infantry were very done up, and that I should not have enough troops at my disposal in the event of a serious attack next day.

At 9 p.m. I received several orders instructing me not to vacate Loos but there never has been the slightest idea of doing so.

At 2 A.m. General Briggs arrived with the 8th Cavalry Brigade, and took over command.

When my Brigade entered Loos it found some field guns, howitzers and infantry, 'A' Echelon ammunition limbers apparently abandoned as well as all the German guns and material captured on the previous day. As far as one could ascertain there were no troops at all covering Loos to the E. and N.E. at the time my Brigade entered the town.

As far as the guns were concerned I believe the field guns came into action the

5.

next day in the position in which we found them. The Howitzers were got away during the night of the 26th/27th covered by a party under 2/Lt Dunville, Royal Dragoons.

In conclusion I should like to add that the 9th Gordons and the Camerons showed a most excellent spirit. They never hesitated for one moment when Col McNeile asked them to go back again and they could not understand why they had ever been ordered to retire.

David M Campbell
Brig-General
6th Cavalry Brigade

18/11/1915.

Reference Map 36c.(N.W.1) 1/10,000.

Report on movements and action of the 6th Cavalry Brigade between 12.30 p.m. on September 26th and 2 a.m. on September 27th, 1915.

At about 12 noon on September 26th General Briggs informed me that two regiments of my Brigade were under the orders of the G.O.C. 15th Division. Soon afterwards General McCracken informed me that he was afraid his troops were retiring from Hill 70 and LOOS, that he had no reserves in hand, that he did not know whether or not he still had troops in LOOS or whether even the front line of the German trenches were in our hands or not. He ordered me to move up two regiments to the British old front line and then to work forward and occupy the German front line between the LENS ROAD REDOUBT and the LOOS ROAD REDOUBT.

At about 12.30 p.m. the 3rd Dragoon Guards under Lt. Colonel Smith Bingham and 1st Royal Dragoons under Lieut.Colonel McNeile moved forward and occupied this line without difficulty and commenced to consolidate the position. The 3rd Dragoon Guards were on the right and the 1st Royals on the left.

At this time the old British front line was occupied by men of the 15th Division who had been collected there after retiring from LOOS.

There were also considerable bodies of the 21st Division retiring up the hill. They were in disorder and without Officers. They said they had an order to retire.

As soon as we had taken over our line I went to Quality Street, in accordance with my orders and telephoned the information to the 15th Division.

At Quality Street I saw Generals Wilkinson, Wallenstein and Matheson. They informed me that so far as they knew there were no British Troops in LOOS but whether the Germans were in it or not no one seemed to know. I now received orders to push my two regiments into LOOS and to hold it

(G.164 from IV Corps). I returned to the front line where I met General Matheson and informed him what my orders were. He said he was sure his men were E of LOOS and he could see the flags. This, however was incorrect as the flags had been left when the men retired.

I ordered the 3rd Dragoon Guards and Royals to advance and occupy LOOS. Taking the Pylons and Crassier as the dividing line - the 3rd Dragoon Guards to occupy the right half of the town including the Crassier and the Royals the left half.

I had no information at all that the 47th Division were forming a defensive flank and so made arrangements to occupy the whole town. The Royals and 3rd Dragoon Guards advanced under considerable shell fire in the steadiest possible manner.

On arrival at LOOS the O.C. Royals found some infantry West of the town and some more including 9th Gordons, Camerons and Argyle and Sutherland Highlanders retiring through the town. These latter regiments numbered about 400 men and they returned with him and re-occupied trenches S.E. and E. of the town.

The 3rd Dragoon Guards connected up with the 141st Brigade on the right and with the Argyle and Sutherland Highlanders on the left.

The line then held by the troops under my command was from CHALK PIT M.6.a.8.8. across the CRASSIER - G.36.c. - round the S.E. and N.E. outskirts of the village to about point 58 - G.29.d.58.

Having visited General Thwaites and ascertained his dispositions and having received a report from Major Campbell Argyle and Sutherland Highlanders that his men were completely done up, I relieved them by one squadron 3rd Dragoon Guards who now came under the command of Colonel McNeile, commanding the left sector.

A Staff Officer of the 3rd Cavalry Division visited me

between

between 6 and 7 p.m. I explained the situation and told him that although I should be alright during the night I thought more troops ought certainly to be sent up as the infantry were very done up, and that I should not have enough troops at my disposal in the event of a serious attack next day.

At 9 p.m. I received several orders instructing me not to vacate LOOS but there never had been the slightest idea of doing so.

At 2 a.m. General Briggs arrived with the 8th Cavalry Brigade and took over command.

When my Brigade entered LOOS it found some Field Guns, Howitzers and infantry "A" Echelon ammunition limbers apparently abandoned as well as all the German Guns and material captured on the previous day. As far as one could ascertain there were no troops at all covering LOOS to the E and N.E. at the time my Brigade entered the town.

As far as the Guns were concerned I believe the Field Guns came into action the next day in the position in which we found them. The Howitzers were got away during the night 26/27th covered by a party under 2/Lieut Dunville, Royal Dragoons.

In conclusion I should like to add that the 9th Gordons and the Camerons showed a most excellent spirit. They never hesitated for one moment when Col. McNeile asked them to go back again and they could not understand why they had ever been ordered to retire.

18/11/15.

(Sgd) D.M. Campbell.
Brig-General.
6th Cavalry Brigade.

1)
       6' Cavalry B^de
        3 Cavalry Div^n

Major Davidson.

   Having read Sir John's despatch on the Battle of Loos in which he says "A Cavalry brigade was put in to garrison Loos" and knowing you to be a man of discretion I thought, for my own satisfaction, I would write and ask you whether the real situation as it was on the afternoon of the 26 when the two regiments of my brigade advanced on Loos, was really known by the authorities. I do not wish to inflict a full account of what

happened or you are no
doubt if the following facts
are known all other
less important details are
known too.

Did you know

1. That when my regiments
reached Loos there were
no infantry on the N or N E
of the Crassier and the
whole of this part might
well have been in the
hands of the enemy. There
was not a soul on Hill 70.
The Royals found some
Gordon Highlanders and
men of other regiments W of
the town and induced
them to now come and
assist in holding the
NE corner.

2. That there were at least one if not two abandoned English Field Artillery Batteries to the W of the town and one if not two abandoned heavier howitzer batteries near the Loos Hulluch Road. The former came into action during the French attack, and the latter were got away during the night of the 26. under a covering party supplied by the Royals.

3. All the German guns captured in Loos have been abandoned. In fact it was only the presence of my brigade which prevented the Germans

walking into Loos and
taking the Division from
the offensive flank in
rear.

I have no wish to detract
in the smallest way from
the splendid attack
made by the 15" Div" and
fully recognise that they,
and they alone, are were
responsible for the capture
Loos & the guns and
material therein captured;
but I do think that the
splendid orderly advance
of the 3" D.[?] & Royals
under heavy shell fire
through broken infantry;
the reoccupation of the
town and thereby the

saving, not only of the guns & material already captured from the Prussians, but also of our own guns and infantry ammunition waggons which have been abandoned, deserves something better than "A cavalry brigade was put in to garrison Roos." If the facts are known but it was deemed advisable to describe our share of the work in the way it was described well & good — the authorities are the best judges, but just for my own satisfaction and in justice to the 3rd D.G's & Royals I should much like to know how much is known to the "Powers that Be".

When I was at home I saw a gun marked "Captured by the Welsh Guards at Loos."
Now I am pretty sure that this gun is one that was in a garden close to 3rd D.G H.Q and of course inside our line of defence! My reason for thinking so being that in their attack the Welsh guards never got up to any such guns at all,

and possibly because
we had pulled this gun
out with a view to its
removal at night and
could not understand
why the W G had put
a sentry over it." If I
am right this gun
belongs to the XV Div"
but that is a small
matter — I should like
very much to see you
again & will look you
up if I come to here.
Best of luck.

Yrs S.
Louis J M Campbell

Copy of letter from O.C. 6th Cavalry Bde.

6th Cavalry Bde.,
3rd Cavalry Division.

My dear Davidson,

Having read Sir John's dispatch on the Battle of Loos in which he says, "A cavalry Brigade was put in to garrison Loos," and knowing you to be a man of discretion, I thought, for my own satisfaction, I would write and ask you whether the real situation as it was on the afternoon of the 26th when the two regiments of my brigade advanced on Loos, was really known by the authorities. I do not wish to inflict a full account of what happened on you and no doubt if the following facts are known all other less important details are known too.

(1) That when my regiments reached Loos there were no infantry on the N. or N.E. of the Crassier and the whole of this part might well have been in the hands of the enemy. There was not a soul on Hill 70. The Royals found some Gordon Highlanders and men of other regiments W of the town and induced them to advance and assist in holding the N.E. end.

2. That there was at least, one, if not two, abandoned English Field Artillery Batteries to the W. of the town, and one, if not two, abandoned English Howitzer Batteries near the Loos Hulluch road. The former came into action during the Guards attack, and the latter were got away during the night of the 26th under a covering party supplied by the Royals.

3. All the German guns captured in Loos had been abandoned. In fact it was only the presence of my brigade which prevented the Germans walking into Loos and taking the Division forming the defensive flank in rear.

I have no wish to detract in the smallest way from the splendid attack made by the 15th Division and fully recognise that they, and they alone, were responsible for the capture of Loos and the guns and material therein captured, but I do think that the splendid, orderly advance of the 3rd Dgs.and Royals under heavy shellfire, through broken infantry, the re-occupation of the town and thereby the saving, not only of the guns and material already captured from the Germans, but also of our own guns and infantry ammunition wagons which had been abandoned, deserved something better than "A Cavalry brigade was put in to garrison Loos." If the facts are known. But it was deemed advisable to describe our share of the work, in the way it was described, well and good. The authorities are the best judges, but just for my own satisfaction and in justice to the 3rd Dgs. and Royals I should much like to know how much is known to the powers that be.

When I was at home I saw a gun marked "Captured by the Welch Guards at Loos." Now I am pretty sure that this gun is one that was in a garden close to 3rd D.G.H.Q. and of course inside our line of defences! My reason in thinking so being that in their attack, the Welsh Guards never got up to any fresh? guns at all, and secondly because we had pulled this gun out with a view to its removal at night and could not understand why the W.G. had put a sentry over it. If I am right, this gun belongs to the 15th Division, but that is a small matter. I should like very much to see you again and will look you up if I come to Aire.

Best of wishes,

Yours sincerely,

(signed) David.M.Campbell.

WAR DIARY.

Army Form C. 2118.

WAR DIARY
or
INTELLIGENCE SUMMARY

(Erase heading not required.)

6th Cavalry Brigade
September, 1915.

Instructions regarding War Diaries and Intelligence Summaries are contained in F. S. Regs., Part II. and the Staff Manual respectively. Title pages will be prepared in manuscript.

Hour, Date, Place	Summary of Events and Information	Remarks and references to Appendices
20th Sept.	Orders were received that 3rd Cavalry Division was placed at disposal of 1st Army and that the 6th Cavalry Brigade were to march to a bivouac in the BOIS-DES-DAMES — MARLES-LES-MINES on the night 20th/21st September via CAUCHY-A-LATOUR — AUCHEL —	
6.30 p.m.	Brigade rendezvous at BELLERY and marched by above route to BOIS-DES-DAMES arriving in bivouac at 4.45 A.M.	
21st Sept.	Brigade remained in bivouac.	
22nd Sept.	Officers patrols were sent out to reconnoitre roads and country in direction of VERMELLES. The Brigade remained in bivouac.	
23rd Sept.	Brigade remained in bivouac.	
24th Sept.	Brigade remained in bivouac. Officers patrols were sent to reconnoitre 8 routes for Cavalry through and over our trenches to German 1st line trenches.	
25th Sept. 5.30 A.M.	Brigade stood to ready to move.	
8.45 A.M.	Brigade moved to VAUDRICOURT.	
11 A.M.	Brigade moved to RUITOIRE	

Army Form C. 2118.

WAR DIARY
or
INTELLIGENCE SUMMARY
(Erase heading not required.)

6th Cavalry Brigade
September, 1915.

Instructions regarding War Diaries and Intelligence Summaries are contained in F. S. Regs, Part II. and the Staff Manual respectively. Title pages will be prepared in manuscript.

Hour, Date, Place	Summary of Events and Information	Remarks and references to Appendices
25 Sept (contd) 2.30 pm	Following patrols were sent out:— Patrol No 1. In direction of LONE TREE (Capt. WORTHINGTON 3rd Dragoon Gds and four men)	
	Patrol No 2. In direction of LONE TREE (Lieut. BENTON 3rd Dragoon Gds and one man)	
	Patrol No 3. In direction of Loos to report on situation at HILL 70 and PUITS 14 (Capt. HOLROYD SMITH 3rd Dragoon Gds and three men)	
	Patrol No 4. (2c no. 3 (Lieut. HARRIES 3rd Dragoon Gds and 3 men)	
3. p.m.	Patrols Nos 1 and 2 reported our infantry held up at LONE TREE HILL. Patrols Nos 3 and 4 reported our Infantry engaging the Germans on HILL 70 and that our infantry were just in possession of PUITS 14 BIS	
3.15 pm	Patrol No 5 was sent in direction of HULLUCH and returned with report (2/Lt BENTON 3rd Dragoon Guards) that fighting was in progress at that place and that LONE TREE HILL to Southern side was held by enemy.	
4.10 pm	Patrol No 6. (Capt. WORTHINGTON and 3 men) patrolled to 'LONE TREE HILL and reported that Germans were surrendering in parties of 200 at that place.	
8 pm	Brigade Hd Settled for night. Very wet night.	

Army Form C. 2118.

6th Cavalry Brigade
September, 1915.

WAR DIARY
or
INTELLIGENCE SUMMARY
(Erase heading not required.)

Hour, Date, Place	Summary of Events and Information	Remarks and references to Appendices
Sept 26.		
5.30 AM	Brigade Saddled up ready to move	
9.20 AM	No 1 Patrol (2/Lt Cubitt - Royal Dragoons) patrolled to Bois Hugo. No 2 Patrol (2/Lt Katinakis 3rd Dragoons) reconnoitred towards the Quarries, G.6.c. and Fosse 8 and reported these places held by enemy.	
11.30 AM	Two Regiments (3rd Dragoon Guards and Royals) of the Brigade were placed under orders of G.O.C. 15th Division. Orders were received from G.O.C. 15th Division that two Regiments were to move forward to old British front line trenches, and then to work forward and occupy German front line between the Lens Road Redoubt and the Loos Road Redoubt. The 3rd Dragoon Guards and Royals moved forward and occupied line as above without difficulty and started to consolidate the position. The strength of these two Units in the line was about 250 each. The N. Somerset Yeomanry were in Reserve with Brigade led horses.	
3 p.m.	Orders were received from IV Corps (G164) for two Regiments to occupy Loos. The 3rd Dragoon Guards and Royals advanced at once and occupied Loos, the 3rd Dragoon Guards	MTM

Army Form C. 2118.

6th Cavalry Brigade
1st September 1915

WAR DIARY
or
INTELLIGENCE SUMMARY
(Erase heading not required.)

Hour, Date, Place	Summary of Events and Information	Remarks and references to Appendices
26 Sept (contd)	3pm (Cap) taking that part of town to the right of and including PYLONS, TOWER, and the CRASSIER, and the Royals left half.	
	Advance to LOOS was carried out under fairly heavy shell fire.	
	About 300 Infantry, made up of Gordons, Camerons, and Argyll and Sutherland Highlanders who were found W. of the town, and retiring through LOOS itself, were collected by O.C. Royals and re-occupied trenches S.E. and E. of the town.	
	The 3rd Dragoon Guards connected up with the 14th Brigade on the right and with the Argyll and Sutherland Highlanders on the left.	
	The line then held by the Brigade was from CHALK PIT M 6 (a) 8.8 across the CRASSIER - G 36 c - round the S.E. and N.E. outskirts of town to about point 58.G.29.d.58	
9pm	Orders received, through 11th Corps, from 1st Army that General Campbell was to command all troops in LOOS and that his force were not to leave LOOS on any account.	

Army Form C. 2118.

4. Cavalry Brigade
September. 1915

WAR DIARY
or
INTELLIGENCE SUMMARY
(Erase heading not required.)

Hour, Date, Place		Summary of Events and Information	Remarks and references to Appendices
26th Sept. (Loos)	11.29 pm	The 1st Somerset Yeomanry who had been ordered earlier in the evening to occupy trenches G23.a. 44 to Loos Rd exclusive G28.d. report trenches held by Scots Guards. General Campbell requested General Briggs to send up 1st Somerset Yeomanry to him at Loos as fires at his disposal was inadequate, and the Infantry which has been collected were without food and done up.	
	12 midnight	The 1st Somerset Yeomanry arrived and took up position on left of 1st R. Dragoons, joining up with Guards Division on their left at 29.d. pot S. to point 58	
27th Sept.	2.30 AM	General Briggs arrived with 8th Cavalry Brigade and took over Command from General Campbell. The 8th Cavalry Brigade took over some of the line previously held by 4th Cavalry Brigade and the line held by the latter Brigade was as follows. 3rd Dragoon Guards from Eastern trenches 36.b.60 inclusive to roads 36.b. 27 Exclusive. Royals from Road 36.b. 27 inclusive to 30.c. point 53 inclusive.	WAM

1247 W 3299 200,000 (E) 8/14 J.B.C. & A. Forms/C. 2118/11.

Army Form C. 2118.

6th Cavalry Brigade
September 1915.

WAR DIARY
or
INTELLIGENCE SUMMARY
(Erase heading not required.)

Hour, Date, Place		Summary of Events and Information	Remarks and references to Appendices
27th Sept. (contd)	2.30 AM (contd)	N. Somerset Yeomanry from 30 C. House just south of point 22 inclusive to 29 D. just south of point 58. Each Regiment had two squadrons in front line and one in support. The infantry were all relieved and sent back. There was considerable shelling and sniping throughout the day.	
	3.45 P.M.	Heavy bombardment by both sides.	
	4. P.M.	Grande division attacked Hill 70, Puits 14 and Chalk Pits. The machine guns of the Brigade Co. operated.	
	6.30 P.M.	The Bombardment became less severe. Continued to improve trenches and defenses of Hoos during night which was very wet.	
28th Sept	4.30 AM	The Brigade stood to in its trenches. 2/Lieut BERRYMAN Royal Dragoons and 3 men were sent in direction of Hill 70 and CHALK PIT 25 A to get information. His report was of value and helped the Units of the Guards Division to estimate accurately the situation in these places. Loos was heavily shelled from 11.30 AM to 4 P.M.	WH

Army Form C. 2118.

WAR DIARY
or
INTELLIGENCE SUMMARY
(Erase heading not required.)

Instructions regarding War Diaries and Intelligence Summaries are contained in F. S. Regs., Part II. and the Staff Manual respectively. Title pages will be prepared in manuscript.

Hour, Date, Place		Summary of Events and Information	Remarks and references to Appendices
28th Sept.	3.45 p.m.	Guards Division attacked Puits 14 from CHALK PITS The machine guns of the Brigade co-operated.	
	7 p.m.	Orders received that the 2nd Brigade 1st Division would relieve the Brigade. Very heavy rain.	
	11.30 p.m.	Relief carried out.	
	1.30 A.M.	Relief completed and Regiments marched back to horses which were at 16 c (36 A)	
29th Sept.	8. A.M.	started to BOIS DES DAMES	
	11. A.M.	Arrived at BOIS DES DAMES	

N.T. Hoysted Capt.

121/7381

3 Cavalry Division

6th Cavalry Brigade

Vol ~~XIII~~ XI

Oct 15

Army Form C. 2118.

WAR DIARY
INTELLIGENCE SUMMARY
(Erase heading not required.)

6th Cavalry Brigade
for October 1915

Hour, Date, Place	Summary of Events and Information	Remarks and references to Appendices
Oct. 1st	Brigade in bivouac in the BOIS DES DAMES.	
3rd 12 noon	Brigade marched into Billets as under: 3rd Dragoon Guards ⎫ Royal Dragoons ⎬ RAIMBERT. "C" Bty. R.H.A. ⎭ Bde H.Q. ⎫ N. Somerset Yeomanry ⎬ FERFAY. 6th Field Ambulance ⎪ 13th Mobile Vet. Section ⎭	
19th 9 a.m.	Brigade moved to Billets as under: Bde. H.Q. .... HONINGHEM. 3rd Dragoon Guards .... BEAUMETZ-LES-AIRE. Royal Dragoons ...... LAIRES — LIVOSSART. North Somerset Yeomanry .... LAIRES. "C" Bty. R.H.A. .... FEBVIN PALFART. 6th Field Ambulance .... PALFART. 13th Mobile Vet. Section .... PALFART.	A.T.H

Army Form C. 2118.

WAR DIARY
INTELLIGENCE SUMMARY
(Erase heading not required.)

8th Cavalry Brigade
for October 1915.

Instructions regarding War Diaries and Intelligence Summaries are contained in F.S. Regs., Part II. and the Staff Manual respectively. Title pages will be prepared in manuscript.

Hour, Date, Place	Summary of Events and Information	Remarks and references to Appendices
Oct. 21st	Brigade moved into permanent billets as under:— Bde. H.Q. remained at HONENGHEM. 3rd Dragoon Guards to FONTAINE-LES-HERMANS — NEDONCHELLE — WESTREHEM. Royal Dragons — LIGNY-LES-AIRE — RELY — LATIRMAND. N. Somerset Yeomanry — NEDON — AMETTE — AUCHY-AU-BOIS. "C" Bty R.H.A. — LAIRES. 6th Field Ambulance — COTTES (ST HILAIRE) 13th Mobile Vet Section — AUCHY-AU-BOIS. Dismounted reinforcements arrived for units as under:— 3rd Dragoon Guards 2 officers 100 other ranks Royal Dragoons 2 officers 100 other ranks The establishment of the above two Regiments was thus increased to 26 officers 651 other ranks.	
Oct. 31st	The Bde. in billets as above.	W.T.H. W.T.Holyn Capt Bde Major 8th Cav Bde

1247 W 3259 200,000 (E) 8/14 J.B.C. & A. Forms/C. 2118/11.

3rd Cavalry Division

Ct. Cav. Bde.
Nov. 1/1915
Vol XII

121/7655

nil
CMG

Army Form C. 2118.

WAR DIARY
or
INTELLIGENCE SUMMARY
(Erase heading not required.)

6th Cavalry Brigade
for November 1915.

Hour, Date, Place	Summary of Events and Information	Remarks and references to Appendices
1st Nov	The following proceeded by motor bus from AUCHY-AU-BOIS to SERCUS to trace out works to be dug there by the 6th Cav Bde:— 3rd Dragoon Guards 2 officers 40 other ranks The Royal Dragoons 2 " 40 " North Somerset Yeomanry 2 " 20 " The above parts billetted in SERCUS.	
3rd	The following proceeded by motor bus from AUCHY-AU-BOIS to join parts which left on 1st:— 3rd D. Gs. 10 officers 80 men Royals 8 " 80 " N.S.Y. 4 " 40 "	
5th	G.O.C. and Staff Captain attended Divisional Staff Ride. The digging party from SERCUS rejoined Brigade.	W.R.H. Gilpin Capt
9th	The following proceeded by motor bus to OUDERDOM to work under Fifth Corps digging communication trenches.	

Army Form C. 2118.

6th Cavalry Brigade
for November 1915.

WAR DIARY
INTELLIGENCE SUMMARY
(Erase heading not required.)

Instructions regarding War Diaries and Intelligence Summaries are contained in F. S. Regs., Part II. and the Staff Manual respectively. Title pages will be prepared in manuscript.

Hour, Date, Place	Summary of Events and Information	Remarks and references to Appendices
Nov. 17. 10 AM.	3rd D. Gs. Officers Oricos 158 men. Royals 3 " 6 " 156 " N.S.Y. 2 " 3 " 81 " The Brigade marched into a new billetting area as under:- Bde Head quarters - - ROYON 3rd D. GS - - OFFIN — LOISON Royals - - CREQUY— TORCY. N.S.Y. - - HESMOND — LEBIEZ C B° R.H.A - - SAINS — LEZ- FRESSIN 6th Fld Ambulance - - TORCY. 13th Mobile Vet Section - - PETIT BEAURAIN.	Reference Map ARRAS 1:80,000.
Nov. 22nd	The digging Party which proceeded to OUDERDOM on Nov 9th returned by Motor bus arriving at ROYON 9.30pm.	
Nov. 23rd	The following proceeded by rail from MARESQUEL at 10.30 AM for POPERINGHE for digging work with 54th Corps. 3rd D. Gs. 5 officers 183 other ranks Royals 4 " 183 " 2nd Lt H. Dent 3rd D. Gs went to OUDERDOM to command Diggers Parties from 3rd Cav Div.	
Nov. 30th	Bde Class digging Party which proceeded to Poperinghe on Nov 23rd...	M Molyneux Capt. Bde Major 6th Cav Bde

WAR DIARY
or
INTELLIGENCE SUMMARY

(Erase heading not required.)

Army Form C. 2118.

6th Cavalry Brigade
30st November 1915.

Hour, Date, Place	Summary of Events and Information	Remarks and references to Appendices
	Following casualties occurred to Brigade Digging Detachment at OUDERDOM NOVEMBER 9th to 30th.	
	KILLED 3 O.R. 3rd dns 1st Royal Dragoons	
	WOUNDED 2 O.R. 3rd Dragoon Guards	
	4 O.R. 1st Royal Dragoons	
	1 O.R. N. Somerset Yeo.y	

6 Cavalry Bde.

Dec 1915
vol. XIII

3rd C.D.

Army Form C. 2118.

6th Cav Bde
For December 1915

WAR DIARY
or
INTELLIGENCE SUMMARY
(Erase heading not required.)

Instructions regarding War Diaries, and Intelligence Summaries are contained in F.S. Regs., Part II. and the Staff Manual respectively. Title pages will be prepared in manuscript.

Hour, Date, Place	Summary of Events and Information	Remarks and references to Appendices
Dec 7th 5 p.m.	The following returned to permanent billets from OUDTROM into Huts had been employed by 7xth Corps digging trenches:— 3rd D.G. 5 officers 180 other ranks Royal Dgns 4 " 174 "	
Dec 12th	The following proceeded under Command of Major P.C. Hardwick, Royal Dragoons by motor bus to LYNDE to proceed continue the work on the LA BELLE HOTESSE LINE 3rd Dragoon Guards 3 Officers and 86 other ranks Royal Dragoons 4 " 89 " A Somerset Yeomanry 2 " 56 "	
Dec 13.	The following proceeded to LYNDE by motor bus to form park whilst left on 10 inst. 3rd Dragoon Guards 1 officer 107 other ranks Royal Dragoons 1 " 107 " A Somerset Yeomanry 1 " 36 "	
Dec 20th	Lt Col H.D. O'Neill Comdg Royal Dragoons, accidentally killed by fall from horse General Staff Ride.	W Montgomery Capt

Army Form C. 2118.

6th Car Bde
December 1915.

WAR DIARY
or
INTELLIGENCE SUMMARY
(Erase heading not required.)

Instructions regarding War Diaries and Intelligence Summaries are contained in F. S. Regs., Part II. and the Staff Manual respectively. Title pages will be prepared in manuscript.

Hour, Date, Place	Summary of Events and Information	Remarks and references to Appendices
Dec 24th	The party under Major Hardwick at LYNDE beyond Ft Bde in personal shells.	
Dec 27 11am	Orders received for dismounted driver to be formed forthwith and to remain concentrated in Little meeting further orders to move. Battalion Known as 6th Battalion the dismounted Many from the Bde placed under command of Lt Colonel A Bent 3rd 9 Foot.	
	Composition of 6th Battalion	
	3rd 9 Fo. { Batt Hd-qrs 53 all ranks
{ 1 Company   320 -
{ Machine gun Detachment 42 -	
	Royals { 1 Company 310 all ranks
{ Machine gun Detachment 42 -
{ 19.4 guns	
	N.S.Y. { 1 Company 330 all ranks
{ Machine gun Detachment 42 all ranks
{ 9.4 guns	
	Total 1171 all ranks, 166 horses, 4.8 vehicles	M.J. Helen RHG O.C. 6 Car Bde

WAR DIARY
or
INTELLIGENCE SUMMARY

(Erase heading not required.)

Instructions regarding War Diaries and Intelligence Summaries are contained in F.S. Regs., Part II. and the Staff Manual respectively. Title pages will be prepared in manuscript.

Hour, Date, Place	Summary of Events and Information	Remarks and references
June 1st	The Machine Gun detachments of the 6th Battalion entrained at HARESQUEL at 12.16 to FOUQUEREUIL to form part of the 3rd Division of the Guards Infantry Corps.	
June 2nd	Transport and all whole of 6th Batt. marched to MARESQUEL and billetted there the night. 9 p.m. 9 a.m.	
June 3rd	6th Batt. entrained at MARESQUEL at 5.30 AM and left for FOUQUEREUIL at 9.15 AM to join 3rd Guards Bde.	
June 4th	Brigadier General Campbell sent Col Lord Bob and Rode Major proceeded to BETHUNE to take over Command of 1st Gds Infy Bde. Col Lord Bob returned on promotion to Bde.	W. T. H. Lytton Capt Bde Major Lt Col L Bde
June 5th & 6th		

Army Form C. 2118.

WAR DIARY
or
INTELLIGENCE SUMMARY
(Erase heading not required.)

6th Cavalry Bde
2nd Feb. 1916.

Hour, Date, Place	Summary of Events and Information	Remarks and references to Appendices
Feb 1st	G.O.C. and Bde Major returned from BETHUNE, General Kennedy comdg 7th Cav Bde having taken over command of 3rd Dismounted Bde.	
Feb 2nd	The 6th Battalion of our Dismounted Bde returned by rail to MARESQUEL, and companies rejoined their units in Armoured Billets. The following casualties occurred between Jan 3rd and Feb 1st in the 6th Battalion.	
	Killed Wounded Sick/missing	
	Officers	
	3rd D.G.s O.R. 6 21 1	
	Royals Officers 1 1 —	
	O.R. 11 39 5	Capt A.H. Maltalent killed
	N.S.Y. Officers — 1 —	Lt R.R. Helme wounded
	O.R. 3 15 1	
	Bde HQ Officers — 1 —	Capt. Poulton R.M.S.C. wounded
	O.R. — 1 —	
	Total Officers 1 3 —	
	O.R. 20 76 7	RFH

Army Form C. 2118.

6th Cav. Bde.
For Feb 1916.

WAR DIARY
or
INTELLIGENCE SUMMARY
(Erase heading not required.)

Army Form C. 2118.

Instructions regarding War Diaries and Intelligence Summaries are contained in F. S. Regs., Part II. and the Staff Manual respectively. Title pages will be prepared in manuscript.

Hour, Date, Place	Summary of Events and Information	Remarks and references to Appendices
Feb 29th	Under orders from Cav Corps the 5 machine gun section of the 6th Cav Bde were formed into a separate unit and designated 6th Cav Bde Machine Gun Squadron. The Squadron went into billets at OFFIN and will in future be known as a complete unit under the Bde Machine Gun Officer for Messing, Discipline and Employment in the field. The strength of the Squadron is as under:— Officers O.R. Horses Bicycles 7 213 299 9	W.S. Holgson Capt Bde Major 6th Cav Bde

1247 W 3239 200,000 (E) 8/14 J.B.C. & A. Forms/C. 2118/11.

Army Form C. 2118.

6th Cavalry Brigade
for March 1916

WAR DIARY
INTELLIGENCE SUMMARY
(Erase heading not required.)

Instructions regarding War Diaries and Intelligence Summaries are contained in F. S. Regs., Part II. and the Staff Manual respectively. Title pages will be prepared in manuscript.

Hour, Date, Place	Summary of Events and Information	Remarks and references to Appendices
March 8th	The G.O.C. inspected the 3rd Dragoon Guards at marching order.	
- 9th	" " " the Royal Dragoons	
- 10th	" " " N.S.Y.	
- 11th	" " " "C" By R.H.A.	
- 20th	The G.O.C. held a Tactical Tour for all Regtl Commanders and Squadron Leaders.	
1st — 31st	Brigade remained at Hanzeinville billets and continued Training.	

W. S. Hodgson Capt.
Bde Major
6th Cav Bde

WAR DIARY
or
INTELLIGENCE SUMMARY

(Erase heading not required.)

Army 8th Corps
April 1916

Hour, Date, Place	Summary of Events and Information	Remarks and references to Appendices
April 19th	G.O.C. 3rd Can Div. inspected N.S.Y. in Reconnaissance and other field work.	
20th	G.O.C. 3rd Can Div. inspected Royal Regiment in flank	
	Guard Scheme	
23rd	G.O.C. and Bde Major attended Divisional Staff Ride RECLINGHEM	
April 11th to 30th	Bde. trained in Hill 60 and continued training	

A.E. Hope Capt
Bde Major

Army Form C. 2118.

3 C

1st Cavalry Bde.
For May 1916

WAR DIARY
—or—
INTELLIGENCE SUMMARY
(Erase heading not required.)

Instructions regarding War Diaries and Intelligence Summaries are contained in F.S. Regs., Part II. and the Staff Manual respectively. Title pages will be prepared in manuscript.

Hour, Date, Place	Summary of Events and Information	Remarks and references to Appendices
May 1st	The North Somerset Yeomanry proceeded by march route to LE TOUQUET and went into camp near the GOLF LINKS. Provision for these Bde Camps at LE TOUQUET had been obtained in order that the Regts of the Bde might make use of the Sands off PARIS-PLAGE for drill there being no suitable ground in the permanent billetting area.	VC 18
11th & 12th	Brigadier General Campbell and Bde Major attended a Corps Staff ride in the neighborhood of ABBEVILLE.	
15th	The Brigade marched to ST RIQUIER and went into billets as under in order to take part in five days Divisional Training.	
	Bde HQrs Signal Troop — ST RIQUIER.	
	3rd D.G's — ONEUX	
	ROYALS — —	
	N.S.Y — —	
	6th M.G. Squadron — —	
	C 135 R.H.A — COULONVILLERS — MAISON ROLLAND	
	— ST RIQUIER.	
	The N.S.Y. and 6th M.G. Squadron joined the Bde at ST RIQUIER on	
16th to 20th	15th having marched from LE TOUQUET CAMP.	
	Bde took part in Divisional Training	
21st	The Bde less C 135 R.H.A. returned to permanent billets	
22"	Brigadier General D.G.M. CAMPBELL handed over command of the Bde on being appointed to command the 21st Division.	

D.J.E. Ryan Major

Army Form C. 2118.

6th Cav Bde
For May 1916

WAR DIARY
INTELLIGENCE SUMMARY

(Erase heading not required.)

Hour, Date, Place	Summary of Events and Information	Remarks and references to Appendices
May 23rd	Brigadier General A.E.W. HARMAN took over Command of the Bde.	A.E. Hogan Major Bde Major
24th	The 3rd D.Gs and 6th M.G. Squadron proceeded to LE TOUQUET Camp.	
27th	Royals moved into new billets at FRESSIN.	
30th	"C" Bty. returned Bde from St RIQUIER, where they remained after Bde left, and went into billets at WAMBERCOURT.	

Army Form C. 2118.

6th Cav. Bde
For June 1916.

WAR DIARY
or
INTELLIGENCE SUMMARY
(Erase heading not required.)

Vol 19

Hour, Date, Place		Summary of Events and Information	Remarks and references to Appendices
June 5th		The 3rd Dgns. returned to Permanent billets from PARIS-PLAGE CAMP.	
June 6th		The Royals march to PARIS PLAGE CAMP.	
June 18th		Notice received that all units of the Bde are to be concentrated in Permanent billets by June 22nd.	
June 21.		The Royals returned to Permanent billets from PARIS PLAGE CAMP.	
June 24th 8.15 p.m.		Bde. assembled at 7 cards 220 yards S. of Pm. Pl. S? VAAST and marched via HESDIN — REGNAVILLE — LABROYE to DOMVAAST	
June 25. 3 a.m.		Bde. went into billets as under:—	
		Bde H.Q. & 6th Signal Troop ⎫	
		C./35. R.H.A. ⎬ DOMVAST	
		6th M.G. Squadron	
		13th Mob. Vet. Sect. ⎭	
		3rd Dgs. — — — — — — MARCHEVILLE	
		Royals — — — — — — BRAILLY	
		N.S.Y. — — — — — — FROYELLES	

R.T. Halpin Major

Army Form C. 2118.

WAR DIARY
INTELLIGENCE SUMMARY
(Erase heading not required.)

6th Cas. Bde.
for June

Hour, Date, Place	Summary of Events and Information	Remarks and references to Appendices
June 25th 9 p.m.	6th Cas. Fld Amb. – – – CORNEHOTTE Bde. assembled at X roads 700 yds N of St X N YVRENCHEUX and marched via YVRENCH – DOMQUER – X roads B of CHAUSEE BRUNEHAUT – DOMART – EN – PONTHIEU to ST LEGER – LES – DOMART Bde. went into billets as under: Wet day –	
June 26th 2 AM	Bde H.Q and 6th Signal Troop ⎫ 3rd Sqn ⎬ ST LEGER – LES – DOMART. 6th M.G. Squadron ⎭ C B. RHA 6th Cas Fld Amb 13th Mob Vet Royals – – – – – – PERNOIS N.S.Y. – – – – – – BELLETTRE	
9.30 p.m.	Bde moved at N.W. entrance of VIGNACOURT and marched to CORBIE EAST AREA.	
June 27. 4·30 AM	Bde went into bivouac at BONNAY at a bout – West of E of D'ANCRE after a very hot march.	

Army Form C. 2118.

WAR DIARY
or
INTELLIGENCE SUMMARY

(Erase heading not required.)

Instructions regarding War Diaries and Intelligence Summaries are contained in F. S. Regs., Part II. and the Staff Manual respectively. Title pages will be prepared in manuscript.

1/5 Cheshire Bde.
For June 1916

Hour, Date, Place		Summary of Events and Information	Remarks and references to Appendices
June 28th	10 am	Bde in bivouac at BONNAY. Very wet day. Divn Operation Order No.1 dated 27/6/16 received ordering Bde to be ready to leave at 7.30 a.m. on 29th inst.	
	5.30 pm	Orders received that move was postponed 24 hours.	
June 29th	10.30 A.M.	Off rendered 3rd Bde was sent under orders received from Divn to reconnoitre route to be followed to the Bde in case of an advance. Lt Anderson Royals was sent to Divisn Hqrs as liaison officer with 29th Infantry Div.	
	2 pm	"A" Squadron Royals under Capt H.T. Mills detailed to Divisional Cavalry with 19th Infantry Division.	
	11.10 A.M.	Bde in bivouac at BONNAY. G.O.C. and 2 Bde Major went to SHAMROCK TREE observation post to reconnoitre BLACKWOOD and surrounding country.	
June 30th	10. A.M.		
	2.30 pm	Regtl Commanders arrived at French Hd.quarters	
	6.30 pm	Bde in bivouac at BONNAY. G.O.C. had a conference with Commanding Officers	

W.T. Holgan Major

1247 W 3299 200,000 (E) 8/14 J.B.C. & A. Forms/C. 2118/11.

Army Form C. 2118.

WAR DIARY
INTELLIGENCE SUMMARY
(Erase heading not required.)

6th Cas. Bde.
for June

Instructions regarding War Diaries and Intelligence Summaries are contained in F. S. Regs., Part II. and the Staff Manual respectively. Title pages will be prepared in manuscript.

Hour, Date, Place		Summary of Events and Information	Remarks and references to Appendices
June 25th		6th Cas 2td Amb. — — CORNEHOTTE	
	9 p.m.	Bde assembled at x roads 700 yds N of K4 in YVRENCH edx	
		and marched via YVRENCH – DOMQUER – x roads B	
		of CHAUSEE BRUNEHAUT – DOMART-EN-PONTHIEU to	
		ST LEGER-LES-DOMART	
June 26th	2 A.M.	Bde went into billets as under: Rest day –	
		Bde H.Q. and 6th Signal Troop	
		3rd Dgs	
		6th M.G. Squadn ST LEGER-LES-DOMART.	
		C. B5. R.H.A.	
		6th Cas 2td Amb	
		13th Mob Vet	
		Royals — — — — PERNOIS	
		N.S.Y. — — — — BELLETTRE	
	9.30 p.m.	Bde assembled at N.W. Entrance to VIGNACOURT and	
		marched to CORBIE EAST AREA.	
June 27th A·30 A.M.		Bde went into bivouac at BONNAY at about 4 a.m. E of D'ANCRE after a very hot march.	

Army Form C. 2118.

WAR DIARY
or
INTELLIGENCE SUMMARY
(Erase heading not required.)

O/C Car Coy
for June 1916

Instructions regarding War Diaries and Intelligence Summaries are contained in F. S. Regs., Part II. and the Staff Manual respectively. Title pages will be prepared in manuscript.

Hour, Date, Place		Summary of Events and Information	Remarks and references to Appendices
June 28th		Bde in bivouac at BONNAY. Very wet day.	
	10 a.m.	Divl. Operation Order No. 1. dated 27/6/16 received ordering Bde. to be ready to move at 7.30 a.m. on 29th inst.	
	5.30 p.m.	Orders received that move was postponed 24 hours.	
	10.30 A.M.	2nd remount 3rd Dgs was sent with orders received from Divn. to reconnoitre route to be followed by Bde in case of an advance.	
	2 p.m.	Lt Anderson Royals was sent to Divn. Hd as liaison officer with 19th Infantry Divn.	
	11.10 A.M.	"A" Squadron Royals under Capt H T Mills detailed Divisional Cavalry with 19th Infantry Division.	
June 29th	10. A.M.	Bde in bivouac at BONNAY. G.O.C. and Bde Major went to SHAMROCK TREE Observation post to reconnoitre BLACK WOOD and surrounding country.	
	2.30 p.m.	Regtl. Commanders arrived at Brigade Headquarters	
June 30th		Bde in bivouac at BONNAY.	
	6.30 p.m.	G.O.C. held a conference with Comdg. Officers	

H. T. Hogan Major

Army Form C. 2118.

WAR DIARY
INTELLIGENCE SUMMARY

for 6th Cavalry Bde
for June 1916

(Erase heading not required.)

Instructions regarding War Diaries and Intelligence Summaries are contained in F. S. Regs., Part II. and the Staff Manual respectively. Title pages will be prepared in manuscript.

Hour, Date, Place	Summary of Events and Information	Remarks and references to Appendices
6.30 p.m.	A. Gordon Boyds moved to HENENCOURT WOOD and came under orders of G.O.C. 19th Infantry Division.	R.T. Hodgson Major Brigadier

Army Form C. 2118.

WAR DIARY
— or —
INTELLIGENCE SUMMARY
(Erase heading not required.)

6th Cav. Bde.
For July 1916.

Vol 2 O

Instructions regarding War Diaries and Intelligence Summaries are contained in F. S. Regs, Part II. and the Staff Manual respectively. Title pages will be prepared in manuscript.

Hour, Date, Place		Summary of Events and Information	Remarks and references to Appendices
July 1st	7.30 A.M.	Bde. formed up in avenue at BONNAY ready to move.	Reference map 1:100000
	7.45 A.M.	Bde. off saddled and stood ready to move at 1 hours notice.	
	12 noon	Message received that there was no chance of the Bde. being required to move before 6pm at the earliest.	
	5.30 pm.	Message received that Bde. was to be prepared to move at 2 hours notice.	
	5.35 pm.	Message received saying that Gunden Royals attached to 1st Ind. Division would join the Bde. tonight.	
	7 pm.	Message received saying that Bde. would not be advancing from concentration area to-morrow.	
July 2nd		Bde. in bivouac at BONNAY.	
	8.40 pm.	Message received saying that Bde. would be ready to move at 2 hrs notice after 9 am 3rd inst.	
	6.35 pm.	Officer & 8 O.R. Cav. Fld. Ambulance proceeded to MORLANCOURT to assist in case of German bombard.	

W.R.Hodgson
Major

Army Form C. 2118.

WAR DIARY
INTELLIGENCE SUMMARY
(Erase heading not required.)

6th Cav. Bde
July 1916

Instructions regarding War Diaries and Intelligence Summaries are contained in F.S. Regs., Part II. and the Staff Manual respectively. Title pages will be prepared in manuscript.

Hour, Date, Place	Summary of Events and Information	Remarks and references to Appendices
July 3rd	Bde in Bivouac at BONNAY.	Reference maps
7.30 pm	Orders received that Bde would probably move WEST to-morrow.	1:100000
July 4th 1 am	Orders received for Bde to march at 5.15 am to the HALLENCOURT area.	
5.15 am	Bde marched by the NEUVILLE – AMIENS – AILLY – SUR SOMME – SOUES – AIRAINES route to ALLERY. Bde halted to off-saddle, water and feed at DREUIL-LES-AMIENS.	
4 pm	Bde went into billets as under:- Bde HQ 6th Signal Troop 3rd DG 13th M.G. Sect. } MEREIESSART Royals M.S.Y. C-506 R.H.A. 6th M.G. Squadron } ALLERY 6th Cav Fld Amb. WIRY-AU-MONT LE HAMEL	
July 5th 5.30 AM	Orders received for 1 officer and 58 O.R. from dismounted Squadron of each Regt to be held in readiness to proceed by rail from LONGPRE to MERICOURT for possible battlefield etc under 15th Corps.	A.S. Holgan Major

Army Form C. 2118.

6th Cav Bde
for July 1916

WAR DIARY
INTELLIGENCE SUMMARY

(Erase heading not required.)

Instructions regarding War Diaries and Intelligence Summaries are contained in F. S. Regs., Part II. and the Staff Manual respectively. Title pages will be prepared in manuscript.

Hour, Date, Place		Summary of Events and Information	Remarks and references to Appendices
July 5th	6 p.m.	Advance party left LONGPRÉ.	Reference maps 1:100000
July 6th	4 p.m.	Orders received that Bde was to be ready to move at 12 hours notice from 6 a.m. July 7th.	
July 7th		Bde in billets ready to move at 12 hours notice.	
	6.30 p.m.	Orders with regard to state of readiness cancelled.	
July 8th	1 A.M.	Orders received for Bde to be ready to return to the QUERRIEUX neighbourhood any hour after 1 p.m. July 8th.	
	12 noon	Orders received for Bde to march at once in rear of 7th and 8th Cav Bde to CORBIE.	
	2.15 p.m.	Bde assembled at EASTERN exit of AIRAINES and marched via SOUES — PICQUIGNY — AMIENS — CAMON — LAMOTTE — VECQUEMONT to CORBIE.	
July 9th	2 a.m.	Bde arrived at CORBIE and went into bivouac NNW WEST of the town.	
		Bde HQ established in PLACE DE LA REPUBLIC.	
	4.30 p.m.	Bde moved into bivouac at VAUX-SUR-SOMME	
July 10th		Bde in bivouac as above.	
July 11th	9 a.m.	1 officer and 70 other ranks from dismounted squadrons proceeded by bus from CORBIE to MERICOURT for salvage duties under 15th Corps.	

K.T. Halyer Major

Army Form C. 2118.

6th Cav Bde
for July 1916

WAR DIARY
INTELLIGENCE SUMMARY
(Erase heading not required.)

Instructions regarding War Diaries and Intelligence Summaries are contained in F. S. Regs., Part II. and the Staff Manual respectively. Title pages will be prepared in manuscript.

Hour, Date, Place	Summary of Events and Information	Remarks and references to Appendices
July 12th	Bde in bivouac at VAUX-SUR-SOMME	Reference map:
9.30 AM	Bde Hqrs and senior Majors of Regts reconnoitred roads for Cavalry by MEAULTE — FILIFORM TREE — BRONFAY FARM — CARNOY to MONTAUBAN.	Trench map sheet 57 d S.E. & S.W.
13th	Bde in bivouac at VAUX-SUR-SOMME	
14th 4am	Bde in bivouac as above ready to move at half an hour notice from 4am	
8pm	State of readiness cancelled during night	
15th 5am	Bde in bivouac as above ready to move at half an hour notice from 5am	
8.30pm	State of readiness cancelled during night	
16th 6am	Bde in bivouac as above ready to move at 12 hours notice from 6am	
12.30pm	State of readiness extended to 4 hours.	
17th	Bde in bivouac as above ready to move at 4 hours notice	
18th	"	
19th 2pm	Bde moved into billets at LAHOUSSOYE. A relief of dismounted men of Bde who had been attached to the 7th and 34th Divisions was carried out.	

W. T. Holgrove(?) LtCol

Army Form C. 2118.

6th Cav Bde
R July 1916

WAR DIARY
INTELLIGENCE SUMMARY
(Erase heading not required.)

Instructions regarding War Diaries and Intelligence Summaries are contained in F. S. Regs., Part II. and the Staff Manual respectively. Title pages will be prepared in manuscript.

Hour, Date, Place	Summary of Events and Information	Remarks and references to Appendices
July 20th 2.30pm	GOC 3rd Can Div held Staff Ride in neighbourhood of BONNAY. GOC Bde, Major OC C Sqn RHA and OC Bt. M.G. Squadron attended. Bde in billets at LA NEUVILLE.	Reference Map 1:100000
21st	Bde in billets at LANEUVILLE.	
22nd	As above	
23rd	As above	
24th	As above	
25. 8 AM	Following party under Lt. Col. WORMALD. D.S.O. Royals proceeded by march route to BECOURT to work under III Corps at digging and improving trenches in the neighbourhood of CONTALMAISON. 3rd Dn 3 officers 93 other ranks Royals 3 . 92 . — N.S.Y 2 - 92 - The party rode up to BECOURT the horses returning to the Bde billets at LA NEUVILLE.	

W J Walker Major

Army Form C. 2118.

6th Cavalry Bde
for July 1916.

WAR DIARY
INTELLIGENCE SUMMARY
(Erase heading not required.)

Instructions regarding War Diaries and Intelligence Summaries are contained in F. S. Regs., Part II. and the Staff Manual respectively. Title pages will be prepared in manuscript.

Hour, Date, Place	Summary of Events and Information	Remarks and references to Appendices
July 27th 8 am	A party similar in numbers to that which proceeded on the 23rd left to join 1st Party for shipping etc. on time	Reference Map 1:100000
MAMETZ - CONTALMAISON		
29th 3:30 pm	Two attachments of Afrino each from 6th R.E. Squadron proceeded to Dmt moved to BECOURT for watering and provisioning strong posts. All horses and limbers returned to Bde Horse Lines detachments were placed under the 15th Division.	
30th 12:30 pm	A party consisting of officers and N.S. other ranks from each Sqdn proceeded to Dmt moved to BECOURT to billet, a similar number of each Regt. digging at CONTALMAISON and MAMETZ.	
6:15 pm	Orders received to the effect that all digging and watering parties were to be relieved on 31st and that the Soixan would move west on August 1st.	

W.S. [signature]

Army Form C. 2118.

6th Cav Bde
for July 1916

WAR DIARY
or
INTELLIGENCE SUMMARY
(Erase heading not required.)

Instructions regarding War Diaries and Intelligence Summaries are contained in F. S. Regs., Part II. and the Staff Manual respectively. Title pages will be prepared in manuscript.

Hour, Date, Place	Summary of Events and Information	Remarks and references to Appendices
July 31st 2.15AM	Orders received for horse and transport to escort up to join head of working parties and 6th R. G. Squadron from BECOURT	Reference Map 1:100,000
9.30AM	Horses and transport of parties returned to above left.	
6 p.m.	Working parties returned Regt in bivouac.	

Casualties July 1916.

Unit	Killed	Wounded	D. of Wounds
3rd Dragoon Guards	—	3	1
1st R. Dragoons	—	7	1
N. Somerset Yeo.	—	6	—
6th M. Gun Sqn (M.Gun Corps)	—	1	—
TOTAL	—	17	1

W.P. Halyer Major
Bde. Major

1247 W 8290 200,000 (E) 8/14 J.B.C. & A. Forms/C. 2118/11.

Army Form C. 2118.

6th Cavalry Bde
for August 1916.

WAR DIARY
INTELLIGENCE SUMMARY
(Erase heading not required.)

Instructions regarding War Diaries and Intelligence Summaries are contained in F. S. Regs., Part II. and the Staff Manual respectively. Title pages will be prepared in manuscript.

Hour, Date, Place	Summary of Events and Information	Remarks and references to Appendices
Aug 1st 6 am	Bde assembled at & rendez double L de LA NEUVILLE and marched via DAOURS – VECQUEMONT – road just S. of AMIENS CITADELLE to LA CHAUSSEE – thence via PICQUIGNY – SOUES to billets and bivouac at SOUES and LAMESGE.	Maps 1/100,000
Aug 2nd 5 am	Bde assembled at W ent of SOUES and marched via AIRAINES – SOREL – LIERCOURT – PONT REMY – BUIGNY L'ABBE – VAUCHELLES to NEUF MOULIN, and went into bivouac as under:-	
	Bde HQ 6th Signal Trp 3rd Bde 6th M.G. Squadron } CAOURS	
	Royals C. 3rd R.H.A. N.S.Y. } NEUF MOULIN.	
	Bde in bivouac as above.	
Aug 3rd 11 pm	Orders received that the Bde would march on 4th and 5th to permanent billeting area ROYON – HESMOND – OFFIN – FRESSIN	

Army Form C. 2118.

6th Cavalry Bde
for August 1916

WAR DIARY
INTELLIGENCE SUMMARY
(Erase heading not required.)

Instructions regarding War Diaries and Intelligence Summaries are contained in F. S. Regs., Part II. and the Staff Manual respectively. Title pages will be prepared in manuscript.

Hour, Date, Place	Summary of Events and Information	Remarks and references to Appendices
Aug 4th 5am	Bde assembled at X roads just N of M of MILLENCOURT and marched via DOMVAST — MARCHEVILLE — CRECY — LIGESCOURT to MAINTENAY. Bde went into horse and cattle as under:- Bde H.Q. and 6th Signal Troop Royals 3rd S.Y. 6th M.G. Squadron C "B" R.H.A. } MAINTENAY 3rd Dgs. — ROUSSENT. Bde assembled in two columns as under and marched to permanent billets:- Western Column. Bde HQrs, 6th Signal Troop, 3rd Dgns, N.S.Y. assembled at X roads 1 road N of MAINTENAY and marched via BOIRE – LE – SEC — B of BEAUR — AINVILLE Eastern Column. Royals, C "B" R.H.A., 6th M.G. Squadron assembled at St REMY – AUX – BOIS and marched via GOUY – ST – ANDRÉ – MARÉSQUEL — AUBIN – ST VAAST	Reference Map 1:100,000 MH MH Ayr Maj.
Aug 5th 7.30am		

Army Form C. 2118.

WAR DIARY
INTELLIGENCE SUMMARY
(Erase heading not required.)

6th Cav. Bde
for August 1916

Instructions regarding War Diaries and Intelligence Summaries are contained in F. S. Regs., Part II. and the Staff Manual respectively. Title pages will be prepared in manuscript.

Hour, Date, Place	Summary of Events and Information	Remarks and references to Appendices
Aug 5. 12 noon	Bde went into billets as under:- Bde H.Q. ⎱ ROYON. 6th Signal Troop ⎰ 3rd Dgs - - - OFFIN — LOISON — Pt BEAURAIN Royals - - - FRESSIN. N.S.Y. - - - HESMOND — LEBIEZ C/J Bty RHA - - - WAMBERCOURT. 6th M.G. Squadron - - - CAVRON. 6th Cav Fld Amb - - - OFFIN. 13th M.V. Section - - - LEBIEZ.	WD
Aug 8. 4pm	Following detail of officers entrained at FRUGES and proceeded to ARRAS for attachment to 64th Inf Bde 21st Div for work in the line:- 3rd Dgs 1 offr 2 other ranks Royals 1 officer 3 " " N.S.Y. 3 " "	WD

Army Form C. 2118.

WAR DIARY
INTELLIGENCE SUMMARY
(Erase heading not required.)

6th Cavalry Bde
for August 1916

Instructions regarding War Diaries and Intelligence Summaries are contained in F. S. Regs., Part II. and the Staff Manual respectively. Title pages will be prepared in manuscript.

Hour, Date, Place	Summary of Events and Information	Remarks and references to Appendices
Aug 9th	Following alterations in billeting area took place	MTH
	Bde HQ & 6th Signal Troop from ROYON to EMBRY.	
	NSY Regt HQ from HESMOND to ROYON	
13th	6th Car Hd Amb from OFFIN to HESMOND	MTH
	The following parts from the Bde proceeded by lorry to II Corps area for laying cables:—	
	3rd Sqn 2 officers 59 other ranks	
	Royals 1 " 60 "	
	N.S.Y. 1 " 61 "	
	Total 4 " 180 "	
20th	Shepards of Nyperes with 21st Div were relieved by a party	MTH
	of same strength. The M.S.O. furnishing an officer & the	
	place of the Royals.	
23rd	A notification was received that the Divison would probably move on the 28th inst.	MTH
24th	The above notification was cancelled.	MTH
31st	The party which left the Bde on the 13th inst. for duty under II Corps was relieved by a party of the	MTH

Army Form C. 2118.

WAR DIARY
INTELLIGENCE SUMMARY
(Erase heading not required.)

6th Can. Bde.
for August 1916.

Hour, Date, Place	Summary of Events and Information	Remarks and references to Appendices
	Same strength. The Relief was carried up in two parties the 1st on 31st and the 2nd party on the 1st Sept. Major Cliff 3rd Bgn went up with this party to command the 3rd Can Div parts	A.D. Holyon Major Bde. Major.

Army Form C. 2118.

WAR DIARY 6th Cav Bde   September 1916

INTELLIGENCE SUMMARY

(Erase heading not required.)

Instructions regarding War Diaries and Intelligence Summaries are contained in F. S. Regs., Part II, and the Staff Manual respectively. Title pages will be prepared in manuscript.

Hour, Date, Place	Summary of Events and Information	Remarks and references to Appendices
5th Sept.	Following detail of Sappers proceeded to Cav to ARRAS to relieve Sapps there doing duty in the line with 21st Div:— 3rd Dgs 1 Sgt 2 OR Royals 3 — N.S.Y. 1 Officer 3 OR	N.T.H.
6th Sept.	Notification received that 3rd Cav Div would be moving on on any day after 9th Sept.	N.T.H.
7th Sept.	The 6th A.G. Squadron, parts of Sappers attached 21st Div and the digging Parks with II Corps rejoined the Brigade.	N.T.H.
9th Sept.	Orders received that Div would move to the AUTHIE valley prior to moving.	NOH
10.30AM 10th Sept.	The Bde marched in two columns to the valley of the AUTHIE River via GOUY STANDRE – SAULCHOY and via LAMBUS ST JOSSE – DOURIEZ	NOH
1 p.m.	Bde Went into Billets and bivouac as under:— Bde HQ. 6th Signal Troop } DOMINOIS Royals C. Bde R.H.A 13 M.V.S	

N.T. Hopper B/Major Bde Cav Bde

Army Form C. 2118.

WAR DIARY
INTELLIGENCE SUMMARY
(Erase heading not required.)

6th Cav. Bde.
September 1916

Hour, Date, Place	Summary of Events and Information	Remarks and references to Appendices
Sept 10th	3rd Dgs. — — — ARGOULES.	
1 pm	N.S.Y. ⎫ SAULCHOY	
	6th M.G. Squadron ⎬	
	6th Cav. Fld Amb. ⎭	M.T.H.
Sept 11th		
2 pm	Bde marched in two columns one by VIRONCHEAUX — CRECY — FOREST L'ABBAYE and the other by LIGESCOURT — CRECY — CANCHY to billets and bivouacs as under:	
5.30 pm	Bde HQ ⎫	
	6th Signal Troop ⎬ DRUCAT.	
	Royals ⎪	
	"C" 106 R.H.A. ⎪	
	13th M.V.S. ⎭	
	3rd Dgs. — LE PLESSIEL	
	N.S.Y. ⎫ NEUIZZY-L'HOPITAL	M.T.H.
	6th M.G. Squadron ⎭	
	6th Cav. Fld Amb. CANCHY.	M.T.H.
Sept 12th		
11 AM.	Bde marched by VAUCHELLES — EPAGNE — PONT REMY — L'ETOILE — FLIXECOURT to LA CHAUSSÉE:	M.T.H.
5 pm	Bde met with bivouac as under:	

Army Form C. 2118.

6th Can. Bde.
September 1916.

WAR DIARY
or
INTELLIGENCE SUMMARY
(Erase heading not required.)

Hour, Date, Place	Summary of Events and Information	Remarks and references to Appendices
Sept. 12th 5 pm	Bde H.Q. 6th Signal Troop 6th M.G. Squadron } LACHAUSSEE EAST. 6th Can. Fd Amb. Royal 13 F.M.V.S. N.S.Y. LACHAUSSEE NORTH. 3rd Dgns C Bty R.H.A. } LACHAUSSEE WEST.	
Sept 13th	Bde remained in above bivouacs.	
10 AM	GOC and Bde Major attended Conference at Divisional Headquarters.	N.T.R.
2.30 pm	GOC held Conference at Bde H.Q. which Comdg Officers of all units attended.	N.T.R.
Sept 14th 8 am	Bde marched by St SAUVEUR — AMIENS northern outskirts — RIVERY — CAMON — LAMOTTE to BUSSY	M.H.
11 am	Bde watered at LAMOTTE.	

Army Form C. 2118.

6th Can. Bde
September 1916

WAR DIARY
or
INTELLIGENCE SUMMARY
(Erase heading not required.)

Instructions regarding War Diaries and Intelligence Summaries are contained in F. S. Regs., Part II. and the Staff Manual respectively. Title pages will be prepared in manuscript.

Hour, Date, Place		Summary of Events and Information	Remarks and references to Appendices
	1 p.m.	Bde halted WEST of BOSSY to allow 2nd Inf Div 2 mile. Can Div to clear the village.	
	2 p.m.	Bde Hqrs mt. bivouac just N of BOSSY.	
	3.15 p.m.	Bde. H.Q. established in BOSSY CHATEAU. Warning order received from Division that Div would be concentrated with 7th 28th Bdes just W. of BONNAY and 8th Bde just W of LA NEUVILLE by 11 a.m. to-morrow 15th inst.	N.T.N.
Sept. 15th	9 a.m.	Brigade marched to a point just S.W. of BONNAY where it arrived, off-saddled and fed.	N.T.N.
	11 a.m.	Brigade ready to move at 30 mins notice.	
	6.45 p.m.	Order received that Bde would bivouac in present positions for the night and be prepared to move at 30 mins notice from 9 a.m. following morning.	N.T.N.
Sept. 16th	6 a.m.	State of readiness altered to 30 mins from 9 a.m.	
	11.40 p.m.	Orders received that Bde would move at 7 a.m. 17th inst to a bivouac just S. of PONT NOYELLES.	N.T.N.

N.G. Stopford Lt. Col
Bde Major
6th Can Bde

Army Form C. 2118.

6th Cavalry Bde
For September 1916

WAR DIARY
INTELLIGENCE SUMMARY
(Erase heading not required.)

Instructions regarding War Diaries and Intelligence Summaries are contained in F. S. Regs., Part II. and the Staff Manual respectively. Title pages will be prepared in manuscript.

Hour, Date, Place		Summary of Events and Information	Remarks and references to Appendices
Sept 17th	7 am	Bde move to relief above. A very thick fog until 9 am.	
	8.45 am	Bde halt side Airaines just S. of PONT NOYELLES.	N.T.R.
	10 am	State of readiness reversed.	
Sept 18th		Bde in bivouac as above. A very wet day.	N.T.R.
Sept 19th		" " " " Wet night	N.T.R.
Sept 20th		" " " " Wet morning.	N.T.R.
Sept 21st	12 noon	Orders received that Bde would move W. of AMIENS the following day.	N.T.R.
Sept 22nd	12.30 pm	Bde marched by VECQUEMONT — LAMOTTE — AMIENS Station — PICQUIGNY to Airaines and billets at SOUES — LE MESGE. arriving 5.45 pm.	N.T.R.
Sept 23rd	9.45 am	Bde marched by FLIXECOURT — N. bank of R. SOMME — DOMART-EN-PONTHIEU to bivouacs and billets at BEAUCOURT — BEAUVOIR-RIVIERE — WAVANS —	N.T.R.
Sept 24th	7.30 am	Bde marched by AUXI-LE-CHATEAU — LE PONCHEL — LABROYE to billets on NORTH bank of L'AUTHIE RIVER between RAYE-SUR-AUTHIE and ROUSSENT both inclusive. Units were billeted as under:— Bde H.Q. & ("A"Signal Troop) DOURIEZ C"B"S, R.H.A. 6th Cav. Fld. Amb.	N.T.R.

Army Form C. 2118.

6th Cavalry Brigade
for September 1916.

WAR DIARY
or
INTELLIGENCE SUMMARY
(Erase heading not required.)

Hour, Date, Place	Summary of Events and Information	Remarks and references to Appendices
Sept. 25th	3rd Dragoon Guards — MAINTENAY.	
	Royals — — RAYE-SUR-AUTHIE	
	North Somerset Yeomanry — SAULCHOY.	
	6th M.G. Squadron — ROUSSENT.	
	13th M.V.S. — SAULCHOY.	A.T.H.
26th	Bde in above area.	M.T.H.
	Following drafts have rejoined the Bde from 2nd Army.	M.T.H.
	Officers O.R.	
	3rd D.Gs. 1 44	
	Royals 1 35	
	N.S.Y. 2 54	
	Having following drafts are still attached to 2nd Army.	
	Officers O.R.	
	3rd D.Gs. 1 21 men	
	Royals — 30	
	N.S.Y. — 29	
29th	Orders received that Bde has to march following villages to-morrow for 1st Indian Cav. Div. on 29th inst. A.T.H.	
	RAYE-SUR-AUTHIE — SAULCHOY — ROUSSENT — DOURIEZ	M.T.H.
29th 9am	March moved with new billets no incident	

Army Form C. 2118.

6 A Cav. Bde
for September 1916.

WAR DIARY
INTELLIGENCE SUMMARY
(Erase heading not required.)

Instructions regarding War Diaries and Intelligence Summaries are contained in F. S. Regs., Part II. and the Staff Manual respectively. Title pages will be prepared in manuscript.

Hour, Date, Place	Summary of Events and Information	Remarks and references to Appendices
Sept 29. (continued)	ROYALS to ST JOSSE — ST AUBIN — LE MOULINEL. N.S.Y. " MERLIMONT — CUC Q. 13th Hrs " CUC Q C'Ds RHA " AIRON ST VAAST. 6th Cav Bde Amb " TRANG DU FLIERS. 6th Cav Bde Headquarters moved to VERTON.	M
Sept 30. 9 am	Casualties September 1916. 	UNIT	KILLED	WOUNDED	MISSING	 	---	---	---	---	 	3. Dragoon Guards	1	8	2	 	Royals	-	7	1	 	N. Somerset Yeo.	-	5	-	 	C.M/Gun Sqn	-	3	-	 The above casualties occurred among shipping parties found by the Bde during the month.	

A.P. Holgan Major
Brit Major
6th Cav Bde.

Vol 23

WAR DIARY.

6th CAVALRY BRIGADE.

1st to 31st OCTOBER, 1916.

Army Form C. 2118.

6th Car Bde
for October 1916

WAR DIARY
or
INTELLIGENCE SUMMARY

(Erase heading not required.)

Hour, Date, Place	Summary of Events and Information	Remarks and references to Appendices
Oct 1st	Bdo in billets as under :-	
	Bde H.Q. — VERTON	
	3rd Bde — MAINTENAY.	
	Royals — S'JOSSE – S'AUBIN – LE MOULINEL	
	N.S.Y. — MERLIMONT – CUCQ	A.M.
	C B5 RHA — AIRON S'VAAST.	
	6th M.G. Squadron — ROUSSENT.	
	6th Cav Fld Amb — RANG-DU-FLIERS	
	13th M.V.S. — CUCQ	
Oct 2nd 8am	The following should men returned at HESDIN fr attachment to Heavy Arty	N.T.R.
	3rd L. 3 officers 46 other ranks	
	Royals 1 " 26 "	
	N.Y. 1 " 54 "	

Army Form C. 2118.

2n 6th Cav. Bde.

October 1916.

WAR DIARY
INTELLIGENCE SUMMARY
(Erase heading not required.)

Instructions regarding War Diaries and Intelligence Summaries are contained in F. S. Regs., Part II. and the Staff Manual respectively. Title pages will be prepared in manuscript.

Hour, Date, Place	Summary of Events and Information	Remarks and references to Appendices

October 20th	Following detail proceeded to Acq to Boozincourt to relieve parts there making under Reserve Army.
	
	      Officers other ranks
	3rd Dgns 1 65
	Royals 2 69
	N.S.Y. 1 70
	Total 4 204
	
	Lt. Col. A. SHIRE Royals proceeded in command of 6th Cav Bde Pats.
	
	The following changes in billeting areas took place.
	3rd Bgn from MAINTENAY to { RANG DU FLIERS
	            AIRON ST VAAST
	            AIRON NOTRE DAME
	            CAMPIGNEULLES-LES-
	            GRANDES.
	
	6th M.G. Squadron from ROUSSENT to VERTON.
	
	6th Cav Fld Amb from RANG DU FLIERS to MERLIMONT PLAGE
		sent 57D/1 3/10/1916
		
		N.T.H
		
		K.T.Hobson
		Major

October 21st		

Army Form C. 2118.

6th Cav. Bde.
October 1916

WAR DIARY
or
INTELLIGENCE SUMMARY
(Erase heading not required.)

Instructions regarding War Diaries and Intelligence Summaries are contained in F. S. Regs., Part II. and the Staff Manual respectively. Title pages will be prepared in manuscript.

Hour, Date, Place		Summary of Events and Information	Remarks and references to Appendices
21st	21st Oct.	"E" 'B'ty R.H.A. with remainder of I. & 8th R.H.A. proceeded to LE PONCHEL and came under orders of the 1st Cav. Division at that place.	
	4 a.m.	The dismtd men who left the Bde on Oct 2nd by omo the Bde on relief of parts which proceeded at 20th inst.	
	23rd "	Major W.T. HODGSON 1st R. Dragoons Bde Major 6th Ca. Bde appointed GSO II 1st Cav. Bri:	SSD
	24th "	Major W.T. Hodgson left 6th Bde to join 1st Cav. Div.	
	28th "	Capt. S.G. HOWES 21st Lancers Staff Capt 6th Cav Bde appointed Brigade Major vice Major Hodgson.	SSD

SHAotr Cpr.

Vol 2

Army Form C. 2118.

WAR DIARY
or
INTELLIGENCE SUMMARY
(Erase heading not required.)

6th Cavalry Brigade
for November 1916

Hour, Date, Place	Summary of Events and Information	Remarks and references to Appendices
Nov 1st – 30th	Bde in billets as on Oct 21st (see Oct War Diary)	JAH
Nov 11th	C Bde RHA in ROUSSENT from Nov 8th to 24th. Working party who were attached to Reserve (Nov 29th) Army from Oct 30th represent the Bde & returned at MONTREUIL. 3rd Dns 1 officer 65 O.R. Royals 2 " 69 " N.S.7 1 " 66 "	JAH
Nov 7th	Capt J. BLAKISTON–HOUSTON 11th Hussars appointed Staff Capt vice Capt S.G. HOWES 2nd Lancers joined the Bde.	JAH
Nov 24th	"C" Battery RHA who were attached to 1st Cav Div rejoined Bde & pads billetted in ROUSSENT.	JAH
Nov 1st – 30th	Bde continued training.	J.J. Hardy Capt

Army Form C. 2118.

WAR DIARY
or
INTELLIGENCE SUMMARY

(Erase heading not required.)

6th Cavalry Brigade
for Dec. 1916

Hour, Date, Place	Summary of Events and Information	Remarks and references to Appendices
Dec 1st – 31st	Brigade remain in billets as in November & continued training	
Dec 11th	G.O.C. 3rd Cav. Bde inspected 6th M.G. Sqn in marching order at VERTON, afterwards setting a scheme against imaginary Enemy at BAHOT.	
Dec 12th	Lt. Col. PALEY DSO. G.S.C.1 2nd Bde. lectured on 2nd Army Scheme on SOMME to all Officers & NCOs of 6th Cav. Bde.	
Dec. 13th	G.O.C. 6th Cav. Bde. inspected Royal Dragoons in marching order on Sarum at MERRIMONT PLAGE	
Dec. 14th	G.O.C. 6th Cav. Bde. inspected N Somerset Yeo. in marching order dismounted at MERRIMONT PLAGE. 3rd Dgs inspection on Dec. 12th was cancelled owing to raining then.	

J H Rose Bgr

Army Form C. 2118.

WAR DIARY
or
INTELLIGENCE SUMMARY

(Erase heading not required.)

6th Gr. Bde
Dec: 1916

Hour, Date, Place	Summary of Events and Information	Remarks and references to Appendices
Dec 6.	C Baton RHA left the 13th XProcken & join 1st Army Artillery School AIRE for temporary duty as Instructional Batt:	SH.

Army Form C. 2118.

6th Cav Bde
Dec 1916

WAR DIARY
or
INTELLIGENCE SUMMARY
(Erase heading not required.)

Instructions regarding War Diaries and Intelligence Summaries are contained in F. S. Regs., Part II. and the Staff Manual respectively. Title pages will be prepared in manuscript.

Hour, Date, Place	Summary of Events and Information	Remarks and references to Appendices
Dec 16th	Training of this Command troop to the 3 Regts. Fr Brigr gone to the SA at Harman 6.c 6th C.B. 1st Squadron & 4 tps 2nd Royal Regts. 3rd N.S.J. & War	J.S.A.
Dec 15th	SitC Inspection 6th Cav by Pioneer Bn.	J.S.A.
Dec 20th	6th Cavalry Pioneer Battalion under Lt Col M R Brickhouse DSO carried N General Pn. Embarred & proceeded to MARESQUEL B.H.Q. 5 officers including 1 M.C. & Regtl. 82 O.R. 22 Horse.	J.S.A.
	formed by in ri. of 2nd R Regts & RAM & Personnel from Cav Depot Ambulance & R.E. Personnel from 3rd Jafar.	Marsh Capt.

Army Form C. 2118.

16th Can Bde
Dec 1916

WAR DIARY
or
INTELLIGENCE SUMMARY
(Erase heading not required.)

Hour, Date, Place	Summary of Events and Information	Remarks and references to Appendices
Dec 20 h (Cont)	3 Companies one for each Regt 7 Officers 247 O.R. 16 Draught Horses to Company Each Company.	SSA
Dec 21st	Pioneer Battalion Entrained MARESQUEL	SSA
	12 noon & Proceeded to ACHEUX &	
	work under XIII Corps.	
Dec 22nd	Bde Exchanged billeting area with	
	8th Cn Bde.	
	Bde HQ. MARESQUEL	
	6th M.G.Coy. MARESQUEL & ECQUEMICOURT	
	3rd Dts. AIX EN ISSART – MARANT – MARENLA.	
	MARLES SUR CANCHE	MM
	ROYALS. PLUMOISON. – BOUIN – AUBIN ST YAAST	
	N Somerset Yeo. OFFIN. LOISON. BEAURAIN CHATEAU	
	C.C.F.A. HESMOND	
	Bde M.V.S HESMOND	N Marshall

Army Form C. 2118.

WAR DIARY
or
INTELLIGENCE SUMMARY
(Erase heading not required.)

6th Cavalry Brigade
for Decr. 1916

Instructions regarding War Diaries and Intelligence Summaries are contained in F. S. Regs., Part II. and the Staff Manual respectively. Title pages will be prepared in manuscript.

Hour, Date, Place	Summary of Events and Information	Remarks and references to Appendices
Dec. 28th	G.O.C. visited 1/1 prisoner Battalion and French Batt. H.Qrs. and Company of N. Somerset Yeo: at P.18 Central. 3rd D. G's Company at J.23.c.84 Roy are " at J.23.a.58. (Reference map Sheet 57D 1/40,000)	MA1
Dec 22nd to Dec. 31st	The remainder of the Brigade in billets as on 22nd December.	MA1

J Blakiston Houn. for Captain

1 Noff Captain 6 Cav. Bde

Army Form C. 2118.

WAR DIARY
OR
INTELLIGENCE SUMMARY
(Erase heading not required.)

6th Cavalry Brigade
Vol 276 January 1917

Instructions regarding War Diaries and Intelligence Summaries are contained in F. S. Regs., Part II. and the Staff Manual respectively. Title pages will be prepared in manuscript.

Hour, Date, Place	Summary of Events and Information	Remarks and references to Appendices
From January 1st	Brigade remained in same billets area Picquigny	JBM
to 2nd 3rd	XIII Corps attached to 6th O.C. A.S.C.	JBM
16th January	Inspection of Transport	JBM
17 February	G.O.C. inspected horses of Regiments	JBM
" "		JBM
24th "		JBM
25 "		
" "	North Somerset Yeomanry	JBM
30 February	7 am Officers & 87 other Ranks left for VILLERS S. AU BOIS	JBM
	8 th 6th Machine Gun Squadron and attached	
16	1st Canadian Corps	

J Blah Johnson Lt Captain
6 Cav: Bde.
H/q Captain

WAR DIARY or **INTELLIGENCE SUMMARY**

Army Form C. 2118.

Vol 7
6th Cavalry Brigade
Sept 1917

Hour, Date, Place	Summary of Events and Information	Remarks and references to Appendices
Sept 1st 2nd	The 13th Coy "C" Bn. RHA & 6th M.G. Sqdn remained in billets in various farms.	
	C Bn RHA attached 106mm Artillery School	J.R.
	A Instructional Battery	
Sept 11th	6 M.G.S.Q attached to Canadian Div.	
	following death of Brigadier General by Lt Col Alfred Burn 3rd Bn.	
	LESTEM D'MOINEUR CROIX JOFFERZA 14 M.G. Sqd.	
	SOMS handed over acting SUTTON	
	MEDAILLE MILITAIRE.	
Sept 17th	A.D.V.S. Col Evap inspected 6 horse troops	
	with men from 11th Regt.	
Sept 24th	Sgt 3rd class Dr McKeon horse 6th Sqdn Can. Gen.	
	Horses M. Corp. to M. Sommer 7th	
Sept 27th	6th Bde hrs to field in terms of A.J. 989. Lt N.G. Neele ?	

Army Form C. 2118.

6th Cavalry Bde
Sept 1917

WAR DIARY
or
INTELLIGENCE SUMMARY

(Erase heading not required.)

Instructions regarding War Diaries and Intelligence Summaries are contained in F. S. Regs., Part II. and the Staff Manual respectively. Title pages will be prepared in manuscript.

Hour, Date, Place	Summary of Events and Information	Remarks and references to Appendices
Sept 2nd 28%	6th Cavalry Bde Bt Remained at Doullens under XIII Corps working on Railway Embankment.	Sgd

A.H. Fasto Major
Bde Major 6th Cav Bde

6th Cavalry Bde

Army Form C. 2118.

WAR DIARY
or
INTELLIGENCE SUMMARY
(Erase heading not required.)

HQ 6th Cavalry Brigade
March 1917.

Vol 28

Hour, Date, Place	Summary of Events and Information	Remarks and references to Appendices
March 1 – 31.	The Bde remained in billets in Neuvy St. Amand.	
March 6	GOC inspected horses of 1st & 3rd Regts & Normand Pro.	
March 9	C Battery RHA rejoined the Bde from 1st Army & here billeted in Les Pinoy. 1 Officer & 10 men from Each Regt of the Bde proceeded to 3rd Army LE PUITS REGNIER to undergo a course in Cavalry Manoeuvring.	
March 14	BC RA En corps inspected horse & stables in of C Batt & RHA at LES PINOY.	
March 15th	6th Cavalry Bde Bde rejoined the Bde & took over from DRAGOONS.	
March 16	DSR Cav Corps held Carry Parade.	
March 20/21st	Brigadier Officer RFC instructor 2 Officers & 1 Sergt RE & 10 o the 3 Regts in addition of aeroplanes bombing places & aeroplanes.	

J.E. Potts Col.

Army Form C. 2118.

WAR DIARY
or
INTELLIGENCE SUMMARY
(Erase heading not required.)

Hour, Date, Place	Summary of Events and Information	Remarks and references to Appendices
March 22nd	The B'th Bn A & B Sektions carried out a route march round [illegible] the Brigadier 3rd Div. F. inspection of the B'n.	J.H.
June 25	A morning parade from the B'n Inter company of Sep Lee Lancaster 3rd Div. 10 h 13 Im terms (Lieut D.H. Watson Royal Small Z Bomber 3rd Div. 3 nd Co.M. Doddington N57) and 120 OR proceeded to Ploy to Meerus & Drove in neighbourhood.	J.H.
March 26th	C Coy 10th Bn movement to Meerusmont 2 days for rifle comp.	J.H.
March 27th	Inoculations from parade for B'th Strength & Officers including 1 attached (Lieut E.S.G. STEEDALL Royal Small Hon GRD BROWNE Royal Small EAI RIDDLE 3rd Div gave FALMASHUS) 1 DC OR proceeded from Base Ar Havaine or 25 Mar	J.H.

1247 W 3250 200,000 (E) 8/14 J.B.C. & A. Forms/C. 2118/11.

Vol 29

CONFIDENTIAL.
****

War Diary of 6th Cavalry Brigade.

APRIL 1917.

Army Form C. 2118.

6th Cavalry Brigade.
April 1917.

WAR DIARY
or
INTELLIGENCE SUMMARY
(Erase heading not required.)

Instructions regarding War Diaries and Intelligence Summaries are contained in F. S. Regs., Part II. and the Staff Manual respectively. Title pages will be prepared in manuscript.

Hour, Date, Place	Summary of Events and Information	Remarks and references to Appendices
April 1st – 4th	The Bde remained in Billets as during March.	
April 5th	The Bde was ordered to concentrate in the area ECOUMILCOURT – CONTES – AVAIN ST VAAST – BOUIN. PLUMOISON thereby closing up on its most Easterly billets & allow Divnl Hd Qrts. Trpts & 17th Cav Bde to come into close billets from the West.	
April 6th	Bde remained in close billets – Bde H.Q. BOUIN.	
April 7th	The Bde marched at 9.15am via X Rds STE-AUSTREBERTHE – NAIL – CONCHY-SUR-CANCHE to billeting area YACOURRIE-LE-BOUIN – PT FORTEL – FORTEL. Bde H Q YACOURRIE-LE-BOUIN. Regtl Hd Qrs LEWIS	
April 8th	The Bde marched to FOSSEUX via X Roads ARBRE – REBREUVIETTE – HERGNY – SUS ST LEGER. SOMBRIN arr 2.30 p.m. Brechlow wagon of the Bde made Bde Transport Officer. Concentration div. boundary under 1st A.C. at BOISETTE – SURLENCOURT	MF Rodolph.

1247 W 3259 200,000 (E) 8/14 J.B.C.&A. Forms/C. 2118/11.

Army Form C. 2118.

WAR DIARY
or
INTELLIGENCE SUMMARY

(Erase heading not required.)

6th Cavalry Brigade
April 1917

Hour, Date, Place	Summary of Events and Information	Remarks and references to Appendices
April 9th	13th MMS. Came under orders ADVS. 6 Q.O. Amm: Waggons from Divn Ammn. Column were attached to Bde on arrival at FOSSEUX. Billets in FOSSEUX were mostly thoroughly Frenchified & about 30% of horses of Bde were to be provided little room for Br Cav Bde. Ref map 1/20000 51B N.W. & S.W. 1/40000 51B & C. Bde There R. at 1h12 when at 5.30 AM. 10.30 AM Bde marched via X Roads P12a (Mercer Src) — WANQUETIN — BRICK WORKS — GOUVES — DUISANS reached W end of DUISANS without inc End of GOUVES. A Sqd. 3rd D.Gs. moved Sth. of Bde at P12 a to rear of 2nd Sqdn in order to be sufficiently in rear of Bde to wait & attack on HANCOURT FEUCHY line about N34 c & d.	

Signature

Army Form C. 2118.

8th Cavalry Brigade
April 1917.

WAR DIARY
or
INTELLIGENCE SUMMARY
(Erase heading not required.)

Instructions regarding War Diaries and Intelligence Summaries are contained in F. S. Regs., Part II. and the Staff Manual respectively. Title pages will be prepared in manuscript.

Hour, Date, Place	Summary of Events and Information	Remarks and references to Appendices
April 9th	Order of March Bde HQ. 6th Sigs & troop 3rd Bde. 10th Hrs hd tp, 1 sec. 6 M.G. Sqn, 1 sec. 6 M.G. Sqn, and 1 sect. C Bty. R.H.A. Royals hd tp. 1 sec. 6 M.G. Sqn. C Bty R.H.A. (less RHA) (Bn. RHA less 1 sec.) Field troop R.E. (Lt Mathers) N someway 2nd Echs. 6 M.G. Sqn. less 3 sections. 1 sec. 6 M.G. Sqn. Pack section 8th Car. Fd Amb.	
2.30 pm	The Bde moved to concentration area in 6.13.d just East of ARRAS.	
4.30 pm	The Bde following 8th Car Bde formed through ARRAS to rendezvous of Cavalry Track Jnction with HY30 (Hyderabad Redoubt divisionally) halted East of ARRAS in 6.28.C.	
	As the 3rd Div. Inf. required the Bde as 8 pm	
1 at 11.30 pm	the Bde moved back to bivouac at ARRAS South of NOUEZ down x Rds L.10.C.	

[signature]

Army Form C. 2118.

6th Cavalry Brigade
April 1917.

WAR DIARY
or
INTELLIGENCE SUMMARY
(Erase heading not required.)

Hour, Date, Place	Summary of Events and Information	Remarks and references to Appendices
April 10th	Prepared to stand at short notice at 5.30 AM.	
6.30 AM	B de move through ARRAS & billets in D.R.P. in H.31.c.	
	A Sub 3rd D.B. have previously gone forward to join 5th Cav B de & to prepare HQ camp over & in German HAYCOURT-FEUCHY line about H.3n.c. & N.h.a. Camps were complete about 4 PM. O.C. advised that 2 officers en route for Foden with Details, in LA BERGERE & MONCHY LE PREUX.	
1.20 / 3 PM	B de move forward to H.33.d. Boring afternoon there was slight shelling to b and H.31.c.	
At 7 PM	B de move back to H.32.a. & bivouaced for night. There was also some constant snow storms.	

J.H. Anstruther.

Army Form C. 2118.

6th Cavalry Brigade
April 1917.

WAR DIARY
or
INTELLIGENCE SUMMARY

(Erase heading not required.)

Instructions regarding War Diaries and Intelligence Summaries are contained in F. S. Regs., Part II. and the Staff Manual respectively. Title pages will be prepared in manuscript.

Hour, Date, Place	Summary of Events and Information	Remarks and references to Appendices
April 11th	At 5.30 AM 3rd Dragoon Guards with 1 Sec MG Sqdn & 1 Sec ECBHA R.H.A moved up to H.33.a. From 2 April 11 to LABERGERE & MONCHY LE-PREUX + 10th in order to keep touch in permanent liaison with 8th Cav Bde who were just on the left & North of 6th C.B. At 7 AM 12th and 13th replaces LANCERS & 7TH HUSSARS to be close frontier with the idea each was to have & therefore to prevent At 8.30 AM CC 3rd Dr. Gds sent forward Patrols 3rd Dr. (C.Lt. Holroyd-Smyth M.C.) in conjunction with The Essex Yeo & 5th Cav Bde & troops from Official to Ring South of MONCHY between MONCHY & CAMBRAI R.E.	Appendix B. [signature]

Army Form C. 2118.

6th Cavalry Brigade
April 1917

WAR DIARY
or
INTELLIGENCE SUMMARY
(Erase heading not required.)

Hour, Date, Place	Summary of Events and Information	Remarks and references to Appendices
April 11th	Orders sent to "B" Sqdn. (Major G.T. Cliff) then to Monchy. B Sqdn took up a position on the Ridge on their objective approximate line from Landmark N.12.6 – N.12.6.7.7 – O.1.C.2.2. Ryan of 3rd D.G. in touch with detachments of LANCER GEFF. During advance to this objective German Machine Gun dugouts on the Ridge at front & a hostile Battery of guns were taken & manned by the 3rd D.G. B Sqn report came had moved to N.4.C. 3rd D.G. supported cavalry this advance. Still expose during this advance to S.H. fire from Monchy and another source of 7.15 AM G.O.C. ordered 3rd D.G. to resist force 3rd D.G.	Appendix B [signature]

Army Form C. 2118.

6th Cav Bde
April 1917.

WAR DIARY
or
INTELLIGENCE SUMMARY.
(Erase heading not required.)

Place	Date	Hour	Summary of Events and Information	Remarks and references to Appendices
N. & C.	11/4/17	10.10 am	O.C. 3rd D.G. reports German counter attack from OOSTMAPPE when he had sent 1 troop & 2 M.G. team. Rifle & M.G. fire on his right flank which seems heavily held by Infantry from hostile Battalion. 3rd D.G. aeroplane reports that German were to trenches on line (A 15.A. horses, & to hostile line north A.R. & M.Gs.	Appendix B.
		12 noon	STROHARTS FACTORY – KEERING CAPSE – PEZRES & then (A 15A Bn were to make by the Inf as advance & then when horses, & to hostile line north A.R. & M.Gs.	
		1.30 pm	R.H.A. rendered 2 sects "C Bn" to N. Batteries owing to the N. Support positions, which had been spotted by hostile Aeroplane. C. Bn H' made C.R.A. then took up position in N. & C.	
		2.35 pm	O.C. 3rd D.G. reports that hostilities were & heavily held & that Enemy were advancing 1000 x East of LA BERGERE. O.C. therefor ordered 1 sct. N. Somerset Bn (Major Tozer) with 1 sect M.G to the H.A. & M.S.T. & to co-op from SM bytes ½ squn. 3rd D.G. right flank. Protected 1/2 N.Art. & 30 & gunners came & a	

[signature]

Army Form C. 2118.

6th Cav Bde
April 1917

WAR DIARY
or
INTELLIGENCE SUMMARY
(Erase heading not required.)

Place	Date	Hour	Summary of Events and Information	Remarks and references to Appendices
N4C	11th	5.45pm	a print of 6th Bde Bedford. Orders recd that 6 Cav Bde would be relieved by 12th Div & then retire, when complete, to 3rd Div H.Q. at N57. Bd 11.30 pm the relief was completed & 3rd Bde 11th N57 & 3 M.G. Sects moved back to their bivo. During night 11/12th the Bde reached their bivouac at L17d. Rain thunderstorm seria in progress. Close liaison was kept with 12th Bde through Major Tomkinson Royals. The Officer long liaison summoned on 15th was L.17760 on Royals Box Headquarters. 2nd Lt. STARKEY NS7 a Cpl & liaison Officer with 3rd Cav. Bde 2nd Cav Div on the right & South of CAMBRAI Road. The 13th & also 3rd Bde were in touch with 8th Cav Bde O.C. 3rd Bde reported & forwarded in Hotchkiss Rifle stating that the lie in of 3rd Bde was the frontal attack with Hotchkiss Rifles which were able there to ascend the Germans prior to counterattack.	[signature]

Army Form C. 2118.

WAR DIARY
or
INTELLIGENCE SUMMARY.
(Erase heading not required.)

6 Cav Bde
April 1917

Place	Date	Hour	Summary of Events and Information	Remarks and references to Appendices
In Hd of LOUEZ L17d.	12		At 10.30 a.m. The Bde moved back to billets in FOSSEUX via HABARCQ - LATTRE ST. QUENTIN. B echelon joined the Bde during the morning at FOSSEUX.	
FOSSEUX	13-15		Bde remained in FOSSEUX.	
	16		Bde moved westwards from FOSSEUX at 8 a.m. via SUS-ST-LEGER - IVERGNY - REBREUVIETTE - NAVAINS - AUXILE-CHATEAU to billets in area LABROYE - LE BOISLE - FERME-IVERGNY - VITZ VILLEROY - TOLLENT - VAULX - LE PONCHEL. Bde HQ to LE BOISLE.	
LE BOISLE	19th	9am	The Bde marched further westwards to a billeting area Bde HQ} MAINTENAY 6 [?] 13 A.M.T.S. 3rd Dr. PT. PREAUX - ARGOULES. SAULCHOY- GRAND PREAUX. Royals [?] from & farms to N.W.D of PRON. M.S.F. NEMPONT - ST. FIRMIN - NAMPONT- ST. MARTIN C.Bty. ROUSSENT C.M.G.Sqn BUIRE-LE-SEC.	

[signature] Capt.

Army Form C. 2118.

WAR DIARY
or
INTELLIGENCE SUMMARY.
(Erase heading not required.)

6th Cav Bde
April 1917.

Place	Date	Hour	Summary of Events and Information	Remarks and references to Appendices
MAINTENAY	2/4/17		Paras 1 & 2 numbered working parties whose by the Bde on March 25th & 27th under CAPT V.E.C. CHERNEGY 3rd D.G. rejoined the Bde at MAINTENAY 2.20 p.m. Included in working party were reinforcements being up to PREVENT where a Reinforcement camp had been started. 3rd D.G. 3 Officers 66 O.R. Royals 4 Officers 72 O.R. NS7 2 Officers 61 O.R. 6MGns 2 Officers 16 O.R. Details of working parties is attached in Appendix A. Issued to new MG formation Order NO 42 Enemently sent a marked Appendix B. Plan. Bde remained in billets to the M Enemy.	App A. App C. App D App B.
MAINTENAY	21/30 3/4		300 Ridley Horses sent the event arrived from Remounts 3rd D.G. 7. 6 M.G.D.H. Royals 62. 6 Lg Troops. NS7 30. M Lyons 30	[signature]

Army Form C. 2118.

WAR DIARY
INTELLIGENCE SUMMARY
(Erase heading not required.)

Place	Date	Hour	Summary of Events and Information	Remarks and references to Appendices
ARRAS	25-31 March		Extracts from War Diary of 6th Can. Bde Co. of 3rd Can. Div. in Bermuda 1st. She he belong for the proceeded by Lor Express for the Purpose of CAPT OFF CARNEGY 3rd Div. On March 25 & 27th Journey & Appear in the Command of Non-Army last Map of March covered. Consisted in Turning a Camp by Track from ROUTE D'AMIENS to ARRAS or 6-26 a 5.5 to first line Trenches M 5 a 8.5 Ref Map 51 B & C 1:20000 Precision Been & taken over by one Co. Div. Working Party.	
ARRAS	1.4.17		Work was Commenced on CAMRON Track	
	2.4.17		Completed.	
	3.4.17		Sub. E. R. Hit. Reserve M C & R. E. Provided 3 CR 3rd Div. Mounted tel. 1 ER NSJ rounded.	
	5.4.17		1 CR 3rd Div. Armin	
			Mani 2 or 3 P&R Dugouts	
	6.4.17		Work on Track & assembly trenches continued on the line North to the been four funnels to headway to clear German wire Track continued through to Route Speaks	

Army Form C. 2118.

WAR DIARY
or
INTELLIGENCE SUMMARY.
(Erase heading not required.)

Instructions regarding War Diaries and Intelligence Summaries are contained in F. S. Regs., Part II. and the Staff Manual respectively. Title pages will be prepared in manuscript.

Place	Date	Hour	Summary of Events and Information	Remarks and references to Appendices
ARRAS	10.4.17		As for as ACHIETTE HOR A 31 f 8.3 @ 2pm Ca. in line however 5 O.R. 3rd Bn. 1 O.R. N.S.F. Appendix A (Copy (t)	
	11.4.17		Shoving forward Australian to long Trench + removing Shields followed attack on ORANGE HILL + three Tanks up front by this point by 10.30 am. (B)(C)(B) Coy. Employed in clearing ARRAS. R.G. Stratton had a R.G. line between ARRAS + FEUCHY.	
	12.4.17		S/Sgt called for R.G. work Kt. Km. South MONCHY LE PREUX Bombin. Off Capt. H. Wilson D.S.O. R.H.6.4 v Lt. Col. Newton Dettrin 3 in 4th. recorner + brought in.	
	13.4.17		O.C. 6 C.B. Coy recet. Recon. from G.S. 3rd Ca. Div to clear MONCHY LE PREUX of M.A. Car Bde nomenel. Shot 2 rds carried out at 4 am 14th inst. Sabege kk carried our. Neghbouring Fosses taken y MONCHY	
	15.17.4.17		1 O.R. N.S.F. killed	
	18.4.17		Lt. No. 156 R.Q.A. Lt. Stockdale 5 N.S.F. 2 O.R. remained at ARRAS.	J. Hilton

1577 Wt. W10791/1773 500,000 1/15 D. D. & L. A.D.S.S./Forms/C. 2118.

WAR DIARY
or
INTELLIGENCE SUMMARY.

Army Form C. 2118.

Place	Date	Hour	Summary of Events and Information	Remarks and references to Appendices
ARRAS	18/4/17		Appendix A (Cont) Carrying on usual work. 30 Officers 63 OR 3rd Dn. 2 Officers 70 OR Ronah 1 Officer 46 OR NSY. Entrained for DOULLENS & proceeded by motor lorries to Cav Corps Remounts Camp FREVENT.	
FREVENT	9/4/17		A convoy of horses to join 6th Cav Bde on 21st April.	

M. Marsden

3rd D. Gds.   6th M.G.Sdn. O.C. A.1 Echelon.2/Lt.RILEY.
Royals.   7th C.F.A.   O.C. A.2 Echelon. Lt.DOUGLAS.
N. S. Y.   Camp Comdt.   Staff Captain.
C.Battery.   Supply Officer. 3rd Field Squadron.
3rd Cavalry Division.

Ref.Map:- 51.B & C. 1/40,000.   April 5th.
          51 B. N.W. & S.W. 1/20,000.

6th CAVALRY BRIGADE CONCENTRATION ORDER No.1.

1. After Zero + 2 hours on Z day, the Brigade will remain standing-to at one hour's notice.
   So soon as the first order to move is received, the 3rd Cavalry Division will move into its first position of readiness as follows:-

   (a) 8th Cavalry Brigade will march via the X roads in P.13.a.- WARQUETIN - BRICKWORKS - GOUVES - DUISANS.- Fork roads L.8.c. - L.1.a&c. on the St.POL - ARRAS Road to G.13.d.1.4. (Sheet 51 B. 1/40,000.)
   The 8th Brigade will close up so that its tail is East of the Rly. in L.1 while its head remains at G.13.d.1.4.

   (b) 6th Cavalry Brigade. will follow 8th Brigade and halt with its head West of DUISANS, and its tail East of GOUVES.
   Order of March: Bde. H.Q., 6th Signal Troop, 3rd D. Gds. 1 Sect.'C' Battery, Royals, 'C' Battery less 1 Section., Field Troop R.E., 6th M.G.Sqdn., less 3 Sections, N. S. Y., Pack Section C.F.A.

   (c) Divnl.H.Q. Details, H.Q. C.R.A., Signal Squadron, H.Q. Field Squadron will follow 6th Cav. Bde. halting West of GOUVES.

   (d) 7th Cavalry Brigade. will follow Divnl.Troops and halt head South of X roads in M.31.d, tail just East of WARQUETIN.

   (e) 'A' Echelons, divisionalized, will remain in Bde. bivouacs, horses harnessed in, but poles down ready to move at 2 hours notice in order of march of Brigades.
   'A'1 Echelons under Lt.M.V. DRUMMOND, 2nd Life Guards.
   'A'2 Echelons, divisionalized, under Capt.YEATMAN, 1st Life Guards.
   'A'1 Echelon will follow 7th Cav.Bde. when it moves forward.
   'A'2 will follow Divnl.Ammunition Column.

   (f) Divnl.Ammunition Column will remain in its bivouac, same orders as for 'A' Echelon, and follow 'A'1 Echelon when it moves.

   (g) Mobile V.Sections will follow 'A'2 Echelon, under orders of A.D.V.S.

   N.B. (1) All troops will clear the roads and villages as far as possible when halted.
        (2) When any unit receives the order to move, it will warn the unit in rear of it.
        (3) So soon as march is resumed all units will close up.

2. (a) Pack Mounted Section,6th C.F.A.will move with the Bde under all circumstances.
   (b) Light Sects.C.F.A's, will be collected so soon as Divn. has carried out its first concentration park just off the road in P.13.a.8.6. and await orders of A.D.M.S.

3. (a) Divnl.Report Centre, North exit of DUISANS.
   (b) Bde. Report Centre at Head of 6th Cav.Bde.

Bde. Major   6th Cav. Bde

SECRET.

3rd Cavalry Division Concentration Order No.3.
----

1.   The subsequent move forward will take place with a view to bringing the Division into the following position of readiness by the time the Infantry attacks are expected to reach the WANCOURT - FEUCHY Line, viz at Z+8 hours.

(a) 8th Cavalry Bde. will move via the St.POL - ARRAS Road to just short of the Western exit of ARRAS in G.31.a.4.7. thence due East to the Road Point in G.31.b.5.7. where it will join the Cavalry Track "A" which it will follow to the Eastern end of H.31.b. (1/30,000)

(b) 6th Cav.Bde. will move into the area vacated by the 8th Bde.

(c) Divl.Troops and 7th Bde. will move into the area vacated by the 6th Bde.

(d) 'A' Echelon, the Div.Ammn.Col. and the M.V.S. will move into the area vacated by the 7th Bde.

(e) No. 7 L.A.C. Battery will receive separate orders.

2.   Div.Report Centre will move up to the Head of the 8th Bde. at the Eastern end of H.31.b

3.   Subsequent to this concentration, troops will move in accordance with 3rd Cav.Div. O.O. No. 1 issued today.

6/4/17.   Sd/ A.E.PAGET, Lt.Col,
                                    G.S. 3rd Cavalry Divn.

....

6th Cavalry Bde. Concentration Order No. 3.

Ref. Map 51 B,N.W. and S.W.   1/30,000
     51 B and C   1/40,000

1.   See above paras 1 (a) (c) (d) (e) and 2.

2.   6th Cav.Bde. will move via DUISANS - Fork Roads L.8.c, - L.9.a. and c. on the main St.POL - ARRAS Road to G.13.d.0.4. and will close up so that its tail is East of Railway in L.9.

3.   Bde. Report Centre at Head of Bde.

4.   Subsequent to this Concentration the Bde. will move into the area vacated by 8th Cav.Bde. vide para 1 (a) of 3rd C.D. C.O. No. 3 (above) and thence in accordance with 6th Cav.Bde. Operation Order No. 1 issued today.

6/4/17.   Captain.
                            Brigade Major 6th Cavalry Bde.

A = 5ᵗʰ D.G's H.Qrs
B = 'A' Sqdn. in support in old German trench.
C = 4 Guns 'C' R.H.A.
D = 'B' Sqdn. 5ᵗʰ D.G's and 2 Troops N.S.Y.
E = Inf. M.G Section.
H = 'C' Sqdn. 5ᵗʰ D.G's.
K = 1 Sub Section M.G.
M = Hotchkiss rifle posts.
P = Details of 12ᵗʰ Inf. Bde.
S = 2 Troops N.S.Y.
W = 1 Sub Section M.G.
Z = German battery of 4 Guns
Y = 2 Hotchkiss rifles and 10 men.
X = Point reached by Patrols.
F = 6ᵗʰ Cav Bde H.Qrs.
▬ = Germans.

SCALE 1:20 000

Appendix "C"

SECRET.   Copy No.....

6th Cavalry Brigade Operation Order No.1.

Ref.Map 51.B. N.W. & S.W. 1/20,000
       51.B. & C.   1/40,000   April 8th, 1917.

1.....The Third Army is attacking the German defences East of ARRAS tomorrow, in conjunction with an attack by the First Army on the VIMY RIDGE.

   These attacks will take place at ZERO hour, which will be notified later.

   12th and 3rd Divisions VI Corps will attack respectively North and South of main ARRAS - CAMBRAI Road.
   Their Reserve Brigades will assault the BROWN Line (WANCOURT - FEUCHY line) at approximately Z + 8 hours.

   Should this attack be successful, the 37th Division will pass through the 12th Division and attack MONCHY-LE-PREUX and the ground North and South of it, between the ARRAS - CAMBRAI Road and the River Scarpe.

2.   So soon as MONCHY-LE-PREUX has been seized, the task of
 (a)   3rd Cav. Div. is to advance and seize, as its first objective, the line VIS-EN-ARTOIS - BOIRY NOTRE DAME (both inclusive) protecting its own left flank.
 (b)   2nd Cav. Div. is, at the same time, to advance and seize the line FONTAINE-LES-CROISILLES - VIS-EN-ARTOIS (both exclusive) on the South bank of the River SENSEE.
 (c)   The 50th Infantry Bde. plus 1 Brigade R.F.A. (17th Div) will follow 3rd Cav. Div. in order to relieve it for a further advance.

3. (a)   8th Cavalry Brigade will move North of MONCHY-LE-PREUX and seize BOIRY NOTRE DAME.
 (b)   6th Cavalry Brigade will move South of MONCHY-LE-PREUX and seize VIS-EN-ARTOIS, gaining touch with the left of the 2nd Cavalry Division (5th Cavalry Bde) and co-operating with that Brigade as well as with the 8th Cavalry Brigade.

   The first bound will be the line St.ROBART FACTORY - BOIS-DU-VERT - BOIS-DU-SART - East end of PELVES
   Dividing line between Brigades : The MONCHY-LE-PREUX - BOIRY NOTRE DAME Road inclusive to the 8th Cavd Brigade.

 (c)   Divisional Troops and 7th Cavalry Bde. will follow 6th Cavalry Brigade, and move in to reserve about H.33 Central.
 (d)   A.1 Echelons under Lt. J. DRUMMOND 2nd Life Guards will follow the 7th Cavalry Brigade and park in H.32 Central.

 (e)   Divl. Ammunition Column will follow A.1 Echelons and park in H.32 Central.

 (f)   A.2 Echelons will follow Divl. Ammunition Column and park East of the Cavalry Track in G.23.C.

4.   In consequence

   3rd Dragoon Guards, plus 1 Section 'C' Battery, will act as Advanced Guard and will seize Southern Edge of Spur in O.15.a. 2.4. - BOIS-DU-VERT - Road in O.3.c.9.6. exclusive.
   When this objective is gained, main body Bde. H.Q., Royals, 'C' Battery (less 1 Section), Field Troop R.E., 6th M/Gun Sqn., (less 3 Sections), N.S.Y., Pack Section 6th C.F.A., will move from CROSSING over WANCOURT - FEUCHY line about N.4.a.9.8 - South of MONCHY to a position about O.7.b.5.5.

5. (a) Advanced Divisional Dressing Station will be established on the main ARRAS - CAMBRAI Road about LES FOSSES FARM in N.11.b.8.4.
    (b) Divisional Collecting Station for walking cases will be established in the Caves in ARRAS where the ARRAS - CAMBRAI Road runs into ARRAS.

6. Advanced Divisional H.Q. will be established in O.7.b.9.6. So soon as 6th and 8th Brigades have completed first bound

    Brigade Report Centres will be established

    (a) at H.33.d.8.4 when 3rd Dragoon Gds. are just East of WANCOURT - FEUCHY line.
    (b) at N.12.b.3.6 when 3rd Dragoon Gds. are moving forward to first objective.
    (c) at O.7.b.9.6. when 3rd D.Gds. have gained their objective.

7. ACKNOWLEDGE.

                                              Captain.
                              Brigade Major 6th Cavalry Brigade.

Issued at 1 am. 9/4/17.

Copies No. 1 to G.O.C.
         2   3rd D.Gds.
         3.   Royals
         4   N.S.Y.
         5.   'C' Battery R.H.A.
         6.   6th M/Gun Sqn.
         7.   6th C.F.A.
         8   Camp Commandant.
         9.   O.C. A.1 Echelon.
        10   O.C. A.2 Echelon.
        12   3rd Cav.Div. (8 copies.)
        11   3rd Field Sqn.
        13   2nd Cav.Div for 5th Cav.Bde. (thro' 3rd Cav.Div.)
        14   8th Cav.Bde.
        15   Staff Capt.
        16)
        17)   File & War Diary.

Army Form C. 2118.

WAR DIARY or INTELLIGENCE SUMMARY.

(Erase heading not required)

Cavalry Brigade
April 1917

Place	Date	Hour	Summary of Events and Information	Remarks and references to Appendices

Appendix 'E'. Casualties

	OFFRS			O.R.			
Date	K.	W.	M.	K.	W.	M.	
5/4/17	3rd Dragoon Guards				3		
6/4/17	1st Somerset Yeo.				1		
8/4/17	3rd Dragoon Guards				5		
9/4/17	1st R. Dragoons				2		
"	1st Somerset Yeo.				1		
10/4/17	3rd Dragoon Guards				1		
"	1st R. Dragoons		1*			3		* Major H.A. Tomkinson
"	"L" Battery R.H.A.					1		
11/4/17	3rd Dragoon Guards	1*	3*		18	66	3	* 2/Lt M.V.T. Mott 2/Lt S.A.S. Fitz-R. Cole 2/Lt M.A. Dulson
"	1st R. Dragoons		-		2	23	-	*½ C.H. Newton - Deakin
"	1st Somerset Yeo.		4*		4	14	-	Major W.A. Kennard, D.S.O. (B.H.Q.s.c.r.), Lt S.W. Applegate M.S. 2/Lt K.G. Jenkins 2/Lt J.H. Hewes
"	"L" Battery R.H.A.				3	15	1	
"	6th M.G. Squadron		2*		1	5	-	* Lt A.R. Cooper, 2/Lt C.G. Lowden
"	1st Cav. Bde. Hd					2	-	
"	6th Signal Troop							

Army Form C. 2118.

6th Cavalry Brigade
April 1917.

WAR DIARY
or
INTELLIGENCE SUMMARY.
(Erase heading not required.)

Instructions regarding War Diaries and Intelligence Summaries are contained in F. S. Regs., Part II. and the Staff Manual respectively. Title pages will be prepared in manuscript.

Place	Date	Hour	Summary of Events and Information	Remarks and references to Appendices
	13/4/17		Lt. M/Sunderson	
	17/4/17		Hauned 7o.	
	19/4/17		Hanned 7o.	
			Appendix 'E' Casualties (total)	
			(accidentally)	
			K.	O.R. Wounded	Missing	
			1	1	1	
				1		
			1		1	

Army Form C. 2118.

6th Cavalry Brigade
May 1917.

Vol 30

WAR DIARY
or
INTELLIGENCE SUMMARY.
(Erase heading not required.)

Place	Date	Hour	Summary of Events and Information	Remarks and references to Appendices
WARENAY	1	—	Bde remained in billets. No moving later hour of April.	
			Bgde Staff Ride took place. Subject Communications of Cav Bde	
	2		Signal test took place.	
			GOC to commander + staff inspection horses of 1st R. Dragoons at Noon.	
	3		GOC inspected horses of 3 BDE teams 3rd Dns at MAILLCROIX.	
			Gen Administration Staff Ride neighbourhood BOISTRAN.	
	4		GOC Staff Capt S. Dowsett and Sketches to BRAS ECM sketch	
			box part	
	5		recce	
			Bde Commander Reported intention to following officers MC. gna	
			Operations were to commenced & reconoit of operation zone	
			MAJOR LE PREUX XXXX B	
			DSO. D G L A BURT 3rd Ds	
			M.C. Capt UEC CARNEGY 3rd Ds.	
			Scn. 1327. Pte(cop) A.G. HARDIES 3rd Dn. (not present)	
			Ptm 1303. Pte BOAST F 3rd Ds.	
			Bdr Corpl 75 KING T 3rd Ds. not present	

[signature] Capt.

WAR DIARY or INTELLIGENCE SUMMARY

Army Form C. 2118.

6th Cavalry Brigade
July 1917

Place	Date	Hour	Summary of Events and Information	Remarks and references to Appendices
5th MAINTENAY			Medal Ribands (Cont). DCM 694 Sgt PACEY LT. N. Somerset Yeo. Military Medal: 64985. Cpl E.H. FORSHAW. =C= Bart R.H.A. 7120. Pte RUDKINS E.J. 3rd D.G. 7874. Pte F DUFFEN 3rd D.G. 1588. Pte (L/Cpl) SYMES H.S. N.S.Y. 363. Sgt A TUCKER N.S.Y. Medaille Militaire 50501. SQMS SUTTON 6 th M.G. Sqdn. Thepford, a Bde parade for presentation of medals 	
	7th		James of 3rd D.G. & R.Mds. went in attendance. The return to be prepared from information to the men of the other 2nd and 3rd sqdns at be shown for contents in areas East & South of PERONNE.	
	12th		Bde. hors ken made friendly with 7th Bde area. There killed for flight 12/13 as over leaf.	

[signature]

Army Form C. 2118.

6th Cavalry Brigade
May 1917.

WAR DIARY
or
INTELLIGENCE SUMMARY.
(Erase heading not required.)

Place	Date	Hour	Summary of Events and Information	Remarks and references to Appendices
	12/13.		B4H.Q. 6 CDA 4.15 pm TORRÉ FONTAINE.	Map
			3rd DG. DOMPIERRE - RAPECHY PONCHES-ESTRUVAL ROISEN	Meadows ABBEVILLE + LENS.
			Royals. BROMMOIS - LE PETIT CHEMIN. ESTRUVAL.	
			N.S.Y. BOURIEZ ST. TOSSÉ	
			C.Bde.A? MOURIEZ	
			6 M.G.Sqn. RAYE SUR AUTHIE FOND D'EVAL.	
			The 13th marched in the pinkeuble 6 villages.	
TORRÉ FONTAINE	13.		B4e A.Q. FROHEN LEGRAND	
			6 C.M.A. }	
			13 H.S. }	
			3rd DG. MEZEROLLES.	
			Royals BEALCOURT - FROHEN LE PETIT.	
			N.S.Y. MILLERS' HOSPITAL.	
			C.Bd.K OUTRE BOIS (N.Bank)	
			6 M.G. Sqn. BARLY.	

Army Form C. 2118.

WAR DIARY
or
INTELLIGENCE SUMMARY.
(Erase heading not required.)

6th Cavalry Brigade
May 1917.

Instructions regarding War Diaries and Intelligence Summaries are contained in F.S. Regs, Part II. and the Staff Manual respectively. Title pages will be prepared in manuscript.

Place	Date	Hour	Summary of Events and Information	Remarks and references to Appendices
FROMENLE GRAND	14	10am.	The Bde. marched as a Bde. to 6Mk Bde HQ E Bn H. } HAVERNAS. C Sqn. 13th Hrs. 3rd Dr. } BERTEAUCOURT LES DAMES. Royals. MST SM(Guards) } HARLOY LES PERNOIS.	Map /Hoppers LENS.
	15.	9.30am	The Bde. marched to billets Bde HQ C Sqn H. 6M. 6 B.H. } BUSSY LES DAOURS E. C. P. H. 13 M.H. 3rd Dns. Royals } LA NÉOVILLE. MST.	ATHENS Sheet
			C Batty ordered to proceed to join 2nd Cav. Div. 6 on 17th.	......

Army Form C. 2118.

6th Cavalry Brigade
May 1917.

WAR DIARY
or
INTELLIGENCE SUMMARY.
(Erase heading not required.)

Instructions regarding War Diaries and Intelligence Summaries are contained in F. S. Regs., Part II. and the Staff Manual respectively. Title pages will be prepared in manuscript.

Place	Date	Hour	Summary of Events and Information	Remarks and references to Appendices
BUSSUS BUSSUEL	16th		Bde. remained in billets. a.a.f. 15th Jan.	11.00.00. AMIENS. Sheet
			C Bty. R.H.A. moved at 8.30 a.m. to HARBONNIERES, en route to ROISEL R.V. 2nd Cav. Bde.	
			Lt Stockdyke with 1st [Bn?] joined horse & 1 OR proceeded to join & Rendezvous F Detachment & 2nd Cav. Bde. signal squadron. ROISEL	
	17th		Bde. march to billets as follows.	
			Bde HQ } BAYONVILLERS	
			R.H.A. }	
			N.S? } HARBONNIERES	
			C.C.P.S. }	
			13 M.V.S. }	
CAYEUX	18th		7 a.m. march from billets via R'ways M'Buire & arrived camp at PERONNE.	
Bonus	19.		Bde. remained in Camp. until the 22nd.	

J. Hartelger

Army Form C. 2118.

WAR DIARY
or
INTELLIGENCE SUMMARY.
(Erase heading not required.)

6th Anty Bde
May 1917

Instructions regarding War Diaries and Intelligence Summaries are contained in F. S. Regs., Part II. and the Staff Manual respectively. Title pages will be prepared in manuscript.

Place	Date	Hour	Summary of Events and Information	Remarks and references to Appendices
BURE	22nd		The Bde commence to relieve 8th & 2nd Cav Bde. Relieve was holding trenches East of JEMEPPY. Br. Hdqrs P.a.m.o 62.C.N.E. 6.Gun 57.C.S.O. from F.6.K.1 atachem & left a section 3rd Cav Bde. Relief done & taking of 6th Cav Bde to the line night May 3rd no casualties (6th Cav Bde W.Diary (Sect Diary)	Appendix A Appendix B
	24		Brig Gen MAKEN HOFFMAN DSO cmdg 14 Cav Bde took over command of the Bde Relief arrangements for Brig Gen Smyth cmdg 3rd Cav Bde. Establishment of Hd.qrs attached. Command of 6th Cav Bde retained handed over to Lt Col Bomer DSO commdg Royal Scots Greys on transfer of D.A. to Command of 7th Dr Gds	App C

1577 Wt.W10791/1773 500,000 1/15 D. D. & L. A.D.S.S./Forms/C. 2118.

Army Form C. 2118

'D' SECTOR

WAR DIARY
INTELLIGENCE SUMMARY
(Erase heading not required.)

Place	Date	Hour	Summary of Events and Information	Remarks and references to Appendices
Field.	23 May.		The 6th Cavalry Brigade began to relieve the 3rd Cavalry Brigade in Sector 'D' of Cavalry Corps front. The trench line to be taken over was from TOMBOIS FARM (exclusive), in F.11.b.2.4 to X.17.d.0.8 (Ref.Map 1/20,000).57D Se) It was divided into Sub-sectors D.1 and D.2, and had three main lines of defence, the Outpost, Intermediate and Second Line. During the night, the 6th Machine Gun Squadron took over from the portions of the 3rd and 5th Machine Gun Squadrons in D.1 Sub-sector, while the 7th Machine Gun Squadron took over from portions of the 3rd and 5th Machine Gun Squadrons in D.2. Sub-sector. The following reliefs also took place : D1.Sub-sector. 1½ Squadrons Royals relieved 1 Squadron 16th Lancers in support of intermediate line. 3rd D.Gds. relieved remaining 2 Squadrons of 16th Lancers in Second Line. D2.Sub-sector. 1½ Squadrons 1st Life Guards took over from 5th Lancers in support of Intermediate line. 2nd Life Guards relieved remaining 2 Squadrons 5th Lancers in Second Line.	
"	24th May.		During the evening Lieut-Colonel A. BURT, D.S.O., took over command of Sub-sector D.1, while Lieut-Colonel Hon.A.F.Stanley, D.S.O. took over the command of the Sub-sector D.2. The following reliefs took place : D.1 Sub-sector. 1½ Squadrons Royals relieved 1 Squadron Royal Scots Greys in the Outpost Line. 3rd D.Gds. relieved 2 Squadrons Royal Scots Greys in Intermediate Line. 1½ Squadrons Royals relieved 1½ Squadrons Royals in support of Intermediate Line. N.S.Y. took over the defences of the Second Line from the 3rd D.Gds.	

Army Form C. 2118.

'D' SECTOR

WAR DIARY
INTELLIGENCE SUMMARY.
(Erase heading not required.)

Instructions regarding War Diaries and Intelligence Summaries are contained in F. S. Regs., Part II and the Staff Manual respectively. Title pages will be prepared in manuscript.

Place	Date	Hour	Summary of Events and Information	Remarks and references to Appendices
Field.	24th May.		**D.2 Sub-sector.** 1½ Squadrons 1st Life Guards relieved 1 Squadron 4th Hussars, in Outpost Line. 3 Squadrons 2nd Life Guards relieved 2 Squadrons 4th Hussars in Intermediate Line. 1½ Squadrons 1st Life Guards relieved 1½ Squadrons 1st Life Guards in support of Intermediate Line. 3 Squadrons Leicester Yeomanry XXXX took over defences of Second Line from 3 Squadrons 2nd Life Guards. The Artillery in 'D' Sector under command of Lieut-Colonel Wainwright, R.A. consisted of : 'C' and 'K' Batteries, R.H.A. B/296 and C/296 Batteries R.F.A. D/296 4.5" Howitzer Battery. 6th Cavalry Field Ambulance relieved C.F.Ambulance of 2nd Cavalry Division at Advanced Dressing Station in EPEHY.	
	25th May		On completion of the relief, Brigadier General A.E.W. Harman, D.S.O. assumed command of 'D' Sector. The whole sector was very quiet with the exception of two localities, The BIRDCAGE in the Outpost Line, and PETIT PRIEL FARM in the Intermediate Line. The former was subjected daily to Trench Mortar fire, while the latter was shelled by Field Guns. Working Parties commenced work both by day and by night and continued during the Brigade's tour in the trenches.	
	XXXX May. 26th.		Patrols were sent out during the night to canal and OSSUS WOOD and towards XXXXX Hill 140. From this date onwards, these localities were patrolled every night. Casualties: 1874 Pte. Wilkinson, D. 3rd Dragoon Guards. Accidentally Wounded.	

Army Form C. 2118.

'A' SECTOR

WAR DIARY
or
INTELLIGENCE SUMMARY.
(Erase heading not required)

Place	Date	Hour	Summary of Events and Information	Remarks and references to Appendices
Field.	27th May.		Nothing of importance occurred. Casualties: 4151 Pte Dysart, D. Royal Dragoons. Wounded.	

	28th May.		Reliefs took place as follows:
			
			D.1 Sub-sector.
			
			1½ Squadrons North Somerset Yeomanry relieved 1½ Squadrons Royal Dragoons in the Outpost Line.
			1½ Squadrons N. S. Y. relieved 1½ Squadrons Royals in support of Intermediate Line.
			Royals took over Intermediate Line, and the 3rd D. Gds. went back to Second Line.
			
			D.2.Sub-sector.
			
			1½ Squadrons 1st Life Guards relieved 1½ Squadrons 1st Life Guards in Outpost Line
			
			Casualties. 3555 Pte Reid, C. Royal Dragoons, Wounded.
			               2871 " Cooper, J.W. " " " Wounded.
			               165570 L.Cpl. Harris, A.V. North Somerset Yeomanry. Wounded.
			               165508 Pte. Emery, H. " " " "
			               165264 " Selman, R, . " " " "
			               165541 L"Cpl. Webber, W.J. " " " " (At duty).
			               165432 Cpl. Barnett, A.H. " " " " "
			               165733 Pte. Sheppard, A.E. " " " "
			               165376 " Kittlety, F.A. " " " "
			               165847 " Smale, F. " " " "
			               165548 L.Cpl. Watts, R.P. " " " "
			
			During the night, the enemy made a raid on the Communication Trench from the QUARRIES to the BIRDCAGE. No.165476 Cpl. DUNN, North Somerset Yeomanry, was on his way down the trench when he was captured by the Raiding Party, and taken to the German line.	

Army Form C. 2118.

"D" SECTOR

WAR DIARY
INTELLIGENCE SUMMARY.
(Erase heading not required.)

Instructions regarding War Diaries and Intelligence Summaries are contained in F. S. Regs., Part II. and the Staff Manual respectively. Title pages will be prepared in manuscript.

Place	Date	Hour	Summary of Events and Information	Remarks and references to Appendices
Field.	29th May.		Nothing to report. Work continued as usual.	
	30th May.		Following reliefs were carried out :-	
			D.1. Sub-sector.	
			1½ Squadrons 3rd D.Gds. relieved 1½ Squadrons N.S.Y. in the Outpost Line.	
			1½ Squadrons 3rd D.Gds. relieved 1½ Squadrons of the N.S.Y. in support of the Intermediate Line.	
			3 Squadrons N.S.Y. took over Intermediate Line from the Royal Dragoons.	
			3 Squadrons of Royals went back to Second line.	
			D.2 Sub-sector.	
			1½ Squadrons of 2nd Life Guards took over the Outpost Line, from 1½ Squadrons 1st Life Guards.	
			1½ Squadrons 2nd Life Guards took over from 1½ Squadrons 1st Life Guards in support of Intermediate Line.	
			3 Squadrons Leicester Yeomanry took over from 3 Squadrons 2nd Life Guards in the Intermediate Line, and 1st Life Guards went back to Second Line.	
			During the relief of the BIRDCAGE, 2 Officers took out a Patrol to the Southern edge of OSSUS WOOD, to lie in wait for any hostile patrols. While carrying out this duty, one of the Officers shot a Sniper, but no patrol appeared.	
	31st May.		4 Officers and 117 Other Ranks from 8th Cavalry Brigade billeted in EPEHY, for work on the Outpost and Intermediate Lines. 3rd D.Gds.	
			Casualties: 3682 Pte Gartell, R. 3rd D.Gds. Wounded.	

Army Form C. 2118.

"D" SECTOR

WAR DIARY
or
INTELLIGENCE SUMMARY.
(Erase heading not required.)

Resume of Work Done (cont).

Instructions regarding War Diaries and Intelligence Summaries are contained in F. S. Regs., Part II. and the Staff Manual respectively. Title pages will be prepared in manuscript.

Place	Date	Hour	Summary of Events and Information	Remarks and references to Appendices
			The new sub-sector H.Q. was almost completed. A new support trench joining 'M' and 'L' Redoubts 140 yards behind the existing communication trench was dug T-heads were made in the Sunken Road just North of CATELET COPSE. *******************	

Brigade Major, "D" SECTOR Captain,

Army Form C. 2118.

'A' SECTOR

WAR DIARY
INTELLIGENCE SUMMARY.
(Erase heading not required.)

Instructions regarding War Diaries and Intelligence Summaries are contained in F.S. Regs., Part II. and the Staff Manual respectively. Title pages will be prepared in manuscript.

Place	Date	Hour	Summary of Events and Information	Remarks and references to Appendices
			RESUME OF WORK DONE.	
			D.1 Sub-sector.	
			Outpost Line. The BIRDCAGE was strengthened and wire increased. A trench was made connecting with the Hotchkiss Post. The trench communicating with the QUARRY was wired continuously on the North and South sides. Wire was also commenced along the suggested communication trench, starting from 'G' Redoubt to the QUARRY.	
			Intermediate Line. All the Redoubts were strengthened. New M.G. Emplacements were made and M.G. Dug-outs were started. In several cases the XXX latter were completed. The new Sub-sector H.Q. was completed. Communication Trenches were dug from 'H' and 'G' Redoubts and a new support trench joining these two communication trenches was started. The SUNK ROAD from the Well to Copse 13 was dug deep enough to allow of men going up to the trenches by day. New wire was put up in front of the Intermediate Line and the old German trench just North of PETIT PRIEL FARM was filled in.	
			D.2.Sub-sector.	
			Outpost Line. The former dispositions were slightly altered. A new XXX and more central H.Q. was dug with room for 1 Support Troop. A new post was also dug. The posts now numbering 4 were all wired. This was only completed in the case of 2 and 3. The new H.Q. of the Outposts was joined to the Intermediate line by a communication.	
			Intermediate Line. All the redoubts were improved and strengthened. New M.G. Emplacements and dug-outs were made. A communication trench 750 yards in length was dug, leading to 'M' Redoubt.	

SECRET.
****

[To D. File]
App A

3rd D.Gds.	6th C.F.A.	L.20/5.
Royals.	13th M.V.S.	
N.S.Y.	Camp Commandant.	
6th M.Gun Sqn.	3rd Cav.Divn. G.S. 'Q'	

Supply Officer.
Transport Officer.
Requisition Officer.
Chaplain.
7th Cavalry Brigade.
~~3rd Cavalry Brigade.~~
Sheet
Ref.Map 1/20,000 /62 C

22nd May, 1917.

1. The 6th Cavalry Brigade will relieve D.1 Sub-Sector of BELL-SMYTH'S Brigade (for details see G.186/1), as follows: Relief to be completed by dawn on May 25th.

(A) <u>Night of 22/23rd May</u>

6th M.Gun Sqn. 3 Officers will report at H.Q. BELL-SMYTH'S Brigade (F.17d.8.8.) at 8 p.m. on 22nd May. They will be met by guides and shewn all Machine gun emplacements.

(B) <u>Night of 23/24th May.</u> machine guns of

6th M.Gun Sqn. will relieve Machine Gun Sqn. in and about the GREEN Line D.1. Sub-sector.
Arrangements for relief will be made between O.C. 6th M.Gun Sqn. and O.C. 3rd M.Gun Sqn.
(3 limbers of 6th M.Gun Sqn. will be required for carrying water, rations, material, etc)
Relief not to commence before 9 p.m. from X Roads in EPEHY F.1.c.9.8., where guides will meet 6th M.Gun Sqn.

3rd Dragoon Gds.)
H.Q. & 3 Sqns.) 4½ Squadrons, under the command of
Royals: 1½ Sqns Lieut.Colonel A.BURT, D.S.O. 3rd D.Gds

will relieve 16th Lancers, who have 1 Squadron in support to GREEN Line, and 2 Squadrons in and about BROWN Line.
(Royals 1½ Squadrons will relieve 1 Squadron 16th Lancers in support to GREEN Line, and 3 Squadrons 3rd Dragoon Gds. will relieve 2 Squadrons 16th Lancers in BROWN Line.)

Representatives of Royals 1½ Squadrons, and of each of the 3 Squadrons 3rd Dragoon Gds. will go forward on the night 23/24th to reconnoitre OUTPOST Line and GREEN Line respectively, under Lieut.Colonel BURT'S instructions.
Guides for these Squadrons and for Officers and N.C.Os. going into front line will be at Reserve Battalion H.Q. D.1 Sub-sector in EPEHY at F.1.c.6.5 at 9.15 p.m.

The Royals 1½ Squadrons moving into support of GREEN Line will come under the command of O.C. D.1. Sub-sector.

Signallers will be sent on to reconnoitre existing lines

(C) <u>Night of 24/25th.</u>

H.Q. & 3 Squadrons 3rd Dragoon Gds., and 1½ Squadrons Royals will take over GREEN Line and OUTPOST Line respectively, under arrangements to be made by Lt.Colonel BURT direct with O.C. D.1 Sub-sector, whose H.Q. are in F.3.b.8.5
H.Q. (2nd-in-Command and reduced personnel) and 1½ Squadrons Royals will move into support of GREEN Line, taking over from the

advanced/

1. (C) Contd.

advanced 1½ Squadrons of the Royals. Guides to be at Reserve Battalion H.Q. EPEHY F.1.c.6.5. at 9 p.m.

H.Q. (2nd-in-Command and reduced personnel) and 3 Squadrons N.S.Y. will take over positions in neighbourhood of the BROWN Line from the H.Q. and 3 Squadrons 3rd Dragoon Gds. Guides to be at Reserve Battalion H.Q. EPEHY F.1.c.6.5. at 9.30 p.m.

Brigade H.Q. 8th Cavalry Brigade will relieve Brigade H.Q. 3rd Cavalry Brigade F.1.d.8.8. Guides to be at Road junction at F.1.c.6.5. at 8.45 p.m.

2. In consequence on the night 23/24th 6th M.Gun Sqn. will move mounted to E.11 so as to arrive there by 8.45 p.m.

H.Q. and 3 Squadrons 3rd Dragoon Gds. and 1½ Squadron Royals will move mounted to E.11, so as to arrive at 9 p.m.
(N.S.Y. will assist 3rd Dragoon Gds. to bring back led horses, at the rate of 1 man to 3 horses, under arrangements of units concerned)

On night 24th/25th
Brigade H.Q. will move, mounted, to E.11 so as to arrive 8.30 p.m.
H.Q. & 1½ Squadrons Royals will move, mounted, to E.11, to arrive 8.45 p.m.
H.Q. & 3 Squadrons N.S.Y. will move, mounted, to arrive 9.15 p.m.
(Camp Party of 3rd Dragoon Gds. will assist N.S.Y. to bring back horses)
NOTE: Brigade H.Q., Royals, and N.S.Y. will send 1 Officer each, mounted, with 3rd Dragoon Gds. on night 23/24th to reconnoitre route from Camp West of VILLERS-FAUCON to E.11.

Mounted troops will on no account reach E.11 before 8.30 p.m., and will not move in large bodies.
Horses will be sent back immediately to permanent bivouacs under Officers to be detailed by units.

3. All units of 6th Cavalry Brigade will come under the orders of the G.O.C. BELL-SMYTH'S Brigade until command passes to General HARMAN on completion of reliefs on night 24th/25th.
Sub-Sectors. Units will report to Brigade H.Q. when relief is complete, and send 4 runners to report at Brigade H.Q. who will remain as permanent orderlies.

4. (a) A Regimental Aid Post will be established at H.Q. of Lieut. Colonels commanding D.1 and D.2 Sub-sectors.
(b) There will be an aid post in EPEHY near Water Tank F.1.c.5.5.
(c) Combined 2nd & 3rd Cav.Div. Dressing Station will be in VILLERS-FAUCON

5. 3rd Field Squadron will remain working in D. Sector.

6. O.C. Units will issue strict orders that no fires are to be lighted East of BROWN Line.

7. Full details regarding D. Sector are contained in 3rd C.D. Defence Scheme (G.186/1 with Appendix A attached.
Details regarding location of Dumps of S.A.A., Grenades, S.O.S. Signals, Very Lights, are contained in Appendix B attached.

8. N.C.Os and men proceeding to trenches will carry blankets and waterproof sheets rolled on banderole on leaving camp.
British Warms and cloaks will not be taken.
Hotchkiss Rifles and ammunition will be carried to E.11 on pack.
1 bandolier only will be taken

9. Transport of Brigade H.Q., Regiments, and M.Gun Sqn. will move by road, under 1 Officer per unit) so as to meet units in EPEHY at 9 p.m. 23/24th and 24/25th. Full instructions regarding route and meeting places will be issued by Staff Captain.

10. ACKNOWLEDGE.

                                               Howes. Captain.
                               Brigade Major 6th Cavalry Brigade.

APPENDIX B.

BELL-SMYTH'S BRIGADE D. Sector.

LOCATION Dumps.	MAP CO-ORDINATES.	S.A.A.	GRENADES No.5.	GRENADES No.20.	No.23	STOKES AMMUN.	S.O.S. "A"	VERY LIGHTS 1"W.	1½"W.	1½"R.	G.	Grd. Flares R.G.	SMOKE CASE
Bde.H.Q.	F.1.c.2.7	91,000	504	410	72	-	21	303	104	78	-	300	26
D.1.Sub-sector.	No.13 Copse F3647	108,000	960	320	-	-	9	300	11	-	-	-	-
D.2 Sub-sector	X.25.c.3.7.	65,500	864	260	60	-	17	60	-	60	60	79	-
D.1 Sub-sector BROWN Line.)	F.1.b.9.5	108,000	348	240	-	-	-	-	-	-	-	-	-
D.2 Sub-sector BROWN Line	W.30.d.4.4.	72,000	-	-	-	-	-	-	-	-	-	-	-
M.Gun Squadron.	W.30.d.4.1	48,000	-	-	-	-	-	-	-	-	-	-	-

	"P" Bombs.	Rockets, G.& S. Rain.
Bde.H.Q.	-	11
D.1.Sub-sector	-	9
B.2.sub-sector	-	6
D.1 Sub-sector) BROWN Line.)	-	-
D.2.Sub-sector) BROWN Line	-	-

3rd C.D. G.186/1

SECRET.
****

3rd CAVALRY DIVISION DEFENCE SCHEME.

1. **BOUNDARIES OF DIVISIONAL FRONT**

    (a)   The boundaries of the Divisional Sector which is known as the "D" Sector, are as follows :-

    (i) On South, the line F.8.c.0.0. - N. Side of MAY COPSE - F.6.c.0.2.
    (ii) On North, the line : N.exit of PEIZIERE - TARGELLE Ravine, X.15.d.7.6. - along N. side of Ravine - X.18.a.7.0.

    (b)   This area is divided into 2 sub-sectors - the Southern sub-sector being known as D.1., and the Northern as D.2.

    (c)   The 2nd Cavalry Division is on our right - the 40th Infy. Infantry Division is on our left.

2. **COMMAND.**
    Each sub-sector will be under the command of a Lieut.Colonel, the whole sector being under a Brigadier-General, whose Headquarters will be at F.1.d.8.8.
    Not more than 2 Lieut-Colonels will be in the line at the same time.

3. **TROOPS ALLOTTED.**
    On taking over from Brig-General BELL-SMYTH'S Brigade, troops will be distributed as under :
    Sub-sector D.1. - 6th Cavalry Brigade.
    -do-   D.2. - 7th Cavalry Brigade.

4. **DESCRIPTION OF DEFENCES.**
    There will eventually be 4 lines :
    (a) The OUTPOST Line.
    (b) The GREEN Line.
    (c) The BROWN Line.
    (d) The BROWN SUPPORT Line.

    (a) consists of a series of posts from the BIRDCAGE in X.29.d.9.8., running northwards to connect with 40th Division about X.17.d.0.7.
    (b) consists of 6 mutually supporting posts, constructed for all-round defence. There are covered by continuous wire and connected by trenches in places.
    (c) and (d) are partially, but not completely wired. 2 Battalions 178th Infantry Brigade are allotted to 3rd Cavalry Division for work on the BROWN Line from 25th to 28th inst. (inclus).

5. **METHOD OF HOLDING THE LINE.**
    (a)   The OUTPOST and GREEN Lines will be held lightly during the day-time, with plenty of automatic rifles and machine guns and with supports at hand, which can work at night and counter-attack, if necessary, by day or night.
    (b)   In order to facilitate reliefs, and to equalise work, the distribution of troops in each sub-sector will be :-
    (i) OUTPOST Line - 1 or 1½ Sqdns. "A" Regiment.
    (ii) GREEN Line   - 3 Sqdns., "B" Regiment.
    (iii) BROWN Line   - 3 Sqdns. "C" Regiment.
    The remaining 2 or 1½ Sqdns. of "A" Regiment will be stationed in rear of (ii) or (iii), as accommodation is available.

6. DEFENSIVE BARRAGES.

S.O.S. Lines are arranged for covering both OUTPOST and GREEN Lines. As the number of guns does not admit of a continuous barrage across the whole front, the S.O.S. lines are arranged so as to cover probable lines of approach, and arrangements are made to concentrate quickly on threatened points.

In the event of the OUTPOST Line being captured, the S.O.S. barrage will be brought back to cover the GREEN Line by Artillery Group Commanders in consultation with the Cavalry Brigade Commander.

As soon as possible, O.sC 6th and 7th M.G. Squadrons will inform C' R.H.A. what portion of these barrage lines they can cover with M.G. barrage. This will enable the Artillery barrage to be thicker on the remainder of the line.

7. PRINCIPLES OF DEFENCE.

(a) In case of local attacks.

The OUTPOST LINE must be held. In the event of the enemy penetrating into any portion of it, he must at once be counter-attacked and ejected.

All Commanders - down to Troop Leaders - must study their positions, and have plans ready for immediate counter-attack with the troops at their disposal at the moment.

(b) In case of attack by the enemy in force.

The GREEN Line is the main line of resistance of the Division and must be held at all costs. Troops holding the OUTPOST Line will do everything possible to delay and break up the enemy's attack. In the event of the enemy penetrating into any portion of the GREEN Line, the Commander of the local reserves to that portion will at once counter-attack with the troops immediately available. Should this be unsuccessful, the Brigade Commander will organise a counter-attack at the earliest possible moment, with such of his reserves and of the Artillery at his disposal as may be necessary. If an operation requiring more strength than is at the disposal of the Brigade Commander is necessary, it will be carried out under orders of the Divisional Commander and after such preparation of Field and Heavy Artillery as the circumstances require. Plans for counter-attacks in any of these eventualities will be prepared in advance by the Commanders concerned.

(c) So soon as the Brigadier considers that he is likely to use the Regiment in the BROWN Line, he will inform the Divisional Commander, who will immediately move up the Brigade in training to the BROWN Line.

8. PATROLLING.

Instructions have already been issued as to employment of patrols - vide 3rd Cav.Div. No. G.240.

Sub-sector Commanders will submit plans for "fighting patrols" to the Brigadier

9. WORK.

The chief task of the Division will probably consist in working on the defences ; this work is classified in order of importance as follows :

(i) Completion of OUTPOST Line (making continuous, wired trench) from BIRDCAGE to join 40th Division about X.17.d.0.7.

(ii) Completion of posts G. - M. as all round works.

(iii) Construction of dug-outs for M.G. Detachments, O.Ps. and Squadron Headquarters.

(iv) Communications to make movement to and from GREEN Line possible by daylight.

10. CONCEALMENT.

All new work will be screened as far as possible. As camouflage becomes available, approaches will also be screened.

11. RELIEFS.

(i) Lieut.Colonels will be relieved every six days under Brigade arrangements.
(ii) Brigadiers will be relieved every seven days.
(iii) The 8th Cavalry Brigade will relieve the 6th Cavalry Brigade after 9 days.
(iv) The 6th Cavalry Brigade will relieve the 7th Cavalry Brigade after 18 days.

Sd/ J.VAUGHAN, Major-General,
Commanding 3rd Cavalry Division.

21/5/17.

APPENDIX 'A'.

1. AMMUNITION.

    S.A.A.   200 rounds per rifle, in addition to the amount
             carried on the man, should be kept in each line
             of defence.

             H.Q. of Front Line system. 100 rounds per rifle.
             Brigade Reserve.   100   "   "   "

    HOTCHKISS.

             2100 rounds in clips.) per Hotchkiss Rifle.
             2000 rounds in boxes.)

             H.Q. of Front Line system 1000 rounds per H.Rifle.
             Brigade Reserve.   1000   "   "   "   "

    MACHINE GUNS.

             3500 rounds in belts) per
             5000 rounds in boxes.) gun.

             H.Q. of Front Line system. 2000 rounds per gun.
             Brigade Reserve   2000   "   "   "

2. BOMBS.

             15 to 20 boxes in Outpost line of sub-sectors.
             36 boxes in GREEN Line of sub-sectors.
             100 boxes in H.Q. of sub-sectors.
             400 boxes in Brigade Reserve.

3. COMMUNICATION.

         All messages sent by Wireless, Signal or over
    the telephone must be sent in code, and never otherwise,
    except in case of S.O.S.
         H.Q. of Sub-sectors are in communication with
    Brigade Headquarters by Wireless.

4. LIAISON WITH ARTILLERY.

         During the day, an Artillery Officer is in an O.P.
    in front line, and is in direct telephonic communication
    with the Artillery Group Commander, and also with
    sub-sector commander's H.Q.
         By night, this Officer remains at sub-sector
    commander's H.Q.

5. S.O.S. SIGNAL.

         S.O.S. Signal is a Grenade bursting into four
    RED lights.

Army Form C. 2118

'D' SECTOR

App B.

WAR DIARY
or
INTELLIGENCE SUMMARY

(Erase heading not required.)

Instructions regarding War Diaries and Intelligence Summaries are contained in F.S. Regs., Part II. and the Staff Manual respectively. Title Pages will be prepared in manuscript.

Place	Date	Hour	Summary of Events and Information	Remarks and references to Appendices
Field.	23 May.		The 8th Cavalry Brigade began to relieve the 3rd Cavalry Brigade in Sector 'D' of Cavalry Corps front. The trench line to be taken over was from TOMBOIS FARM (exclusive), in F.11.b.2.4 to X.17.d.0.8 (Ref. Map 1/20,000). It was divided into Sub-sectors D.1 and D.2, and had three main lines of defence, the Outpost, Intermediate and Second Line. During the night, the 8th Machine Gun Squadron took over from the portions of the 3rd and 5th Machine Gun Squadrons in D.1 Sub-sector, while the 7th Machine Gun Squadron took over from portions of the 3rd and 5th Machine Gun Squadrons in D.2. Sub-sector. The following reliefs also took place : D.1. Sub-sector. 1½ Squadrons Royals relieved 1 Squadron 16th Lancers in support of Intermediate line. 3rd D.Gds. relieved remaining 2 Squadrons of 16th Lancers in Second Line. D.2. Sub-sector. 1½ Squadrons 1st Life Guards took over from 15th Lancers in support of Intermediate line. 2nd Life Guards relieved remaining 2 Squadrons 5th Lancers in Second Line. During the evening Lieut-Colonel A. BURT, D.S.O., took over command of Sub-sector D.1, while Lieut-Colonel Hon.A.F.Stanley, D.S.O. took over the command of the Sub-sector D.2.	57/2 S.e
"	24th May.		The following reliefs took place : D.1 Sub-sector. 1½ Squadrons Royals relieved 2 Squadron Royal Scots Greys in the Outpost Line. 3rd D.Gds. relieved 2 Squadrons Royal Scots Greys in Intermediate line. 1½ Squadrons Royals relieved 1½ Squadrons Royals in support of Intermediate Line. N.S.Y. took over the defences of the Second line from the 3rd D.Gds.	

Army Form C. 2118.

"A" SECTOR

WAR DIARY
or
INTELLIGENCE SUMMARY.
(Erase heading not required.)

Instructions regarding War Diaries and Intelligence Summaries are contained in F.S. Regs., Part II. and the Staff Manual respectively. Title pages will be prepared in manuscript.

Place	Date	Hour	Summary of Events and Information	Remarks and references to Appendices
Field.	27th May.		Nothing of importance occurred. Casualties: 4161 Pte Dysart, D. Royal Dragoons. Wounded.	

	28th May.		Reliefs took place as follows:-
			
			 D.1 Sub-sector.
			
			 1½ Squadrons North Somerset Yeomanry relieved 1½ Squadrons Royal Dragoons in the Outpost Line.
			 1½ Squadrons N. S. Y. relieved 1½ Squadrons Royals in support of Intermediate Line.
			 Royals took over Intermediate Line, and the 3rd D. Gds. went back to Second Line.
			
			 D.2.Sub-sector.
			
			 1½ Squadrons 1st Life Guards relieved 1½ Squadrons 1st Life Guards in Outpost Line
			
			 Casualties. 3655 Pte Reid, O. Royal Dragoons, Wounded.
			             2871 " Cooper, J.W. " "
			             165570 L.Cpl. Harris, A.V. North Somerset Yeomanry. Wounded.
			             165508 Pte. Emery, H. " "
			             165284 " Selman, R. " " (At duty).
			             165541 L."Cpl. Webber, W.J. " "
			             165452 Cpl. Barnett, A.H. " "
			             165765 Pte. Sheppard, A.E. " "
			             165576 " Kittlety, F.A. " "
			             165847 " Smale, F. " "
			             165548 L.Cpl. Watts, R.P. " "
			
			 During the night, the enemy made a raid on the Communication Trench from the QUARRIES to the BIRDCAGE. No.165476 Cpl. DUNN, North Somerset Yeomanry, was on his way down the trench when he was captured by the Raiding Party, and taken to the German line.	

Army Form C. 2118.

D. SECTOR

WAR DIARY
or
INTELLIGENCE-SUMMARY.
(Erase heading not required.)

Instructions regarding War Diaries and Intelligence Summaries are contained in F.S. Regs., Part II. and the Staff Manual respectively. Title pages will be prepared in manuscript.

Place	Date	Hour	Summary of Events and Information	Remarks and references to Appendices
Field.	24th May.		**D.2 Sub-sector.**	
			1½ Squadrons 1st Life Guards relieved 1 Squadron 4th Hussars, in Outpost Line.	
			5 Squadrons 2nd Life Guards relieved 2 Squadrons 4th Hussars in Intermediate Line.	
			1½ Squadrons 1st Life Guards relieved 1½ Squadrons 1st Life Guards in support of Intermediate Line.	
			5 Squadrons Leicester Yeomanry took over defences of Second Line from 5 Squadrons 2nd Life Guards.	
			The Artillery in 'D' Sector under command of Lieut-Colonel Wainwright, R.A. consisted of :	
			'C' and 'K' Batteries, R.H.A.	
			B/296 and C/296 Batteries R.F.A.	
			D/296 4.5" Howitzer Battery.	
			6th Cavalry Field Ambulance relieved C.F.Ambulance of 2nd Cavalry Division at Advanced Dressing Station in EPEHY.	
	25th May		On completion of the relief, Brigadier General A.E.W. Harman, D.S.O. assumed command of 'D' Sector.	
			The whole sector was very quiet with the exception of two localities,	
			The BIRDCAGE in the Outpost Line, and PETIT PRIEL FARM in the Intermediate Line. The former was subjected daily to Trench Mortar fire, while the latter was shelled by Field Guns.	
			Working Parties commenced work both by day and by night and continued during the Brigade's tour in the trenches.	
	26th May.		Patrols were sent out during the night to canal and OSSUS WOOD and towards Hill 140. From this date onwards, these localities were patrolled every night.	
			Casualties: 1874 Pte. Wilkinson, D. 3rd Dragoon Guards. Accidentally wounded.	

Army Form C. 2118.

WAR DIARY
INTELLIGENCE SUMMARY.
(Erase heading not required.)

A SECTOR

Place	Date	Hour	Summary of Events and Information	Remarks and references to Appendices
Field.	29th May.		Nothing to report. Work continued as usual.	
	30th May.		Following reliefs were carried out :-	
			D.1. Sub-sector.	
			1½ Squadrons 3rd D.Gds. relieved 1½ Squadrons N.S.Y. in the Outpost Line.	
			1½ Squadrons 3rd D. Gds. relieved 1½ Squadrons of the N.S.Y. in support of the Intermediate Line.	
			3 Squadrons N.S.Y. took over Intermediate Line from the Royal Dragoons.	
			3 Squadrons of Royals went back to Second line.	
			D.2 Sub-sector.	
			1½ Squadrons of 2nd Life Guards took over the Outpost Line, from 1½ Squadrons 1st Life Guards.	
			1½ Squadrons 2nd Life Guards took over from 1½ Squadrons 1st Life Guards in support of Intermediate Line.	
			5 Squadrons Leicester Yeomanry took over from 5 Squadrons 2nd Life Guards in the Intermediate Line, and 1st. Life Guards went back to Second Line.	
			During the relief of the BIRDCAGE, 2 Officers took out a Patrol to the Southern edge of OSSUS WOOD, to lie in wait for any hostile patrols. While carrying out this duty, one of the Officers shot a Sniper, but no patrol appeared.	
	31st May.		4 Officers and 117 Other Ranks from 8th Cavalry Brigade billeted in EPEHY, for work on the Outpost and Intermediate Lines.	
			Casualties: 3682 Pte Gartell, R. 3rd D.Gds. Wounded.	

Army Form C. 2118.

D. SECTOR

WAR DIARY
INTELLIGENCE SUMMARY.
(Erase heading not required.)

Summary of Events and Information

RESUME OF WORK DONE.

D.1 Sub-sector.
Outpost Line.

The BIRDCAGE was strengthened and wire increased. A trench was made connecting with the Hotchkiss Post.
The trench communicating with the QUARRY was wired continuously on the North and South sides.
Wire was also commenced along the suggested communication trench, starting from 'G' Redoubt to the QUARRY.

Intermediate Line.

All the Redoubts were strengthened.
New M.G. Emplacements were made and M.G. Dug-outs were started.
In several cases the LMX latter were completed.
The new Sub-sector H.Q. was completed.
Communication Trenches were dug from 'H' and 'G' Redoubts and a new support trench joining these two communication trenches was started.
The SUNK ROAD from the Well to Copse 15 was dug deep enough to allow of men going up to the trenches by day.
New wire was put up in front of the Intermediate line and the old German trench just North of PETIT PRIEL FARM was filled in.

D.2 Sub-sector.
Outpost Line.

The former dispositions were slightly altered.
A new MXM and more central H.Q. was dug with room for 1 Support Troop.
A new post was also dug. The posts now numbering 4 were all wired.
This was only completed in the case of 2 and 3.
The new H.Q. of the Outposts was joined to the Intermediate line by a communication.

Intermediate Line.

All the redoubts were improved and strengthened. New M.G. Emplacements and dug-outs were made.
A communication trench 750 yards in length was dug, leading to 'N' Redoubt.

Resume of Work Done (cont).

Army Form C. 2118.

WAR DIARY
INTELLIGENCE SUMMARY.

D Sector

(Erase heading not required.)

Instructions regarding War Diaries and Intelligence Summaries are contained in F. S. Regs., Part II. and the Staff Manual respectively. Title pages will be prepared in manuscript.

Place	Date	Hour	Summary of Events and Information	Remarks and references to Appendices
			The new sub-sector H.Q. was almost completed. A new support trench joining "M" and "L" Redoubts 140 yards behind the existing communication trench was dug. T-heads were made in the Sunken Road just North of CATELET COPSE.	

****

M. Sparks, Captain,
D Sector
Brigade Major 6th Guards Brigade.

App C

ESTABLISHMENT FOR BRIGADE H.Q.
"D" SECTOR.

Detail.	OFFICERS	SERGTS	O.R.	TOTAL	RIDING	DRAUGHT	TOTAL	LIMBERS	MOTOR CARS	
ADVANCED H.Q.										
G.O.C.	1			1						
Brigade Major.	1			1						
A.D.C.	1			1						
Intelligence Offr.	2			2*						*) From Bde
Bombing "	1			1*						) finding Bde.
Sniping "	1			1*						) H.Q.
Batmen.			8	8						
Cook.			1	1						
M.M.P.		1	6	7∅						∅ 3 from other Bde.
Gas N.C.Os.		1		1						
Clerks.		1	2	3+						+ 1 O.R from other Bde.
'Q' Branch at Wagon Lines.										
Staff Capt.	1			1	1		1			
Supply Officer.	1			1						
Transport Offr.	1			1x	1		1			x from other Bde.
Extra Offr.	1			1	1		1			
Batmen.			4	4						
Supply Sergt.		1		1						
Clerks.			2	2						
Issuers.			8	8*						* 3 from other Bde.
Transport Cpl.			1	1	1		1			
Drivers.			2	2		4	4	1		
Chauffeurs.			2	2					2	
TOTAL.	11	4	36	51	4	4	8	1	2	

ESTABLISHMENT FOR SIGNAL TROOP
"D" SECTOR.

Detail.	OFFICERS	SERGTS	O.R.	TOTAL		
Signal Officer.	1			1		
Sergt.		1		1		
Opls.			4(a)	4	(a) 1 from each Bde. not finding Sub-sector H.Q.	
Post Office Telegraphist.			3(b)	3	(b) 1 from one Bde. not finding Sub-sector H.Q.	
Buzzer exchange operator.			3(c)	3	(c) 2 from one Bde not finding Sub-sector H.Q.	
Sappers & Ptes.			8	8	(b & c to be arranged by O.C. 3rd. Signal Squadron.)	
Motor Cyclists.			3	3		
Orderlies.※			8	8	※From D.1 & D.2 Sub-sectors	
TOTAL.	1	1	7	22	31	

WAR ESTABLISHMENT for Dismounted Regiment
A Regiment of H.Q., and 3 Squadrons.

	Officers	W.O's.	S.Sergts & Sergts	Drivers	Rank & File	Total	Horses	Bicycles	Vehicles	
Headquarters.										
Lieut-Colonel,	1					1				
Adjutant.	1					1	3			
Sniping Officer, & Snipers.	2 A		1			3				A. One sniping Off. from another Regt.
Signalling Officer.	1					1	1			
Bombing Officer.	1					1	1			
Intelligence Officer.	1					1	1			
Quartermaster (or Q.M.S.)	1					1	1			
Regtl. Sgt. Major.		1				1				
Q.M.Sgt. (not if Q.M. is up)							1x			x. Riding.
Signalling Sergt.			1			1				
Clerks.			1	1		1				
Armourer Sergt.			1			1				
Transport Sergt.			1			1				
Cook Sergt.			1			1				
Stretcher Bearers.					4	4				
Medical Officer.	1					1	2			
Orderlies for M.O.					2	2				(1 from R.A.M.C.)
Shoeing Smiths.					1	1				
Signallers.					6	6				
Batmen.					7	7 A				
Water Cart Orderly.					1	1				
2 Packs.					2	2	2⊕			⊕ Pack hr
	9	1	6		23	39	3			

Horses and extra batmen for officers as required.

	Officers	W.O's.	S.Sergts & Sergts	Drivers	Rank & File	Total	Horses	Bicycles	Vehicles
Transport.									
Bicycles for orderlies.								2	
Pack horse.					1	1	1		
Cart Water.				1		1	2		1
Cart Officers' Mess.				1		1	2		1
				2	1	3	5	2	2
Recapitulation:-									
Headquarters.									
H.Q.	9	1	6	2	24	42	8	2	2
3 Squdns. (see Appx.A)	9	3	12	12	285	321	24	-	6
TOTALS.	18	4	18	14	309	363	32	2	8

(A) Headquarter details found by each Regiment
not finding Sub-sector H.Q.

Details.	Officers.	Staff Sergts & Sergeants.	O.R.	Total.
2nd-in-Command.	1	-	-	1
R.Q.M.S.	-	1	-	1
Sniping Sergt.	-	1	-	1
Clerk.	-	-	1	1
Shoeing Smith.	-	-	1	1
Batman.	-	-	1	1
Armourer Sergt.	-	1 *	-	1
TOTAL.	1	3	3	7

* from one only of the 2 Regiments not finding Sub-sector H.Q.

(B). TRANSPORT to be found by each Regiment not
finding Sub-Sector Headquarters.

Details.	Water Duties O.R.	Drvrs.	Total.	Horses. Draught	Total	Vehicle
Cart, water.	-	1	1	2	2	1
Cart, Officers' Mess.	-	1	1	2	2	1
Medical Orderly (with water cart.)	1 *	-	-	-	-	
TOTAL.	1	2	2	4	4	2

* Should be a corporal.

Appendix A.

Proposed WAR ESTABLISHMENT for a Dismounted Squadron.

Detail.	PERSONNEL.					HORSES.		VEHICLES.
	OFFICERS.	W.O.'s.	S.Sgts & Sergts	DRIVERS.	Rank & File	TOTAL.	DRAUGHT.	TOTAL.	
O.C. Sqdn. (Major or Capt.)	1					1			
Subalterns.	2					2			
S.Q.M.S.		1				1			
Sergeants.			4			4			
Signallers.					3	3			
Batmen.					3	3			
Corporals.					7	7			
Privates.					70	70			
Stretcher Bearers.					4	4			
Snipers.					8	8			
Total.	3	1	4		95	103			

Transport.

Wagons L.G.S. for Trench Stores.				2		2	4	4	1
Wagons L.G.S. for Supplies.				2		2	4	4	1
TOTALS.	3	1	4	4	95	107	8	8	2

WAR ESTABLISHMENT OF A DISMOUNTED MACHINE GUN SQUADRON – (12 GUNS.)

Detail.	PERSONNEL.					HORSES.			BICYCLES	VEHICLES. L.G.S.
	OFFICERS.	W.O's	STAFF SERGTS. and SERGTS.	DRIVERS	RANK & FILE.	TOTAL.	DRAUGHT.	PACK.	TOTAL.	
Commander.	1					1					
Officers.	6					6					
Sqdn. Sgt. Major.		1				1					
Sergeants.			6			6					
Armourer.			1			1					
Shoeing Smith.(Corporal).					1	1	1		1		(Riding).
Drivers.				8		8	16		16		4
Gunners.					84	84					
Signallers.					3	3				1	
Batmen.					7	7					
Range Takers.					6	6					
Pack.					1	1		1	1		
TOTAL.	7	1	7	8	102	125	17	1	18	1	4

Army Form C. 2118.

6th Cavalry Brigade
June 1917

WAR DIARY
or
INTELLIGENCE SUMMARY.
(Erase heading not required.)

Place	Date	Hour	Summary of Events and Information	Remarks and references to Appendices
Field	1		Following relief of 4th Cav Bde the following took place during 1st/2nd inst. 8th M.G. Sqn took over sufficient ground from Canal Bank. 1st Sqdn 10th Hussars relieving 1st Sqdn 3rd D.G.'s & determined subjects in the Royal Horse Guards relieving 1st R Dragoons in 2nd line. Lt Col. Lord Tottenham 10th C.R.E.M.P.O. relieving Lt Col A Burn DSO in command of 2nd support.	
	2		1st to 3rd 16th Hussars relieved remaining 1 sqdn 3rd DG's in support line. Royal Horse Guards relieved N Somerset Yeo. in support. Extract line. 7th Cav Fld Amb relieve 6th Cav Fld Amb at Advanced Dressing Station in IZRAY.	
	3		Brigadier General B P Portal C.B. D.S.O relieves Brigdr. A.E.W. Harman D.S.O. at C.O.D. Lock. Casualties 1st June to 3rd June. Officers CCM Hilton Green 1st R Dragoon wounded 1st June. 15.698 Pte Atkins D 3rd D.G. wounded	

Army Form C. 2118.

WAR DIARY
or
INTELLIGENCE SUMMARY.
(Erase heading not required.)

6th Cavalry Brigade
June 1917

Place	Date	Hour	Summary of Events and Information	Remarks and references to Appendices
BURE	4th		6th Cavalry Bde having been relieved from the line took over the duties of Res. Bde from 8th Cav Bde. Duties of Res. Bde were to provide mounted & regl & dismounted:— (1) Troops that had been taken from 2nd line. (2) To ambulances & regnl posns of Van Bdes & Dismounts of June especially to LEMPIRE sector on the Southern boundary of sector with 2nd Cav Bde. (3) To be winded on & tops kept & process the Ludwig Both of remounted Indian Div. To acts as Bde of reinforce 2nd Cav Bde & 4th Cav Div. Copy of order to Bde to be attached.	App A.
	7		The 13th Corps are on a tactical scheme in accordance with App A orders issued to be seen by Brt Commanders Army landed of the Avenue.	
	8		The arch the Bde was led from A Bombardo & roles at regain the LEMPIRE sector line from B Post to B intersect Seekers I inch Regt were put at disposal of 2nd Regent of Kennedy	[signature]

WAR DIARY or INTELLIGENCE SUMMARY

Army Form C. 2118.

C.B. Cavalry Brigade
June 1917

Place	Date	Hour	Summary of Events and Information	Remarks and references to Appendices
BURE	6.		1 MGer & 5 OR Essex from 3rd DT & Royals attended a 4 days course in Stokes mortars under Capt Brutton until 10th - 7th Batt. at 9th Cav Bde.	
			7 Lts 2 R.W.Kt 3rd DT & Lt. Hon R H CUBITT Royals attached the Corps 3rd Aus. Lt.H. from Royals & 3 OR (one from each Regt of 7th Bde) left to join 6th Army Sniping School for a course of 12 days see Bouchon.	
			1 NCO + the 15 Cr Lom to Camp as Reserve BT.	
	12.		4 Officers + 150 OR (50 from Each Regt) remained in vicinity of EPEHY as a working party. This party was under command of Capt G M GIBBS NSY Yeomanry Each night.	
	3.10pm		6 Officers and Staff Mounted REPEHY to relieve 7th M.G. on the line Deuberbeck. (2 Officers Royals (Capt F.H.T. TURNER) & 35 m. 5 rank & File	
	10pm		14 Men of Escorts for to Intermediate Dugouts + 3 Sqn Hqrs 2 mill & rifle	
			to 2 machine	
	11.		14 Lt Mrs Royals (Capt TURNER) relieved 1 Off & 5 Escorts Pn in Outpost Line Hqs + 3 Sq. from 3rd DT (Mgr of G T CLIFF) relieved Hqs + Sqly 1/1st Scots in	
			Lt Bromhead at 1pm N.S. Hart Capt

Army Form C. 2118.

6th Cavalry Brigade
June 1917

WAR DIARY
or
INTELLIGENCE SUMMARY.
(Erase heading not required.)

Place	Date	Hour	Summary of Events and Information	Remarks and references to Appendices
BURBE	11		1½ A.M. Regt. relieved forward 1½ Sqdns Royals in 'Intermediate' trenches. H.Q. & 3 Sqdns N.S.7 (Hqrs CM BEAMESE) relieve H.Q. & 3 Sqdns 2nd Dgs in 2nd line. During afternoon gr. Col. Sir Edward Stracey & Hon. F.W. Stopford Royal proceeded to EPEHY via CACHY in 3 religious stoves one the command of D. So Subaltern. Copy of Relief orders atd. Casualties 10543 Pte CAMPBELL J. 12 Royal Dragoon wounded 5898. Pte MCGREGOR F " " 9492. Pte HARRIS E " " 9059. Pte HUNTER G " " 6370. Pte J. THOMPSON " "	App B.
FIELD	14			

[signature]

Army Form C. 2118.

WAR DIARY
or
INTELLIGENCE SUMMARY.
(Erase heading not required.)

6th Cavalry Brigade
June 1917

Place	Date	Hour	Summary of Events and Information	Remarks and references to Appendices
FIELD	15		Enemy patrol attempted to bomb wiring party in D.2 outpost No 1. Par was were driven off by Royals holding that post.	
	17th		Relief in D.2 Sector. 14th Hussars N. Somerset Yeo relieving 1st Royal Dragoons in outpost line. 14th Hrs N.S.Y relieved 1st Sqn Royals in intermediate support. Royals relieved 3rd N Somt Yeo in Intermediate Support line. 3rd N.S.Y relieved N.S.Y in 2nd line.	
	22		Casualties 165881 Pte RIDLEY H.G. N.S.Y. wounded (shell shock). Brig.Gen A.H. Harman D.S. joined 16th Cavalry Bgde. relieving Brig.Gen Lymn Smith. Bgde Hd.Qrs. no. 9 Fleet Rd.	
	21.		In at by Div HQ N Somerset Yeo relieve 1st Col 1st Somerset Yeo + 1st Royal Dragoons in outposts HQ D.2. Major H.A. Tomlinson Royals proceeded to See. Common of Regt. i. D.2. 6 Carts Amt. 2 officers. 20 OR relieve 8th Cav. Div. Amt as returned Advanced Station POZY.	

Signed [signature] Capt.

Army Form C. 2118.

6th Cavalry Brigade.
June 1917

WAR DIARY
or
INTELLIGENCE SUMMARY.
(Erase heading not required.)

Place	Date	Hour	Summary of Events and Information	Remarks and references to Appendices
FIELD	22		Lt Col A Burt DSO 3rd D.G. took over command of 6th Cav Bde vice Lt Col	
	23		Rshops in D.G. sub sector. 3rd D.G. 14 platoons relieved NSY 15 sqn in front line 3rd D.G. 14 platoons relieved 15 sqn NSY in Intermediate support. NSY relieved 3 sqn Royals & 15 sqn 3 sqn D.G. in Intermediate line. Royals took over on same line.	
	25		During early morning 25th a raid was carried out on enemy trenches from X 24 C 1.7 & X 24 a 2.4. The raid was made by 2 parties A Party commanded by Lt Anderson Royals assisted by 2nd Lt J Denville Royals Regt sow officer B Party commanded by Lt C.S. Kehoe Royals assisted by 2nd Lt Rice NSY senior officer. In preparation of the Second of Smith & Royals & NSY were two box ??? were used. parties of Smiths ??? had taken two Royals supper fire 3rd D.G. kpt hostile fire & the wire cut. Bangalore torpedoes. Lt Col Mr Normande D.S.O. Royals was directing officer	[signature]

Army Form C. 2118.

6 Cavalry Brigade
June 1917

WAR DIARY
or
INTELLIGENCE SUMMARY.
(Erase heading not required.)

Place	Date	Hour	Summary of Events and Information	Remarks and references to Appendices
Field	23/6/17		The Right (A) party was operating North of the OCUS Erone Road. The Left (B) party north of the Road. The Right party was near the enemy wire while a Bangalore Torpedo was successfully fused & exploded and the party on the advance. Eventually the party reached enemy trenches which were found empty but had to withdraw owing to flying trenches. The time limit. The Left party on the first line of the enemy wire tried and followed the main line of wire and found some W.L. posts holding a back through the wire & a Rifle Bay entered the enemy trenches. Three Germans were seen & driven off. Two automatic Rifles in shell holes were closed up. The O.C. C party remained in the German trenches for some moments during the time three Germans were accounted for. The enemy bombarded our trenches in K.4 & 2.H.a.3.B. with black mortar on right & left divns. killed. Several of this our men, as both fore coming from their direction. Eng. 29 R Commandant of the contribution J.G. Fabian O.C.

A.D.S.S./Forms/C. 2118.

WAR DIARY or INTELLIGENCE SUMMARY

Army Form C. 2118.

6 Stanley Brigade
June 1917

Place	Date	Hour	Summary of Events and Information	Remarks and references to Appendices
July	25.		The prisoner was taken to our lines before he could be brought in to the intelligence headquarters showing the Germans the lay of the 2nd Battalion Infantry Regt.	

Casualties. 3rd Bn. 4480 Sgt HICK W.T. Killed
13038 L/Cpl BOAST F " "
5444 Pte COMER E Wounded

1st Royal/Dragoon Lewis R.B. HERNE Killed.
8865 Pte NISBET A " "
8889 Pte LEITCH T " "
2nd Lt. T.S. DUNDAS Severely Wounded.
3075 Sgt MANDER R.F. Wounded.
1542 Pte WILKINSON A " "   911 Pte GERRELL R Missing.
3755 " EVANS G " "   7898 " MILES T " "
5768 " BARTLETT C " "
16003 " LAUDER T " "   M.S.7 2/Lt V.C. RICE Wounded.
5930 " COGLAN H " "
6185 " BENNETT J.J. " "

[signature] Capt.

Army Form C. 2118.

WAR DIARY
or
INTELLIGENCE SUMMARY.
(Erase heading not required.)

6 Cavalry Brigade
June 1917

VOL 31

Place	Date	Hour	Summary of Events and Information	Remarks and references to Appendices
June	27		1/3 S/ho 4th Hussars relieve 1/3 S/ho 3rd Lancers in Intermediate Support line. HQ 1/3 S/ho Lancers & 14 S/ho 4th Hussars relieve HQ & 3rd S/ho Royals in 2nd line. 1/3 S/ho 4th Hussars relieve 1/3 S/ho 3rd Lancers in support line. HQ 2nd S/ho Lancers relieve HQ & NCO in intermediate line. Casualties. 3753 Pte McPherson R.H. at Wounded. 6098 - McMull W. Royals =.	
	28.			
	28.3		Bat. remained in camp at BURE.	
	28		Casualties. Injured by the Vessels. 2nd Lt F. PARKS 3rd Bn Lancers. Sgt. for MARSH A 3rd Bn. 15386 Pte Cox H. 7291 - TROTMAN A. 6519 - STEPHENSON AW	

[signature]

3rd D.G's.	6th Signal Troop.
Royals.	Camp Commandant.
N.S.Y.	Supply Officer.
'C' Battery.	Transport Officer.
6th M.G.Sqn.	2/Lt.J.P.BRILL,
6th C.F.A.	'D' Sector (for information).
13th M.V.S.	3rd Cav.Div. G.S.

APPENDIX A

6th Cavalry Brigade Order
for concentration and move to first position of readiness.

Ref.Map.Sheet 62C. N.E. 1/20,000.

1. (a) The Brigade will concentrate with its head at J.23.c. Central North of BUIRE - TINCOURT Road at ZERO hour, and march under the command of Lieut.Colonel A.BURT, D.S.O. 3rd Dragoon Gds. to a position of readiness about E.12. S.W. of EPEHY.
    (b) Order of March. Brigade H.Q., 6th Signal Troop, 3rd D.G's., 6th M.G.Sqn., Royals, N.S.Y.
    (c) Route: Via LONGAVESNES - VILLERS FAUCON.
    (d) 'C' Battery R.H.A. will march independently via VILLERS FAUCON and will rejoin the Brigade about E.12. 1½ hours after the Brigade has left Camp.
    (e) On arrival at E.12 units will dismount, leaving 1 man to 3 horses, and will remain in position of readiness, split up in small bodies.
    (f) Led horses will proceed to K.15.b. under 2nd-in-Command of units, moving independently.
    On arrival here, they will come under the orders of 2nd-in-command N.Somerset Yeomanry, who will keep in touch with the Brigade by sending an Officer with 2 orderlies to the Brigadier.
    He will be responsible for keeping the Brigadier informed of the whereabouts of the led horses in the event of their having to move from K.15.b.

2. Transport Wagons as under will accompany the Brigade :
    (a) 3 L.G.S. Wagons   6th M.G.Sqn.
    1 L.G.S. Wagon per regt. (for carrying ammunition, bombs, etc.)
    Brigade Tool Limber.
    1 Water Cart per unit. (full).

    (b) Transport will concentrate at ZERO hour outside of BUIRE-TINCOURT Road just N.E. of N.S.Y. lines, where it will come under the orders of 2/Lieut.J.P.BRILL, 3rd D. Gds., and march in order of march of units to E.18.b.Central Route: TINCOURT - LONGAVESNES - VILLERS FAUCON.

3. 6th M.G.Sqn. will move on pack.

4. Rations. On man. unexpended portion of days ration, and 1 Iron ration.
    On horse. Unexpended portion of days oat ration.
    Water bottles will be filled before starting.

5. Each Limbered Wagon per Regiment will carry:

5,000 rounds S.A.A.	15 Very Pistols (less those carried on man).
12 Strip Boxes Hotchkiss Ammn. i.e. 3,600 rounds.	3 Hotchkiss Rifle Strip filling boxes machines.
360 Mills Hand Grenades.	
1 1½" Pistol illuminating.	3 boxes 1" Very Flares.
	1 box 1½" flares.

    Each Limber per Regiment will be packed at once on above scale.

3rd D.G's.	13th M.V.S.
Royals.	Supply Officer.
N.S.Y.	Transport Officer.
"C" Battery, R.H.A.	6th Signal Troop.
6th M.G.Sqn.	Camp Commandant.
6th C.F.A.	2/Lt. J.P.BRILL.

1. The 6th Cavalry Brigade will be in reserve to the Sector held by the 3rd Cavalry Division ('D'Sector) and will remain in present area to continue training.

2. It is improbably that the services of the Brigade will be required unless the enemy make a serious attack, penetrate the Intermediate Line, and threaten or capture portions of the Second Line.

3. The role of the Brigade will be :

    (a) Counter-attack, or
    (b) Reinforce troops in the Second Line.

For effectively carrying out either task, the main considerations are that all leaders should know the ground well, and that the troops should arrive at the dismounting positions promptly.

4. In consequence Regimental, Battery, and Machine Gun Officers will reconnoitre the route from the present Camp to S.W. of EPEHY, and dismounting positions about Square E.6 and E.12.

5. Dismounting positions should be selected as far forward as possible consistent with cover and reasonable immunity from shell fire. They should be half way up a slope and not just behind a crest or at the bottom of a valley, either of which the enemy might be able to search.

6. So soon as Regiments and M.G.Sqn have dismounted, they will at once move off on foot, to a position of readiness previously selected i.e.

3rd Dragoon Gds.	at	E.12.a.9.9.
Royals.		E.12.c.9.4.
N.S.Y.		E.12.c.9.4.
6th M.G.Sqn.		E.12.a.9.9.

Led horses will move to a position near water West of ROISEL. The O.C. Led horses will keep touch with events and be ready to move according to Brigadier's orders.

6. The state of readiness required from the Brigade will be that it shall be ready to move at 4 hours notice from the time of receipt of orders at Brigade H.Q. Should it appear probable that the services of the Brigade may be required, a warning order will be sent, directing the Brigade to be ready to move at 1 hours notice.
    The Brigade will therefore be ready to move at 4 hours notice from 6 p.m. 5th June.

7. Fighting troops will move at full War Strength.

8. There is a Divisional Dump of Ammunition, Bombs, Very Lights, etc., at E.16.c.3.1.
    The attached orders will come into force on following message being received from Brigade H.Q.:

    "The Brigade will concentrate at ZERO hour".

                                               Captain,
5/6/17   Brigade Major 6th Cavalry Brigade.

6. When the Brigade concentrates at ZERO Hour, the G.O.C. will proceed to Divisional H.Q. VILLERS FAUCON.
Each Regiment, 'C' Battery R.H.A. and 6th M.G.Sqn., will send one galloper to meet G.O.C. at Divisional H.Q.

7. When any Unit moves it will warn the next in rear of it.

8. Light Section C.F.A. will march independently to Western exit of VILLERS FAUCON.

9. The remainder of the Brigade not referred to in these orders will remain in present Camp. Units will take only sufficient Officers to Complete War Establishment.

From the Dismounting Position in E.12. Squadron Leaders and two Troop Officers will proceed with Dismounted Squadrons. The remaining Officers will accompany Led Horses.

O.C. 3rd Dragoon Gds. will detail a Captain to take command of 6th Cavalry Brigade Details left in camp, and all units will send 2 orderlies to report to him when the Brigade moves.

10. All tool pack horses and those carrying Hotchkiss Rifle Ammunition will be collected at Dismounting Point Position under a Senior N.C.O per Regiment, who will report to the Staff Captain for orders.

11. O.C. N.S.Y. will detail 1 Transport Sgt., and 1 Shoeing Smith to accompany Transport.

12. Captain H.McCOLL JOHNSTON A.V.C. willcproceed with Brigade H.Q. to dismounting point, and will remain afterwards with LedHorses.

13. The Brigade Report Centre will be on the main BUIRE-TINCOURT Road at J.23.central during concentration, and at E.12.9.3. when the Brigade reaches the first position of readiness.

14. ACKNOWEEDGE.

5/6/17.

Sgt S.G. Howes
Captain.
Brigade Major 6th Cavalry Brigade.

3rd Dragoon Gds.
Royals.
N.S.Y.
6th M.Gun Sqn.
6th C.F.A.
"D" Sector (2 copies)
7th Cav.Bde.Details.
Supply Officer.

L.20/29

Ref.Map. 1/20,000 62C. N.E., 62B. N.W.
57C.S.E. 57B. S.W.

9th June, 1917.

1. Troops of 6th Cavalry Brigade will relieve troops of 7th Cavalry Brigade in D.2. Sub-sector on nights 10/11th and 11/12th June, in accordance with attached Movement Table.
Reliefs will not commence before 9.30 p.m.

Lieut.Colonel F.W.WORMALD, D.S.O., Royals, will take command of D.2. Sub-sector from Lieut.Colonel E.H.BRASSEY, M.V.O. 1st Life Guards, on completion of relief on night 11/12th June.

2. (i) On night June 10/11th

A PARTY.
  (a) 6th M.Gun Sqn. will move mounted to E.12. to arrive at 8.45 p.m.
  (b) 1½ Squadrons Royals and H.Q. and 3 Squadrons 3rd Dragoon Guards will move mounted to E.12, to arrive at 9 p.m.
  (c) Sniping Officers of Royals and N.S.Y. and Sniping Sergt. Royals will arrive at E.12. at 8.30 p.m.

(ii) On night 11/12th June.

B. PARTY.
  Lieut.Colonel WORMALD, D.S.O. and Regimental H.Q. Royals, and 1½ Squadrons Royals.
  H.Q. and 3 Squadrons N.S.Y.
  will move mounted to E.12. to arrive at 9 p.m.

Note. Billeting parties of 1 Officer and 1 O.R. per Sqn will report to Brigade H.Q. F.1.d.8.8 at 3 p.m. on 10th from 3rd Dragoon Gds., and 3 p.m. on 11th from N.S.Y.

Units will march independently from Camp with intervals between Squadrons.

(iii) 'C' Battery R.H.A. will relieve 'K' Battery R.H.A. under orders of C.R.H.A.

3. Blankets and waterproof sheets will be carried en banderole.

4. Establishment for trenches will be as laid down in L.20/25.

5. Dismounted men of the Brigade now working in 'D' Sector will rejoin their Regiments under orders which will be issued by G.O.C. 'D' Sector.
These men should be counted in Establishment for trenches.

6. One Officer per Squadron and sufficient men to leave 1 man to 4 horses will proceed extra to Establishment, to take charge of Led Horses, which will remain at E.12, and bring back relieved personnel of 7th Cavalry Brigade.
Horses of Sub-sector H.Q. will be sent back direct.
O.C. 3rd Dragoon Gds. will detail a Captain on night 10/11th and O.C. Royals a Major or a Captain on night 11/12th to take charge of led horses.

7. (a) Transport for A Party will assemble on BUIRE - TINCOURT Road opposite N.S.Y. lines, at 2 p.m. June 10th, and will march under Lt.& Qr.Mr.LINES,Royals, to Southern exits of VILLERS FAUCON E.28.a., where he will report to the Staff Captain 'D' Sector.
(b) Transport for B Party will assemble on BUIRE - TINCOURT Road opposite N.S.Y. lines, at 2 p.m. on 11th, and will march under Lt.& Qr.Mr. SHAKESPEARE,N.S.Y., to VILLERS FAUCON,E.28.a. and report to Staff Captain D.Sector.
Transport as laid down in L.20/25 will remain at VILLERS FAUCON
All available Lewis Handcarts should be sent up.

ACKNOWLEDGE.

Brigade Major 6th Cavalry Bde.

APPENDIX 'A'

1. <u>Ammunition</u>.- Only that carried on the man.

    Regiments will take 7 leather carriers for Hotchkiss Rifle Strips (full) per Hotchkiss Rifle.

2. All Trench Stores will be taken over from 7th Cavalry Brigade, but units will take up :-

    All Very Pistols.
    All Vigilant Periscopes.
    All Hotchkiss Rifle belt fillers.
    All Voils Observors.
    All Trench Stretchers.

    Signal Stores as detailed by O.C. 6th Signal Troop.

3. <u>Rations</u>.

    <u>A PARTY</u>   On man: 1 Iron Ration, and unexpended portion, and Rations for 11th inst. will be drawn at VILLERS FAUCON.

    <u>B. PARTY</u>   On man: 1 Iron Ration and unexpended portion. Rations for 12th will be drawn at VILLERS FAUCON.

4. <u>MAILS</u>.

    Mails will be sorted in Camp by Post Orderlies. O.C. 6th M.Gun Sqn. will detail 1 limber daily to report at Brigade H.Q. at 2 p.m., to convey all mails for trenches to the Wagon Lines.

MOVEMENT TABLE FOR RELIEFS IN 'D' 2 SUB-SECTOR.

Serial No.	Date	Unit.	To relieve similar unit	Place	Remarks.
1.	Night 9/10 June.	8th M.Gun Sqn Advanced Party.		D.2. Sub-Sector.	Advanced Party to reconnoitre all M.G. emplacements 7th M.G. Sqn. in D.2. To report H.Q. 'D' Sector F.1.d.8.8. at 8 p.m. where guides from 7th M.G. Sqn. will meet.
2.	Night 10/11 June.	6th M.Gun Sqn.	7th M.Gun Sqn.	D.2. Sub-sector.	To relieve all machine guns in D.2. under arrangements to be made between Os.C. 6th & 7th M.Gun Sqns.
3.	Night 10/11 June.	1½ Sqns. Royals. H.Q. & 3 Sqns. 3rd Dragoon Gds.	1½ Sqn. Leicester Yeo. H.Q. & 3 Sqns. 2nd Life Gds.	Intermediate Support. 2nd Line.	Sufficient Officers and N.C.Os will be detailed from these Sqns. to go into Outpost and Intermediate Line respectively, so as to ensure that on next night at least 1 Officer or N.C.O. in each post should know his surroundings. Officers & N.C.Os. reconnoitring Intermediate Line will go up on night 10th/11th, and not by day 11th. Guides will be at forked Roads in EPEHY F.1.c.6.5. at 9.15 p.m.
4.	Night 10/11 June	Sniping Officers Royals & N.S.Y. Sniping Sgts. Royals.		D.2. Sub-sector.	To meet Sniping Officer of D.2. at H.Q. D.Sector F.1.d.8.8. at 9 p.m. and be shewn D.2. Sub-sector.
5.	Night 11/12 June.	1½ Sqns.Royals.	1½ Sqns.Leicester Yeo.	D.2. Outpost.	
		H.Q. & 3 Sqns 3rd D.Gds. (Serial No.3. above)	H.Q. & 3 Sqns 1st Life Gds.	Intermediate Line.	Under orders of O.C. D.2.Sub-sector.

P. T. O.

MOVEMENT TABLE FOR RELIEFS IN D.2. SUB-SECTOR. (Contd.)

Serial No.	Date	Unit.	To relieve similar unit.	Place	Remarks.
6.	Night 11/12th June.	Lt.Col.WORMALD Regt.H.Q. Royals.	Regtl. H.Q. I.L.G.	H.Q. D.2 Sub-Sector.	Under orders of G.O.C. 'D' Sector. Guides to be at Forked Rds. EPEHY F.1.c.6.5. 9.15 p.m.
7.	Night 11/12th June.	Remaining 1½ Sqns Royals. H.Q. & 3 Sqns K.S.Y.	1½ Sqns Royals H.Q. & 3 Sqns 3rd D.Gds.	Intermediate Support 2nd Line.	Under orders of G.C. D.2 sub-sector. Guides to be at Forked roads EPEHY at F.1.c.6.5. at 9.15 p.m.

Army Form C. 2118

WAR DIARY

INTELLIGENCE SUMMARY

(Erase heading not required.)

Instructions regarding War Diaries and Intelligence Summaries are contained in F.S. Regs., Part II. and the Staff Manual respectively. Title Pages will be prepared in manuscript.

Place	Date	Hour	Summary of Events and Information	Remarks and references to Appendices
Field.	1st June.		During the morning a German Sniper was shot from the BIRDCAGE. The following reliefs took place :- D.1. Sub-sector. The 8th M.G. Squadron took over Gun Emplacements from 6th M.G. Squadron. 1½ Sqdns. of Xth Hussars relieved 1½ Sqdns. 3rd Dragoon Gds. in support of Intermediate (line. Royal Horse Guards relieved 1st R. Dragoons in 2nd Line.	

"	2nd June.		Lieut-Colonel Lord TWEEDMOUTH, C.M.G., M.V.O., D.S.O., relieved Lieut-Colonel A. BURT, D.S.O. in command of D.1. Sub-sector.
			
			 D.1. Sub-sector.
			
			     1½ Sqdns. of Xth Hussars relieved 1½ Sqdns. 3rd Dragoon Gds. in Outpost Line.
			     1½ Sqdns. " " " " " moved up in support of Intermediate Line.
			     Royal Horse Guards relieved North Somerset Yeomanry in Intermediate Line.
			     Essex Yeomanry relieved Royal Horse Guards in 2nd Line.
			
			 D.2. Sub-sector.
			
			     1½ Sqdns. 2nd Life Guards relieved 1½ Sqdns. 2nd Life Guards in Outpost Line.
			     1½ " " " " " " " " " " in support of Intermediate (line.	

"	3rd June.		7th Cav. Field Ambulance relieved 6th Cav. Field Ambulance at Advanced Dressing Station in EPEHY.
			 Brigadier General E.P. PORTAL, C.B., D.S.O., relieved Brigadier General A.E.W. HARMAN, D.S.O., in command of 'D' Sector.
			 Casualties:-
			     June 1st 1917. 2/Lieut. C.C.H.HILTON-GREEN, 1st Royal Dragoons. Wounded.
			     " 2nd " 15698 Pte. Atkins, D, 3rd Dragoon Guards. "	

Army Form C. 2118.

WAR DIARY
or
INTELLIGENCE SUMMARY
(Erase heading not required).

"D" SECTOR.

Instructions regarding War Diaries and Intelligence Summaries are contained in F.S. Regs., Part II. and the Staff Manual respectively. Title pages will be prepared in manuscript.

Place	Date	Hour	Summary of Events and Information	Remarks and references to Appendices
FIELD.	3/6/17	9.a.m. to 2.30p.m.	EPEHY was shelled with 8" shells from the direction of LE CATELET, most of the shells falling in the vicinity of the Cemetry.	
		6-7 p.m.	QUARRY in X.17.c. was shelled with 5.9". 14 hostile aeroplanes flew over our lines during the day.	
		11.15p.m.	Alternative red and white lights were sent up by the enemy in the vicinity of LA VENDHUILE.	
		11.30p.m.	Two gas signals were sent up, one by the Division on our right, the other by that on the left. No gas came over and they were subsequently cancelled. It is understood that a Klaxon horn sounded by an aeroplane was mistaken for a Strombos. Work. D.1 Sub-sector. Communication trench QUARRY - BIRDCAGE deepened. Wiring of BIRDCAGE proceeded with, 200 yards of wiring from G. Post to QUARRIES completed. G, H & J Posts, parapets improved and undercutting filled in.	
			D.2 Sub-Sector. Communication trench from L. Post to new Outpost Headquarters commenced. Work done on support trench M - L Posts. New M.G. emplacements made at X.28.a.9.8. & X.22.c.4.4.	
	4/6/17	8 a.m.	G. Post and PETIT PRIEL FARM shelled with 18 4.2's. 4 - 4.2's were fired into MALASSISE FARM during the morning.	
		11/30a.m. to12/30 p.m.	20 - 77mm shells fired into X.17.c.	
		11 p.m.	A gold and silver rain rocket was seen to go up in the enemy's lines between OSSUS and HONNECOURT. This was again mistaken for one of our gas signals. Green and red rockets were also fired and a searchlight turned on as if searching for aircraft.	
			Work. D.1. Sub-Sector. Deepening and wiring communication trench BIRDCAGE - QUARRY. Wiring G. Post to QUARRY. Improvement work on G, H & J Posts.	
			D.2 Sub-Sector. Improvement work on K, L & M Posts. Work on C, T & L Posts, to Outpost H.Q. continued. Hotchkiss rifle emplacement made 100 yds S.S.E. of corner on No.1 Post. Work on new M.G. emplacement X.28.a.9.8. continued.	
			Casualties reported. 31236 Pte.Robinson, P. 10th Royal Hussars. Wounded	
			15886 Pte Ashwin J.F. Essex Yeomanry. "	
			29 Tptr.Tpr. Coleman. 2nd Life Guards. "	

Army Form C. 2118.

WAR DIARY
or
INTELLIGENCE SUMMARY.

"D" Sector.

(Erase heading not required)

Instructions regarding War Diaries and Intelligence Summaries are contained in F.S. Regs., Part II. and the Staff Manual respectively. Title pages will be prepared in manuscript.

Place	Date	Hour	Summary of Events and Information	Remarks and references to Appendices
FIELD.	5/6/17.		LITTLE PRIEL FARM shelled intermittently. CATELET COPSE and the BIRDCAGE were slightly shelled during the morning. BIRDCAGE. QUARRY were shelled during the night. Major SIMON, R.E. was killed during the night while examining the wire of the BIRDCAGE. A patrol went out during the night to reconnoitre a suspected emplacement at X.23.d.4.0. They got within 20 yards of it and heard voices from it, but found no wire. They waited over an hour but were not fired on and could not confirm the presence of a machine gun. A small post 100x N. of this was found untenanted and disused. A patrol also reconnoitred the dummy guns at X.23.b.central. They found the place strongly wired and there appeared to be a trench 40 yds behind the wire which was occupied. Following reliefs took place during the night:-	
			D.1 Sub-sector.	
			1½ Sqdns Essex Yeomanry relieved 1½ Sqdns 10th Hussars in OUTPOST Line.	
			1½ " " " 1½ " " in INTERMEDIATE SUPPORT.	
			10th Royal Hussars " Royal Horse Guards in INTERMEDIATE Line.	
			Royal Horse Guards " Essex Yeomanry in 2nd Line.	
			D.2 Sub-Sector. Lt.Col.E.A.BRASSEY, M.V.O., 1st Life Guards relieved Lt.Col. H.COMBE, D.S.O. Leicestershire Yeomanry.	
			1½ Sqdns Leicestershire Yeo. relieved 1½ sqns 2nd Life Guards in OUTPOST Line.	
			1½ " " " 1½ " " in INTERMEDIATE SUPPORT.	
			1st Life Guards " Leicestershire Yeo in INTERMEDIATE Line.	
			2nd Life Guards " 1st Life Guards in 2nd Line.	
			Work. Owing to relief no new work was done in OUTPOST Line. In D.2 Sub-sector, work was continued on communication trench L. Post to new OUTPOST H.Q. This is now 3' deep.	
			Casualty reported. 1918. Cpl. Faithorn, 1st Life Guards, wounded (accidental).	

Army Form C. 2118.

WAR DIARY
or
INTELLIGENCE SUMMARY.

D. SECTOR.

(Erase heading not required.)

Instructions regarding War Diaries and Intelligence Summaries are contained in F. S. Regs., Part II. and the Staff Manual respectively. Title pages will be prepared in manuscript.

Place	Date	Hour	Summary of Events and Information	Remarks and references to Appendices

FIELD.	5/6/17.	10.15 a.m.
		8 p.m.
			4 - 4.2's were fired into G. Post from the direction of LA TERRIERE.
			20 - 77mm shells fell in L. Post.
			A patrol went out at midnight from X.23.c. and heard the enemy working in OSSUS WOOD.
			Work. D.1. Sub-sector.
			  Deepening communication trench to BIRDCAGE and strengthening wire of same.
			Strengthening wire G. Post to QUARRY.
			G. Post improvement of trenches. 2 Hotchkiss rifle positions made in SUPPORT trench.
			H. Post. Improvement in trenches. J. Post. Trenches improved, 10 yards of communication trench dug in CAPELET COPSE. Hotchkiss rifle position and fire step dug in C.T. S. of COPSE. 35 yards of trench dug behind fire trench in CRUCIFORM Sector to provide sleeping accomodation for men.
			D.2. Sub-sector.
			  Improvement of C.T. to M. Post. Work on C.T. L. Post to new OUTPOST H.Q.
			It is 518 yds long, 400 yds are now 5' deep, 72 yds 3'6" deep, 46 yds 2'9" deep.
			Work on sap to gun emplacement commenced X×22×c×5×# X. at X.28.a.8.8.
			Emplacement for A.A. gun completed X.22.c.0.8. Sap and emplacement commenced at X.22.c.3.4.
			Casualty. 3726. Tpr Butcher W. 1st Life Guards. Wounded.
				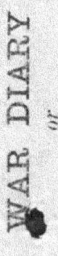

Army Form C. 2118.

WAR DIARY
or
INTELLIGENCE=SUMMARY.
(Erase heading not required)

Instructions regarding War Diaries and Intelligence Summaries are contained in F. S. Regs., Part II. and the Staff Manual respectively. Title pages will be prepared in manuscript.

Place	Date	Hour	Summary of Events and Information	Remarks and references to Appendices
FIELD.	7/6/17.	3.5 a.m.	20 H.E. shells fired into X.28.b. and d. 2 enemy machine guns were very active during the day. They appeared to be firing from the enemy's outpost line in X.23.d. and X.24.c.	
		5.15 a.m.	A German coming out from N. side of OSSUS WOOD to a trench in X.24.c. was shot by our snipers. An Officers patrol went out from No. 1 Post to reconnoitre the salient in the enemy's line at X.23.d.8½.4½. They got close to the salient and saw a post on the road. The enemy was heard talking and the post appeared to be strongly held. The wire did not look very formidable, but the grass in front had been cut. The wire is continuous to N.N.E. & S.S.E. but no sign of a trench could be seen.	
		2.40 a.m.	A golden rain rocket was sent up in the German lines. One sentry sounded a Strombos horn but the alarm was not taken up.	
			Work. D.1 Sub-sector. Repairing and draining trenches after rain. Construction of communication trench in CATELET COPSE continued.	
			D.2 Sub-sector. Repairing and draining. Further 50 yards of communication trench to M. Post completed. Communication trench from L. Post to new OUTPOST H.Q. completely dug from X.22.c.2.3. - X.22.d.7.8. Sap to machine gun position X.22.c.4.2. completed.	
			Casualty. No. 31191 Pte Bell, D. 10th Royal Hussars, accidentally killed.	

Army Form C. 2118.

WAR DIARY
or
INTELLIGENCE SUMMARY.
(Erase heading not required.)

Instructions regarding War Diaries and Intelligence Summaries are continued in F. S. Regs., Part II. and the Staff Manual respectively. Title pages will be prepared in manuscript.

Place	Date	Hour	Summary of Events and Information	Remarks and references to Appendices
FIELD.	8/6/17.		Hostile shelling very below normal. A patrol left No. 2 Outpost and followed the valley to the South side of CANAL WOOD, past the three dummy guns. They report wire runs West along CANAL WOOD on its South side till it reaches the dummy guns, it there runs due South. They heard work going on in CANAL WOOD.	
			Work. For the most confined to drainage etc, owing no reliefs. D.2 Sub-sector. Communication trench L. Post - New OUTPOST H.Q. continued from INTERMEDIATE Line towards PIGEON RAVINE. 70 yards of communication trench to M. Post completed.	
			Reliefs. D.1 Sub-sector. 1½ Sqns Royal Horse Guards relieved 1½ Sqns Essex Yeomanry in OUTPOST Line. 1½ " " " " " 1½ " " " in INTERMEDIATE SUPPORT. Essex Yeomanry " 10th Royal Hussars in INTERMEDIATE Line. 10th Royal Hussars " Royal Horse Guards in SECOND Line.	
			D.2 Sub-sector. 1½ Sqd Leicestershire Yeomanry relieved 1½ Sqns same regiment in OUTPOST Line. The latter went into the INTERMEDIATE SUPPORT.	
			Casualty. 255266. Pte Wearn, Leicestershire Yeomanry. Accidentally wounded.	

Army Form C. 2118.

WAR DIARY
or
INTELLIGENCE SUMMARY

(Erase heading not required.)

Instructions regarding War Diaries and Intelligence Summaries are contained in F. S. Regs., Part II. and the Staff Manual respectively. Title pages will be prepared in manuscript.

Place	Date	Hour	Summary of Events and Information	Remarks and references to Appendices
FIELD.	9/6/17.		LITTLE PRIEL Farm and the BIRDCAGE QUARRY shelled intermittently. M. Post shelled with 15 rounds 77mm in the afternoon. CATELET Valley swept at intervals with machine gun fire. An Officers patrol went out a quarter of a mile in front of the outposts of D.2 Sub-sector and encountered no wire.	
		11 p.m.	A patrol visited the 12 willows at F.5.d.1.5. and remained till 2 a.m. but observed nothing. Lt. Colonel GIBBS, 10th Royal Hussars, relieved Lt. Colonel Lord Tweedmouth, Royal Horse Guards in command of D.1 Sub-sector.	
			Work. D.1. Sub-sector. Improvement of trenches. Communication trench G. Post to QUARRY half dug.	
			D.2 Sub-sector. New telephone shelters made in L. Post. Work on Communication trench L. Post - new OUTPOST H.Q. continued. Owing to operations of 2nd Cavalry Division all work E. of INTERMEDIATE line ceased at 2 a.m.	

Army Form C. 2118.

WAR DIARY
or
INTELLIGENCE SUMMARY
(Erase heading not required.)

Instructions regarding War Diaries and Intelligence Summaries are contained in F. S. Regs., Part II. and the Staff Manual respectively. Title pages will be prepared in manuscript.

Place	Date	Hour	Summary of Events and Information	Remarks and references to Appendices
FIELD.	10/6/17.		LITTLE PRIEL Farm shelled at noon and at 4.30 p.m. with 77mm guns from LA TERRIERE. 13 - 77mm shells were fired at G. Post about 3.45 p.m. 5 - 77mm shells fell in No. 13 Copse about the same time. All were duds. A patrol went out about 200 yards along the Northern edge of CANAL WOOD but gained no information.	
		10.8 p.m.	An S.O.S. Signal was sent up from TOMBOIS FARM, followed by heavy shelling of TOMBOIS VALLEY. about 20 rounds of shrapnel and H.E. fell on G. Post and communication trench from it to D.1 Headquarters. No damage was done. Ground W. of H. Post and near D.1 Headquarters heavily shelled between 10.30 p.m. and 11p.m. chiefly with shrapnel.	
		12.45 a.m.	Enemy sent up red lights at F.6.a. and F.6.c.	
		12.30 a.m.	S.O.S. Signals sent up at GUILLEMONT FARM, followed by heavy artillery firm shelling till 1.15 p.m.	
			Working party on Communication trench G. Post - QUARRY lost 10 killed and wounded by one shell.	
			Casualties.	
			24957. Pte Dolman W.H. 22363. Pte Auton A. 31185. Pte Topham A. 6317. Pte Scott E. 32918. Pte Ward S.P. 32421. Pte WilfordT.A. 68683. Pte Clayton 9600. Pte Allen B. 24724. Pte Brown. R. 22714. Pte Williams W. } 10th Hussars Killed.	
			54359. Pte Taylor W. 12026. Pte Brewer L. 4184. Pte Scott G.S. 19789. Xxx Cpl Godden A. 24729. Pte Goodson } 10th Hussars wounded.	
			1072. Tpr Aston E. Royal Horse Guards. (wounded)	
			31038. Pte Bates, 10th Royal Hussars. Wounded accidentally.	
		Reliefs.	Following reliefs were carried out in D.2 Sub-sector. 8th Machine Gun Sqdn relieved 7th Machine Gun Sqdn. 1½ Sqns Royals relieved 1½ Sqns Leicestershire Yeomanry in INTERMEDIATE SUPPORT. 3rd Dragoon Guards relieved 2nd Life Guards. Details 2nd Life Guards and Leicestershire Yeomanry relieved Details 8th Brigade Dismounted Party.	

Army Form C. 2118.

WAR DIARY
or
INTELLIGENCE SUMMARY.

D. SECTOR.

(Erase heading not required.)

Place	Date	Hour	Summary of Events and Information	Remarks and references to Appendices
FIELD.	11/6/17.		Following reliefs took place:-	
			D. 1 Sub-sector.	
			1½ Sqns Royal Horse Guards from INTERMEDIATE SUPPORT relieved 1½ Sqns same regiment in OUTPOST line.	
			D. 2 Sub-sector.	
			1½ Sqns Royals relieved 1½ Sqns Leicestershire Yeomanry in OUTPOST line.	
			3rd Dragoon Guards relieved 1st Life Guards in INTERMEDIATE line.	
			1½ Sqns Royals relieved 1½ Sqns Royals in INTERMEDIATE SUPPORT.	
			North Somerset Yeomanry relieved 3rd Dragoon Guards in 2nd line.	
			Details 1st Life Guards and Leicestershire Yeomanry relieved Details 6th Cavalry Brigade Dismounted Party.	
			Owing to reliefs no new work was carried out.	

Army Form C. 2118.

WAR DIARY
or
INTELLIGENCE SUMMARY.
(Erase heading not required.)

D. SECTOR.

Instructions regarding War Diaries and Intelligence Summaries are contained in F.S. Regs., Part II. and the Staff Manual respectively. Title pages will be prepared in manuscript.

Hour, Date, Place	Summary of Events and Information	Remarks and references to Appendices
FIELD, 12th June.1917.	Brigadier General A.G.Seymour relieved Brigadier General B.P.Portal, C.B. D.S.O., in Command of D. Sector. Operations. Hostile artillery. During the day PIGEON RAVINE, GATELET COPSE, LITTLE PRIEL FARM, and TOMBOIS FARM were shelled at intervals. At 2.30 p.m. G. Post was shelled with 9 - 77mm shells. At 3.5 p.m. X.23.c and at 5.30 p.m. X.22.c. were shelled by 4.2s. F.O.O. reports this gun to be close up, but exact position not yet located. Between 7 and 8 a.m. No. 15 Copse was shelled with H.E. Our artillery. During the day enemy trenches at F.6.a. and his posts near OSSUS WOOD were shelled. Work. D.1 Sub-sector. Hotchkiss emplacements dug in G. M. Cruciform and T Posts improved. Wiring - K. Post to Outpost No. 1 (100 yards). D. 2 Sub-sector. 66 men (N. Somerset Yeo) worked on trench from L. Post to new Outpost H.Q. 200 yards of communication trench from L. Post to BARRICADE. M. Post improved. Dug-out built.	

Army Form C. 2118.

WAR DIARY
or
INTELLIGENCE SUMMARY.
(Erase heading not required.)

D. SECTOR.

Instructions regarding War Diaries and Intelligence Summaries are contained in F.S.Regs., Part II. and the Staff Manual respectively. Title pages will be prepared in manuscript.

Hour, Date, Place	Summary of Events and Information	Remarks and references to Appendices
FIELD, June 13th, 1917.	**Work.** 100 men (J.E.M.) wired about 400 yards from K. Post towards No. 1 Post. Outposts D.2. 104 men strengthened parapets and made traverses. M. Post. Tactical rays of wire passed out towards our infantry on our left. (114 men). G. Post. Communication trench to QUARRY advanced. L. Post. Communication trench to new Outpost H.Q. continued. (66 men). **Operations.** From No. 1 Post an officers patrol. From No. 3 Post a patrol went out to reconnoitre the enemys wire. Both heard small enemy wiring parties, and both were fired on by M.G. without casualty. **Artillery.** Our artillery shelled the enemys positions at intervals throughout the day. Hostile artillery was more active than formerly against our front system, from PETET PRIEL FARM to VILLERS GUISLAIN. **Hostile defences.** Sentries in BIRDCAGE report hearing sounds of stakes being driven in ground from their right front to OSSUS WOOD during the night.	

Army Form C. 2118.

WAR DIARY
or
INTELLIGENCE SUMMARY

D. SECTOR.

(Erase heading not required.)

Instructions regarding War Diaries and Intelligence Summaries are contained in F.S. Regs., Part II and the Staff Manual respectively. Title pages will be prepared in manuscript.

Hour, Date, Place	Summary of Events and Information	Remarks and references to Appendices
FIELD, June 14th, 1917.	Operations. A patrol located an enemy L.P. near a tree which stands just S. of OSSUS WOOD about X.29.b.5.3. where a small P.M. can be seen.	
	Movement. Considerable movement was observed throughout the day in S.25. in the HINDENBURG LINE. 100-150 men in marching order were seen marching W. from BELLEVUE FARM and later 2 motor cars and 2 lorries. An aeroplane photo shows an enemy sap running W.S.W. from X.30.a.4.6. as far as X.30.a.2.3.	
	Reliefs. D.1 Sub-sector. 2 Sqdns X.R.H. relieved 1½ Sqdns R.H.Gds in OUTPOST LINE. 1 Sqdn X.R.H. " 1½ " R.H.Gds in INTERMEDIATE SUPPORT. Royal Horse Guards relieved Essex Yeomanry in INTERMEDIATE LINE. Essex Yeomanry relieved 10th Royal Hussars in 2nd LINE. D.1 Sub-sector.	
	Work. Communication trench between G. Post and QUARRY dug for another 100 yards. BIRDCAGE communication trench deepened and widened.	
	D.2 Sub-sector. Wiring continued. Communication trench from L. Post to new Outpost H.Q. improved and partially drained.	
	Casualties. No.10543 Pte Campbell, J. 1st Royal Dragoons wounded. No. 5898 Pte Groeger F. " " " No. 9492 Pte Harris E. " " " No. 9059 Pte Hunter G " " " No. 6370 Pte J. Thompson " " "	

Army Form C. 2118.

WAR DIARY
or
INTELLIGENCE SUMMARY
(Erase heading not required.)

D. SECTOR.

Instructions regarding War Diaries and Intelligence Summaries are contained in F. S. Regs., Part II. and the Staff Manual respectively. Title pages will be prepared in manuscript.

Hour, Date, Place	Summary of Events and Information	Remarks and references to Appendices
FIELD 15th June 1917.	Operations. 1.30 a.m. an enemy patrol attempted to bomb a wiring party in front of No. 1 Post, but they were driven off by our covering party. Officers patrols went out to reconnoitre (a) the new enemy sap, opposite the BIRDCAGE, where a working party was located. (b) CANAL WOOD - they were much hampered by the persistent firing of Very lights. Our artillery.- shelled enemy front line and FRANQUE WOOD. Hostile artillery - no more than usual. Movement. Many instances were observed of one man pointing out the country to another - presumably indicating a relief. Work. D.1 Sub-sector. Wire laid for 120 yards from I Post along immediate S. of WXXXX road to OSSUS WOOD. Birdcage. Bombing post commenced to protect trench between front and reserve trenches. G. Post to QUARRY continued by 200 men. D.2 Sub-sector: Wiring vontinued and trenches improved. Relief. Lieut Colonel F.H.D.C.Whitmore and H.Q. Essex Yeomanry relieved Lieut Colonel W.O.Gibbs and H.Q. X.Royal Hussars in Command of D.1 Sub-sector.	

Army Form C. 2118.

WAR DIARY
or
INTELLIGENCE SUMMARY.   D. SECTOR.
(Erase heading not required.)

Instructions regarding War Diaries and Intelligence Summaries are contained in F.S. Regs., Part II. and the Staff Manual respectively. Title pages will be prepared in manuscript.

Hour, Date, Place	Summary of Events and Information	Remarks and references to Appendices
FIELD 16th June 1917.	OPERATIONS. D.1 Sub-sector. An officers patrol went out from BIRDCAGE at 11.15 p.m. There were no sounds of work or any other signs of occupation of the enemys new sap. A snipers nest was found, and the advanced patrol reported the flight of 3 occupants. D.2 Sub-sector. A patrol of 1 N.C.O. and 3 men went out at 11.15 p.m. from No. 2 Post to locate a suspected M.G. emplacement. Our Artillery. Bombared enemy positions at intervals throughout the day and shelled a house, suspected to be an O.P. Direct hits were obtained. Hostile artillery. Intermittent shelling on PETIT PRIEL FARM, No. 12 Copse, L. Post, CATELET VALLEY. A considerable number of blinds were reported. A certain amount of movement was observed throughout the day on the HINDENBURG LINE. A hostile aeroplane was brought down in flames E. of HONNECOURT. WORK. D.1 Sub-sector. BIRDCAGE. Bombing post in support trench deepened, slits made for Stokes Gun ammunition. New arrowhead sap dug out towards German Sap. J. Post. Wire carried out 200 yards along Sunken Road towards OSSUS WOOD. G. Post to QUARRIES. Communication trench carried right through. D.2 Sub-sector. Work as usual on wiring and improving trenches. Casualties. No.31031 Pte E.Shaw, 10th Hussars, Accidentally wounded.	

Army Form C. 2118.

WAR DIARY
or
INTELLIGENCE SUMMARY. D. SECTOR.
(Erase heading not required.)

Instructions regarding War Diaries and Intelligence Summaries are contained in F.S. Regs., Part II. and the Staff Manual respectively. Title pages will be prepared in manuscript.

Hour, Date, Place	Summary of Events and Information	Remarks and references to Appendices
FIELD. 17th June 1917.	OPERATIONS. D.1 Sub-sector. At 11.50 after a bombardment by Stokes Mortars lasting 5 minutes a fighting patrol went out to the enemys new sap. As it approached, about 12 of the enemy jumped out of the trench and lay down in the open. Both sides opened fire. Our patrol entered the trench and threw bombs, which were seen to burst in the midst of the enemy. After 10 minutes, according to a prearranged plan, our party withdrew, without suffering any casualties. The enemy at once bombarded the BIRDCAGE, heavily for 15 minutes with artillery and trench mortars, luckily with little effect. The sap appeared to be about 8 ft deep towards our side, and only about 2 ft deep on the side facing the Germans, so that, if we took it, they could fire into it. A strong officers patrol was also sent to reconnoitre the enemys front line about X.30 central, where the enemy was suspected of constructing another sap. They discovered a converted shell hole - probably a forward M.G. emplacement. 3 Germans crawled out of it to a post about 15 yds in rear, which was just in front of their wire. It was entrenched and strongly held. Enemy reinforcements moved to it across the open, whence it is assumed that the post and the emplacement in front of it are both isolated positions, and not connected by a sap to the fire trench. D.2 Sub-sector. An officers patrol from No. 1 Post reconnoitred an enemy post where the enemy had been seen digging during the day. It was unoccupied. Our artillery. Throughout the day shelled the enemys front line N. and S. of OSSUS WOOD. Stokes Mortars of X.R.H. & E.Yeo under Capt. Wootton and Lieut Lowther moved up to the BIRDCAGE. Hostile artillery as usual. AVIATION. Enemy activity above normal. At 9 a.m. an air fight took place between a Squadron of our battle planes and an unknown number of enemy aeroplanes. One enemy aeroplane fell in flames in the lines. At 12.5 p.m. one E.A. flew over our lines for 10 minutes. At 3 p.m. 8 E.A. flew over our lines at a great height for ½ an hour. RELIEFS. 1½ Sqdns N.S.Yeo relieved 1½ Sqdns R.Dragoons in OUTPOST line. " 1½ Sqdns " " 1½ " " INTERMEDIATE SUPPORT. Royal Dragoons relieved 3rd Dragoon Guards in INTERMEDIATE Line. 3rd Dragoon Guards " North Somerset Yeo " BROWN (2nd line) CASUALTIES. Lieut. G.Glynn, 10th Hussars wounded. (shell shock). 2/Lieut.A.Lowther. " (shell shock). No.165888 Pte W.G.Ridley, N.S.Yeo. Wounded. (Shell shock).	

Army Form C. 2118.

WAR DIARY
or
INTELLIGENCE=SUMMARY.   D. SECTOR.
(Erase heading not required.)

Instructions regarding War Diaries and Intelligence Summaries are contained in F.S. Regs., Part II. and the Staff Manual respectively. Title pages will be prepared in manuscript.

Hour, Date, Place	Summary of Events and Information	Remarks and references to Appendices
FIELD. 18th June 1917.	Our artillery. Bombarded enemy positions at intervals. At 4.30 p.m. our 13 pdrs shelled a new enemy position in X.23.d.2½.5½. Hostile artillery. As usual. A hostile battery was observed in action near the road at S.9.a.4.2.	
	Movement. Throughout the morning men were seen at F.6.a.6.5. observing our positions through field glasses. Movement was observed all day at trench X.30.o. At 6 p.m. a man was seen observing our line through glasses from a hole at S.2.b.0.6.	
	Hostile defences. What appear to be two concreted emplacements can be seen about S.21.d.2.8.	
	Work. BIRDCAGE - QUARRY - shelters built. B. Sap deepened in BIRDCAGE. 40 men worked on wire from I. to OSSUS WOOD. It has now reached a point 550 yards from CATELET COPSE. 100 men improved and thickened wire from K. to No. 1 Outpost. 40 men improved tactical rays at No. 4 Outpost. L. Post shelter for reserve S.A.A. begun.	
	Reliefs. 1 Sqdn Royal Horse Guards relieved 1 Sqdn Essex Yeo in 2nd or Brown line. 1 " " " " 1 " Essex Yeomanry " 1 " Royal Horse Guards in Intermediate line.	

Army Form C. 2118.

WAR DIARY
or
INTELLIGENCE SUMMARY.   D. Sector.
(Erase heading not required.)

Instructions regarding War Diaries and Intelligence Summaries are contained in F.S. Regs., Part II. and the Staff Manual respectively. Title pages will be prepared in manuscript.

Hour, Date, Place	Summary of Events and Information	Remarks and references to Appendices
FIELD June 19th 1917.	<u>Our artillery.</u> During the day shelled VENDHUILE, KINGSTON QUARRIES, OSSUS WOOD, LA TERRIERE, and line of dug-outs in S.20.a. <u>Hostile artillery.</u> (i) Active during morning, an unusual number of blinds reported. (ii) Intermittent bombardment throughout the day of our positions between CATELET VALLEY and TOMBOIS FARM with 4.2 cm and 77 mm. (iii) Between 9.50 and 10.30 a.m. a 13 cm gun, from direction of VENDHUILE, shelled PETIT PRIEL FARM with 20 rounds, of which half were blind. <u>Movement.</u> 3.0 p.m. 2 men were seen in hole E. of road X.23.b.5.5. observing our positions through glasses. A good deal of movement was seen in trenches S. of OSSUS WOOD. Two periscopes were noted in trenches X.30.d., and shortly afterwards our positions opposite were shelled. In the evening large parties of men and transport were seen entering VENDHUILE from LE CATELET. <u>Hostile defences.</u> Signs of fresh digging between F.6.a.6.1. and F.6.a.7.2. Trip wire has been put up 20 yards in front of enemy front line at X.30.c.4.3. near the road. A stake or post is visible in enemys wire in front of new enemy sap opposite BIRDCAGE. A.M.G. reported firing up PIGEON RAVINE at 11 p.m. <u>Work.</u> Trench dug for BIRDCAGE SUPPORT to a sap X.29.b.9.1. - not yet complete. New communication trench before GLYNN QUARRY to BIRDCAGE SUPPORT X.29.d.2.5. Stokes Mortar emplacements and ammunition reserves begun in BIRDCAGE. Cover for men in QUARRY. <u>Reliefs.</u> Capt Wootton (Stokes guns) returned to 105th Brigade H.Q.	

Army Form C. 2118.

WAR DIARY
or
INTELLIGENCE SUMMARY.   D. SECTOR.
(Erase heading not required.)

Hour, Date, Place	Summary of Events and Information	Remarks and references to Appendices
FIELD. 20th June 1917.	Operations. Our artillery normal. Enemy artillery. was unusually active during the day mostly with 4.2 cm. G. and H. Posts, PETIT PRIEL FARM, and QUARRY in X.29.d. were shelled. In the morning a 13 cm H.V. gun put 30 shells in F.5.a. from direction of LA PANNIERE, of which 50% were blind. Movement. 1. Enemy trenches opposite BIRDCAGE were seen to be occupied during the day. 2. Men were seen observing our positions through glasses from holes at S.26.a.2.5. and S.20.b.5.5. The two occupants of S.20.b.5.5. were relieved every two hours. 3. Movement reported in CANAL WOOD. 4. Six men were seen in front of German wire opposite BIRDCAGE apparently taking ground measurements. 5. Working party observed in S.20.a. apparently putting up an overhead telegraph line. 6. A large fire was seen in VILLERS OUTREAUX and another in AUBENCHEUL. Work. Wiring and improvement of trenches as usual. Work continued on new communication trench from GLYNN QUARRY X.29.b.9.2.k to BIRDCAGE. Emplacements for Stokes Guns, dug-outs for ammunition, shelters and dug-outs for men continued. Reliefs. D.1 Sub-sector. 1 Sqdn 10th Hussars was relieved by 2 Sqdns Leicester Yeomanry in INTERMEDIATE SUPPORT. 2 Sqdns Essex Yeo were " " 2 " 1st Life Guards " 2nd Line. 1 Sqdn R.Horse Guards was " " 1 " 1st " " "	

Army Form C. 2118.

WAR DIARY
or
INTELLIGENCE SUMMARY.

(Erase heading not required.)

Place	Date	Hour	Summary of Events and Information	Remarks and references to Appendices
In the field	21/6		**RELIEFS.** Outpost Line. 2 Squadrons, Leicester Yeomanry, relieved 2 Squadrons X.R. Hussars. Intermediate line. 2 Squadrons Life Guards relieved 2 Squadrons Royal Horse Guards. " " 1 " " 1 " Essex Yeomanry. Intermediate Support.1 " Leicester Yeomanry relieved 2 Squadrons Leicester Yeo. Second line. 3 Squadrons 2nd Life Guards relieved 3 Squadrons 1st Life Guards. During this night an officer's patrol was sent out by the Leicester Yeomanry from the BIRD CAGE under Lieut.TOULMIN to reconnoitre a suspected sap at X.30 Central,at 1-10 a.m. the patrol returned hurriedly and warned the garrison of an impending attack. At the same moment the enemy commenced a violent bombardment of the BIRD CAGE BIRD LANE and BIRDCAGE QUARRY, and shortly afterwards a party of the enemy were seen advancing from about X.30 Central. None of this party reached our wire, being driven off by rapid fire from rifles and Hotchkiss rifles, and no estimate of the numbers can be given. In the meantime a second party of the enemy approached from OSSUS WOOD in X.29.d.6.9.. This party was caught by their own T.M.Barrage which was "plastering" our wire along that side and none of the enemy succeeded in reaching our trenches. Of this party 3 wounded prisoners were brought in, two of whom have since died (a report of the examination of the 3rd is annexed) and 7 enemy dead were counted along the front of our wire, including one officer. The enemy's bombardment was intense for 30 minutes and lasted altogether for about 45 minutes. From the above evidence it would appear that:- (1) The enemy intended an attack on the BIRDCAGE from two sides simultaneously. (2) The attack from X.30 Central failed owing to the timely warning given by the patrol. (3) The attack from OSSUS WOOD was broken by the enemy's own T.M.Barrage. CASUALTIES.Officers. Killed and Lieut.P.M.Toulmin, Leicestershire Yeomanry. Killed. O.R. 29889 Pte Butcher, 10th Hussars. Wounded. 6804 Sgt Price S. -do- 4796 Pte Gorch F. -do- 255173 Cpl Knight W.Leicestershire Yeomanry. Killed	

Army Form C. 2118.

WAR DIARY
or
INTELLIGENCE SUMMARY.
(Erase heading not required.)

Instructions regarding War Diaries and Intelligence Summaries are contained in F. S. Regs., Part II. and the Staff Manual respectively. Title pages will be prepared in manuscript.

Place	Date	Hour	Summary of Events and Information	Remarks and references to Appendices
In the Field	21/6		Leicestershire Yeomanry. (ctd)	
			255519 Pte Green A.W. Killed.	
			255401 " Howard R. "	
			256041 " Hart C.C. "	
			256062 " Rhodes G.E. "	
			255510 " Lester F. "	
			268885 " Huss R.W. "	
			256050 " Dormer J.R. "	
			255025 Sgt Talbot A.R. "	
			255176 L/Cpl Rowlinson L. Wounded.	
			255110 Pte Rawson A.M. "	
			255471 " Warner H. "	
			255600 " Bent F.M. "	
			255091 L/Cpl Hutt W. "	
			255412 Pte Shorter W. "	
			255671 L/Cpl Smith J.E. "	
			255201 Pte Bowley F.F. "	
			255796 Pte Harrison S.W. " (Shell Shock).	
			258081 " Thompson W. " "	
			7th M.G.Sqn. 3695 Spr Abbis F.W. "	
			3004 " West S. "	
			3730 " Keith A. " (Shell Shock).	
	22/6.		Brigadier General A.E.W.HARMAN, D.S.O., relieved Brigadier General SEYMOUR, D.S.O., in Sector D.	
			The 5th C.F.A., relieved the 8th C.F.A, in the advanced dressing station at EPEHY.	
	23/6.		RELIEFS. D.1.Sub-Sector.	
			Intermediate Support Line—2 Squadrons 2nd Life Guards relieved 1½ Squadrons Leicestershire Yeomanry.	

Army Form C. 2118.

WAR DIARY
or
INTELLIGENCE SUMMARY.
(Erase heading not required.)

Place	Date	Hour	Summary of Events and Information	Remarks and references to Appendices

In the Field	24/6.		D.2. Sub-Sector. Outpost and Intermediate,} 3rd Dragoon Guards relieved the North Somerset Yeo. Support.
			
			 Intermediate Line. North Somerset Yeomanry relieved 2 Squadrons Royal Dragoons and 1 Squadron 3rd Dragoon Guards.
			
			 Second Line. Royal Dragoons took over the second line.
			
			 During the night 24th/25th a raid was carried out on the enemy trenches from X.24.c.1.7. to X.24.a.2.4. The raid was made by two parties. The right party was operating South of the OSSUS WOOD road and the left party North of the road. The right party reached the enemy's wire and laid a Bangalore torpedo which eventually failed to explode at once and the party was delayed. Eventually the party reached the enemy's trenches and killed some Germans but had to withdraw owing to having exceeded the time limit. The left party cut the first line of the enemy's wire and prepared to blow up the main line of wire but found some white posts marking a track through the wire by which they entered the enemy's trenches. Three Germans were killed by the advanced scouts and an automatic weapon in a shell hôle was blown up. The whole party remained in the hostile trenches for some minutes during which time several Germans were accounted for. The enemy bombarded his own trench in X.24.a.3.8. with trench mortars and it is believed killed several of his own men as hostile fire coming from that direction ceased at the commencement of his bombardment. One prisoner was taken but died before he could be brought in. Other identifications were procured showing the Germans to belong to the 2nd Battalion 124th Infantry Regiment.
			
			 CASUALTIES.
			 3rd Dragoon Guards. 4480 Sgt Hicks W.T. Killed.
			                               13038 L/Cpl Boast F. "
			 1st Royal Dragoons. 5444 Pte Comer E. Wounded.
			                       Lieut. R.B.HELME. Killed.
			                       8865 Pte Nisbet A. "
			                       8809 " Leitch J. "
			                       2/Lieut. J.S.DUNVILLE Wounded (severely).	

Army Form C. 2118.

WAR DIARY
or
INTELLIGENCE SUMMARY.
(Erase heading not required.)

Place	Date	Hour	Summary of Events and Information	Remarks and references to Appendices
In the field	25/6		CASUALTIES (ctd).	
			3075 Sgt. Marder F. Wounded.	
			15412 Pte. Wilkinson A. "	
			5735 " Evans G. "	
			5768 " Bartlett C. "	
			10003 " Lauder J. "	
			5730 " Coglan M. "	
			6185 " Bennett J.T. "	
			911 Pte Grizzell R. Missing.	
			7698 " Miles T. "	
			North Somerset Yeomanry. 2/Lieut. V.C. RICE Wounded.	
			2nd Life Guards. 2729 Tpr. Eddowes "	
			A carrying party was shelled between BIRD CAGE QUARRY and "I" Post.	
			CASUALTIES.	
			Leicestershire Yeomanry. 255140 Pte Dyer A.E. Wounded.	
			255821 L/Cpl Dickinson C. "	
			255825 Pte King H.A. "	
			255250 " Rowe W.H. "	
			256071 " Willcox J. "	
			41780 " Giltus H.J. "	

Instructions regarding War Diaries and Intelligence Summaries are contained in F. S. Regs., Part II. and the Staff Manual respectively. Title pages will be prepared in manuscript.

Army Form C. 2118.

WAR DIARY
INTELLIGENCE SUMMARY.
(Erase heading not required.)

Instructions regarding War Diaries and Intelligence Summaries are contained in F. S. Regs., Part II. and the Staff Manual respectively. Title pages will be prepared in manuscript.

Place	Date	Hour	Summary of Events and Information	Remarks and references to Appendices
	26/6		1½ Squadrons 3rd Dragoon Guards relieved 1½ Squadrons 3rd Dragoon Guards & Vice Versa.Sub-Sector) Outpost D2) Casualties:- 2/Lieut J.S.DUNVILLE,Royal Dragoons. Wounded 25/6/17. Died of wounds.	
	27/6		2 Squadrons Royal Scots Greys relieved 2 Squadrons 2nd Life Guards. Intermediate Line D.1 Sub-Sector.	
			1 Squadron " " " 1 Squadron Leicestershire Yeomanry. 2nd Line.D.1.Sub-Sector.	
			Headquarters and 16th Lancers " Headquarters and 2 Squadrons Leicestershire Yeomanry, 2nd Line.D.1. Sub-Sector.	
			1½ Squadrons 4th Hussars " 1½ Squadrons 3rd Dragoon Guards. Intermediate Line,D.2. Sub-Sector.	
			1½ " " " " 1½ " Royal Dragoons,2nd Line, D.2.Sub-Sector.	
			Headquarters and 5th Lancers " Headquarters and 1½ Squadrons Royal Dragoons, 2nd Line) D.2. Sub-Sector.	
			Casualties:- 2592 S.C.M. Bay, C.H. 7th M.G.Squadron. Wounded, and at duty. 3434 Tpr. Harmer,P. -do- -do-.	
	28/6.		2 Squadrons Royal Scots Greys relieved 2 Squadrons 2nd Life Guards. Outposts D1 Sub-Sector.	
			1 Squadron " " " 1 Squadron Royal Scots Greys. Intermediate Line, -do-	
			Headquarters and 16th Lancers " Headquarters and D.1. Sub-Sector.	
			1½ Squadrons 3rd Dragoon Guards " 1½ Squadrons 3rd Dragoon Guards. Outposts D2 Sub-Sector.	
			1½ " " " " 1½ " 4th Hussars. Intermediate Line B2 -do-.	
			Headquarters and 5th Lancers " D2 Sub-Sector Headquarters and North Somerset Yeomanry. Intermediate Line D2 Sub-Sector.	
			Casualties:- 5753 Pte Morrison W. Royals. Wounded. 6098 " McNeill W. " "	

Army Form C. 2118.

WAR DIARY
or
INTELLIGENCE SUMMARY.
(Erase heading not required.)

6th Cavalry Bde
31 July 1917

Instructions regarding War Diaries and Intelligence Summaries are contained in F. S. Regs., Part II. and the Staff Manual respectively. Title pages will be prepared in manuscript.

Place	Date	Hour	Summary of Events and Information	Remarks and references to Appendices
BURE	1-2		The Bde. remained in bivouac near BURE.	
	3		Bde. marched to SUZANNE area	
SUZANNE	4		Bde. marched at 9.30 A.M. to billets in area:— Bde HQrs N.S.7 6 C.P.A. 13 M.G.S. } HEILLY 3rd D.G. } BURE Royal.) 10th Hsrs 5th Lancers } MÉRICOURT L'ABBÉ	
HEILLY	5		The Bde. marched at 10.15 A.M. to billets Bde HQrs 3rd D.G. 6 C.P.A. 13 M.G.S. } ORVILLE Royal. 10th Hsrs.} AMPLIER N.S.7 AUTHIEULE	
ORVILLE	6		The Bde. marched at 10.30 A.M. to billets. Bde HQ Royal 6 C.F.A. 13 M.G.S. } REBREUVIETTE 3rd D.G. N.S.7 6 Hsrs } ESTRÉE WAMIN. In 1st Army area	
REBREUVIETTE	7		The Bde. marched at 11.30 A.M. to billets. In 1st Army area Bde HQ. 6.M.G.Sqn. 6 C.P.A. 13 M.G.S. } AUCHEL 3rd D.G.} MARLES LES MINES. Royal.) N.S.7 } LA PUGNOY	

Army Form C. 2118.

WAR DIARY
or
INTELLIGENCE SUMMARY.
(Erase heading not required.)

1st Cav: By Bde
6th Cav: Bde July 1917.

Place	Date	Hour	Summary of Events and Information	Remarks and references to Appendices
AUCHEL	7-16		The 13th remained in AUCHEL area until July 16th. Musketry training and services and infoot ranges & Remounts were trained.	
AUCHEL	16		The 13th marched at 4 am to HAZEBROUCK area, & came under the order of Cavalry Corps the Regiment under 1st Army for administration. B Sqdn LES LAURIERS (East ¾ of Bois de la NIEPPE (on HAZEBROUCK – MERVILLE Rd) 3rd Sq. LE CORBIE. C.M.Gun LETO-QUET. R Hd Qrs. } HAZEBROUCK. C Sqdn R.H.A. LAROTTE 13 Amb Sect. M.S.Y. } HAZEBROUCK. 6 C.F.A. } LES LAURIERS. 13 M.H.S. } LES PUREBECQUES.	Ref map. HAZEBROUCK 5a. Hazebrouck + 36 A. 1/40000
AUCHEL	15		C 13 r.a R.H.A. rejoined the Bde. from the cke. sen. ENEMY.	

[signature]

Army Form C. 2118.

6 Country B40
July 1917

WAR DIARY
or
INTELLIGENCE SUMMARY.
(Erase heading not required.)

Instructions regarding War Diaries and Intelligence Summaries are contained in F. S. Regs., Part II. and the Staff Manual respectively. Title pages will be prepared in manuscript.

Place	Date	Hour	Summary of Events and Information	Remarks and references to Appendices
LES LAURIERS			During week 20-28. G.O.C. inspected the whole of the Bn. in Musketry order	
"	23		3rd R.B. proceeded to Rombly range for 1 days musketry.	
"	26		Route " " " "	
"	27		MSY " " " "	
			Regt also made ARE Rifle range, for use for Vickers & musketry	
"	24		3 officers per Regt + 6 Hotchkiss teams per Regt proceeded to CAMIERS S.A. School for 10 days training. Major Tomkinson Royals and Capt McCMORE 3rd R.B. proceeded to CAMIERS. Each as commanding officer + anywhere replacement of No Team from 3rd Cav. Div.	
"	25		2 officers per Regt + 6 H.R. teams proceeded to Carriere to change with party that had been in 2nd.	

A. Hooks Capt.

Army Form C. 2118.

WAR DIARY
or
INTELLIGENCE SUMMARY.
(Erase heading not required.)

Instructions regarding War Diaries and Intelligence Summaries are contained in F. S. Regs., Part II. and the Staff Manual respectively. Title pages will be prepared in manuscript.

6th Cy. Bde
July 1917.

Place	Date	Hour	Summary of Events and Information	Remarks and references to Appendices
LES LAURIERS	28		Lt STARKEY M.S.Y., 2Lt STEDALL R.D.F.S., 2Lt STORK 3rd D.G., with 3 NCOs per Regt. proceeded to HQ Physical & Bayonet Training School ST POL for 12 days course.	

J. Shodo Capt.

Army Form C. 2118.

Vol 33

6th Cavalry Brigade. August 1917

WAR DIARY
INTELLIGENCE SUMMARY.
(Erase heading not required.)

Place	Date	Hour	Summary of Events and Information	Remarks and references to Appendices
LES LAURIERS	1st		The Brigade remained in the same billets as on 18th – 31st July.	Ref. Map
			Brigade H.Q. LES LAURIERS (East end of BOIS DE LA MIEPPE – on HAZEBROUCK–MERVILLE road)	
			3rd Dragoon Guards – LE CORBIE 6th M.G.S – LE TOUQUET	HAZEBROUCK STA 1/40,000
			(1st Royal Dragoons – HAVERSKERQUE C Battery R.H.A, LA MOTTE BAUDET	36A 1/40,000
			(N Somerset Yeomanry)	
			6th C.F.A. LES LAURIERS	
			13th M.V.S LES PURES BECQUES	
	6th		A working party detailed under proceeds by lorry to H.15.c.3.7? (Sheet 28 1/40,000)	
			To work under 5th Army :–	
			3rd Dragoon Guards { Capt. McLMORE* O.C.R.	* 2nd in command of 6th Cav. Bgde
			{ 2nd Lt E.C. STEEDMAN 50	Pack Company
			1st Royal Dragoons { 2/Lt D.S. STEWART* 52	* O.M. 3rd Cav. Div. Dun. Park
			{ Lt D.H. WATSON	
			N. Somerset Yeomanry 2/Lt O/R P. WILLIAMS 50	
	8th		H/Col A. BURT D.S.O.(Temp. Commanding 6th Cav. Brigade) + Brigade Major attended a Divisional Staff Ride in the neighbourhood of Mt des CATS.	Ref. Map HAZEBROUCK STA

WAR DIARY or INTELLIGENCE SUMMARY

Army Form C. 2118.

Cavalry Brigade August 1917

Place	Date	Hour	Summary of Events and Information	Remarks and references to Appendices
Roolaumont	14th		42 Dismounted Personnel attached to 6th M.G.S. proceeded to the Base on transfer to Infantry M.G. Corps.	
	21st		O.C. A.S.C. 3rd Cavalry Division inspects the transport of the Brigade.	
	26th		Following party proceeded by lorry to H. 14. b. 4.8 (Ref Map Sheet 28 1/40,000) in relief of party which proceeded on 6th August.	
			O.R.	
			3rd Dragoon Guards Lt W.G. BAGNALL* 50 * In command of	
			2/Lt L.F. BOWATER 6th Brigade Company	
			1st Royal Dragoons Lt P.R.D. COOKE 50	
			N. Somersets Yeomanry 2/Lt F.T. TURPIN 50	
	15th		2nd Lt W.H. ALLEN North Somerset Yeomanry proceeded on 24th August in relief of 2/Lt W.O. STEWART, Royal Dragoons as O.M.B. 3rd Cav. Div. Disn. Bttn.	
			Lt L. HELLYER 3rd Dragoon Guards proceeds to G.H.Q. S.A. School (HOTCHKISS Rifle Brnch) as HOTCHKISS Rifle Instructor.	
	30th		G.O.C. Lt/Col F.W. WORMALD D.S.O. (Royal Dragoons) + Brigade Major attended a Staff Tour in the neighbourhood of MONT DES CATS. (Ref map HAZEBROUCK SA 1/20,000)	
			Lt/Col F.W. WORMALD acted as G.O.C 6th Cavalry Brigade for the purpose of the Tour.	
	31st		C Battery R.H.A. left the Brigade + proceeds to ST OMER for attachment to 5th Army	S.C.D.

Army Form C. 2118.

WAR DIARY
INTELLIGENCE SUMMARY.

Cavalry Brigade
August 1917

Place	Date	Hour	Summary of Events and Information	Remarks and references to Appendices
LES LAURIERS	31st		Major F. KING 6th Machine Gun Squadron proceeds to Machine Gun School CAMIERS for 1 month's advanced machine gun course. Barrage fire	
	1–31st		The Brigade remained in billets as on 1st inst.	

(CRed)
Capt.
Staff Captain Cavalry Brigade

Army Form C. 2118.

HQ 6th Canadian Infantry Brigade
Sept 1917 Sheet 1
Appx 34

WAR DIARY
or
INTELLIGENCE SUMMARY.
(Erase heading not required.)

Instructions regarding War Diaries and Intelligence Summaries are contained in F. S. Regs., Part II. and the Staff Manual respectively. Title pages will be prepared in manuscript.

Place	Date	Hour	Summary of Events and Information	Remarks and references to Appendices
LES LAURIERS	1-30		The Brigade remained in billets during September stationed Camp Hdqrs.	
Le Champ 36A h40000 K14d			Regts with Inspection of MT horse harness and packs. Field Exercises & Exercises with Troops	
	25"		Bgde Field exercise together one to two weeks. Coln. Inn Cn. Div. Inspector N. Command to review Kilts light marching order. With Cycliste Skis at Arms	
	26		Bgde Parade with various exercises. G.O.C. In Cn. Div. inspected Royal Dragoons & Katchen exercise march SERCUS.	
	27		G.O.C. In Cn. Div. Inspected 3 m.S.B. In Kabul exercises ReineG SERCUS.	

J. Stark Lm

Army Form C. 2118.

6th Cavalry Bgde
Sept 1917.   Sheet 2

WAR DIARY
or
INTELLIGENCE SUMMARY.
(Erase heading not required.)

Place	Date	Hour	Summary of Events and Information	Remarks and references to Appendices
Des Laurieres	29		F.O.C. inspected horses of Bde Sigs	
	30		6th Cav Bde & 7 DG were reviewed to Lafaux Farm	
			Went to KANTERSINGHE Wagon Lines	
			Total Casualties of Whole Bde for Sept.	
			2nd Lt TURPIN F.T. North Somerset Yeo. rejoined 5/9/17	
			Lt DE PROTION 1st Royal Dragoons. Proceeded on Duty 28/9/17	
				J. Roberts Capt.

Army Form C. 2118.

WAR DIARY
or
INTELLIGENCE SUMMARY.
(Erase heading not required.)

6th Army Bde Brigade
October 1917

Place	Date	Hour	Summary of Events and Information	Remarks and references to Appendices
LES LAURIERS	1-18		The Brigade 6th C Bde RHA remained in billets as during the part of July, August & September. C Battery RHA were ngd to 5th Army as an instructional Battery. Their billets near ST HOMER 3 miles N of HOMER.	
	9th		Capt S.C. DEED MC from 1st or 10th Hussars Staff Capt 6th CA Bde and Capt U.E.C. COBEREGY MC B.d.Co L.t d. yin ee officer proceeded to LEROS to the x Staff appointments	
	13th		Major A.H. RYCROFT MC late ADC to late 3rd Brigade Lorne appointed Brigade Major 6th Army Brigade	
	11th		Capt R.M. WOOTTEN. 6th Anzac Ming Brigade joined 6th CA Bde as our appointment as Staff Capt v.c. Capt S.C. DEED MC.	
	2nd		Sm plus men of 3rd Bn Royal N.S.7 proceeded to Base and in Atlock Regt & Bannymaki Heights & 3rd O.R. N.S.7 30 o.R. To Base 3rd & 26 o.R. Regt 30 o.R.	A. Mor G.U.

Army Form C. 2118.

WAR DIARY
or
INTELLIGENCE SUMMARY.
(Erase heading not required.)

6th Cavalry Brigade
October 1917

Place	Date	Hour	Summary of Events and Information	Remarks and references to Appendices
LES LAURIERS	19th		The Bde left LES LAURIERS billeting area & marched on TG & B billets B.H.Q. & Sgnl troop TANGRY. 13 MBs. 3rd DR. { AESTRUS, GUERNONVAL, CONTEVILLE. Royal { EPS, HERREVAL, NEUER BM BOYAVAL.	Ref map MIGRUVAL ST POL MUROW
TANGRY	22nd		The Bde & 15oct 3rd Cav. Res. Park at 9 left TANGRY area & marched { N.S.7 { VALHUON, BRIDER, GROSSART. (M.G.Sqdn TROISVAUX 6 CM AUCHIER & LE HAMEL. K.Billets B.H.Q. & Sgnl troop REBREUVE 13 MBs 3rd D.R. { VACOUZIE LE BOUCO. FORTEL. Pt. FORTEL. HOPITAL. Royal { BOUBERS-SUR-CANCHE. LIGNY SUR CANCHE. CONCHY SUR CANCHE. MONCHEZ. (M.G.Sqdn BONNIERES 6 CM CANETZMONT. No 15 oct 3rd Cav. Park REMREMETTE ROZIERE WAMIN.	Ref map WISSOO LENS

S.J. North
Capt.

Army Form C. 2118.

6th Cavalry Brigade
October 1917

WAR DIARY
or
INTELLIGENCE SUMMARY.
(Erase heading not required.)

Place	Date	Hour	Summary of Events and Information	Remarks and references to Appendices
REBREUVE	Oct 23rd		The Brigade marched to billets as under:-	
			Bde H.Q. } FRANQUEVILLE.	
			6 Inniskg Drgns } GORENFLOS. 3rd Drs. RIBEAUCOURT.	
			13 M.R.S } FRANSU. DOMQUEUR. LE PLOUY.	
			R.C.H.A. BERNEUIL. ST HILAIRE. N.S.7 MONTRELET.	
			LANCHES. EPECAMPS. BONNEVILLE.	
			GORGES. VACQUERIE. FIEFFES.	
			C.M.G.Sqn. ERGNIES. BRUCAMPS	
			6 C.F.A. BOMESMONT.	
			No1 Sect. 3rd Cav. Res. Park. to move daylerten. YAUCOURT - BUSSUS.	
			BUSSUS BUSSUEL.	
				J Atonlo Cpr.

Army Form C. 2118.

6th Infantry Brigade
October 1917

WAR DIARY
or
INTELLIGENCE SUMMARY.
(Erase heading not required.)

Place	Date	Hour	Summary of Events and Information	Remarks and references to Appendices
GORENFLOS	26th		The Bde marched independently to final destinations - no incidents.	Maj J Howard absent on leave.
			Bde HQ LONGUET 3rd Bn LONGPRÉ Royal LONG.	MOUFFLERS. MOUCHELLES LES DOMART
			C & Signalling Troop COCQUEREL. LÉCATELET.	
			13 MTS. LIÉTOIRE	
			NS7 FONTAINE 6 CPA PONT-REMY.	
			FAUCOURT SUR SOMME.	
			DUNCQ - ERONDEALS.	
			BRAY LES MAREUIL.	
			LIERCOURT. BAILLEUL.	
LONGUET	27.		A Bde & working party skeleton & no under. 6 get the Bde area to proceed to huts & bivouac east of PÉRONNE. Park	
			Erecting skittles & huts.	
			1/c 3rd Cav Bde Pioneers: Bn Major E.T. CLIFF 3rd Bde + 40 OR 3rd Bn + 40 horse	
			Adjutant " " " Lt. C.R. KNITTAL 3rd Bn + 6 horse	
			1 Gun NCO " Cpl STONER NS7	
			1/c 1 Bde Sig Co. Capt HEFER TRAFFORD Royal.	
			Lt BOWER Lt WILKINS 3rd Bde and 101 OR 3rd Bn + 4 horse	
			Lt H. SMITH Lt D.A.F.HARRIS + 99 OR Royal + 6 horse	
			Lt K.G. JENKINS + 17 REF & URGE + 97 OR NS7 + 4 horse.	

Napier OC

Army Form C. 2118.

WAR DIARY
or
INTELLIGENCE SUMMARY.
(Erase heading not required.)

6th Cav Bde
Oct 1917

Place	Date	Hour	Summary of Events and Information	Remarks and references to Appendices
LONGUET			C.M.B.R.A. L.H.N.E. ELLIS + 28 O.R. 2 Horses	
			6 CEA 1 Officer 25 O.R. 1 Horse	
			Lt G Babington N.S.I. Am attached to Bde HQ F.	
			a course in Staff duties.	
			Bgdr. AKM Hannay D.S.O. took over temp. command of 3rd Cav	
			Div & Lt/Col Sir T Vaughan cos. Bde.	
			Lt Col A Burt D.S.O. 3rd Dr took over command of 6 Cav Bde	
	17		during temp. absence of Bgdr H to Harman D.S.O.	

Army Form C. 2118.

6th Cavalry Brigade
Nov 1917

WAR DIARY
or
INTELLIGENCE SUMMARY.
(Erase heading not required.)

Place	Date	Hour	Summary of Events and Information	Remarks and references to Appendices
LONGUEIL	1-9.		The Brigade remained in billets as during later part of October.	Ref. my 11/11/1917 APPENDIX
	10th		Cav. Corps HQ resumed the Brigade on Nov 10th from 4th Army.	
	12		Batteries marched on Nov 12th & placed with remainder of 6th Cav. Bde R.H.A. to IX Corps Command area.	
	14		133 men of 6th Bde to join Br. Bdes. & other Cav. Divisions when Bde. train between [ill.] 6th Bde Coy upon to the [ill.]	
	17		The Bde HQ & Bde marched to [ill.]	

Bde H.Q. — BEAUCOURT
6th Dn. } BEAUCOURT
Essex Yeo. } SOR L'YALLUE
[ill.] 13 MGS
N.S. BEHENCOURT
MONTIGNY

Chief Officers
AMIENS
LENS
6 CSH BAPAUMECOURT

15 April 1917

Army Form C. 2118.

WAR DIARY
or
INTELLIGENCE SUMMARY.
(Erase heading not required.)

1/6th North'd Fusiliers November 1917
6 Infantry Bde

Place	Date	Hour	Summary of Events and Information	Remarks and references to Appendices
BEAUCOURT	18.		The Brigade marched on evening of Nov 18th to billets thatwere in BRAY — viz: Bde H.Q. Rot. 3 (Bn & 6th 13th M.G.) 2nd Bn CAPPY NS7 Bois d'LIMPÉ Camp 6 Cav Div Rear Camp CAPPY.	Refer to 1/6 NF Athens.
SUZANNE	20.		The Brigade commenced to entrench. Miners worked up for @ 8.30 AM. Ready to move to fwd locations at 11AM. Move to SUZANNE effected & during afternoon huts in CAPPI offloaded. Bde on moving to rendezvous nr RIV WIRE Bde HQ 6.30 AM 22d. 2 Kos & Co of men to NW FINS for reconstruction on 21 & 22. Bde zone begin on officer + Bde Intelligence officer also sent to NW Fins together.	59c 1/Oct1917 M Stordy Lt Col

Army Form C. 2118.

6th Cavalry Brigade
Nov 1917

WAR DIARY
or
INTELLIGENCE SUMMARY.
(Erase heading not required.)

Instructions regarding War Diaries and Intelligence Summaries are contained in F. S. Regs., Part II. and the Staff Manual respectively. Title pages will be prepared in manuscript.

Place	Date	Hour	Summary of Events and Information	Remarks and references to Appendices
SUZANNE	21		The Brigade moved 1 at 15th horses ready drawn at 2.15 up to horse lines	
	22		The Bde rest orders that they should move up a 23 mins	
	23		The Bde marches 6 billets as follows:— Bde HQ) HERISSART. Royal Horse 12 M I S) TALMAS PUCHEVILLERS. NAOURS HAVERNAS. I Y5 7 CONTAY 6 N.L. Res RUBEMPRE. 6 Cav. La Vicogne.	
TALMAS	23 - 30th		Bde remains in billets as above. The Bde are ordered to send a Dismounted Bde Recce. Bde Inf. Bn. from 3rd Dismounted Bde from own 13th Brigading Battalion. An mounted fmk. Bn to hrs on Nov 30th 130 mm to proceed to TEMPLEUX LE GUERARD K 40 73rd & 13th 24th Div. 11.11 pm. 6th Cav. details. Transport tent. Sup. transfer to 19th Contay to march to TREBIE by Br. nov 30/12 De by no 12 mm. to the reserve of the ready from nov 11 1917. De. be mounted. Orders to detrain have await their arrival & report hrs.	[signature]

Army Form C. 2118.

WAR DIARY
or
INTELLIGENCE SUMMARY

6 Cavalry Brigade

December 1917

M 37

Place	Date	Hour	Summary of Events and Information	Remarks and references to Appendices
TALMAS.	1.		The 6th Cav Battalion & E.M.Bty. entrained at following places:	

At TALMAS 6.30 AM
At TALMAS 6.30 AM HERISSART 9.30 AM & ENTRAY 8.30 AM proceeded to BERNES where they remained in reserve under orders of VII Corps.

Transport proceeded to Route to Cerisy & Pujio 1/2 her man took three stretchers & B. Bolton Pride & 3 M.G. fighting lorries accompanied Force in emergency.

Lt Col Bp was made commander of Lt. Co. F.N. Norwood DSO

	3rd DG	1 AF	217 CR	S. Robin	20 LD	6 CM	6 CR	2. LD
Ranks								
Ranks	O.M.	390. OR		6 Return	20. D	Bottom	100 R	4 LD
MS7		216		5	16			
Strength	76	93		2	20			
								JS Arnott Capt

Army Form C. 2118.

WAR DIARY
or
INTELLIGENCE SUMMARY.

(Erase heading not required.)

(6th Infantry Bde) Dec 1917.

Instructions regarding War Diaries and Intelligence Summaries are contained in F. S. Regs., Part II. and the Staff Manual respectively. Title pages will be prepared in manuscript.

Place	Date	Hour	Summary of Events and Information	Remarks and references to Appendices
TALMAS	2.		The Batter part of Bde trekking area was renunciated & Route - Bde HQ 6 CPA 4.13 MPS moun on 820 am. 3rd Bn. {HERISSART PUCHEVILLERS NS7 CANTAY. Route. ALLONVILLE {6 CPA ALLONVILLE CARDONNETTE RAINNEVILLE ENTRE RUBEMPRE	
MOLLIENS AU BOIS	10.		Brig Sir ATH. HARMAN S.O. returned to 6 th Cur Bde on for Lngton leave returned from England.	
	10.		87 Hours Route. 46 Horses (including an Ishioi) were dispatched by rail from Longueau Station at 7:30 pm. to MARSEILLES. From there to Egypt. (In joint force Cars with 24 O.R. sent on this to MARSEILLES) (Shechelm)	

WAR DIARY or INTELLIGENCE SUMMARY

Army Form C. 2118.

Place	Date	Hour	Summary of Events and Information	Remarks and references to Appendices
MOLLIENS AU BOIS	1.		81 Horses, sick from 3rd Bn, & NSR and 13 Horses 6 M.G.S.Bn. Entrained at LA FAUX ESTRANGES from 11th mort.	
		10 am	27 OR such Regt & OR 6 M.G.S.Bn.	
			Lt Col AHA Inglis with relief of HQ for 75th Dismounted Brigade proceeded to VERMAND to relieve Lt Col F.W. HERMAN D.S.O. & reliving HQ of 6th Dismounted Bde.	
	2.		The 13th marched from billeting area as under. The roads were deep in snow but as much marched independently surprise in their own was no matter.	
			BdyHQ) LONGUET. 3rdBn. ALLYLEHAUTCLOCHER.	
			6th Typed hosp) COQUEREL. BUSSUS BOSSUEL.	
			13 MGS ÉPAGNE. Rand. MILLERS SOUSMONT.	
			6 M.G.S.Bn. EMCOURT. BRUCAMPS - ERGNIES. MICHAELLES LES DAMES.	
			NSR LONG L'ÉTOILE. MOUMERS. CRA. YVAVUMPT BUSSUS	

Army Form C. 2118.

WAR DIARY
or
INTELLIGENCE SUMMARY.
(Erase heading not required.)

1st Cav Bde
Dec 1917.

Place	Date	Hour	Summary of Events and Information	Remarks and references to Appendices
LONGUET	21-31.		The Bde remained in billets without incident.	
			CASUALTIES:—	

UNIT.	K.	W.	M.	TOTAL
3 D Gds { Offs.	—	1 ⓐ	—	1
OR.	1	2	—	3
N. Som { Offs.	—	—	—	—
Yeo. OR.	—	1	—	1

ⓐ Capt. W.G. BAGNELL.

J.Kr..../Capt.

Army Form C. 2118

WAR DIARY
or
INTELLIGENCE SUMMARY
(Erase heading not required.)

6th Cavalry Brigade Jun 1918

Vol 38

Place	Date	Hour	Summary of Events and Information	Remarks and references to Appendices
LONGPRÉ	1.		The Brigade remained in billets as in Dec 21st	H40000 62c.
			The 6th Dismounted Bde (nomenclature changed from 6th Dismounted Bde) LE FERGUIER remained in trenches in neighbourhood of	
	7.		Lt Col A BURT DSO 17th Lancers on 3rd Dragoons Guards relieved Lt Col A H A ING DSO + AO N Somerset Yeo in command of 6th Dismounted Brigade.	
	9.		2nd A.R. Cavalry Corps held a horse jumping parade. A Woorman number were our car 3rd Dr. to Royal 11 MSY.	
	16.		3rd Dragoons Inniskillings were relieved in trenches by 1st Dismounted Division & 6th Dismounted Bde less 7 officers 228 OR, 3 Lancers 6/7 Dragoons Going to Belair and 7 officers 238 OR returned at LONGPRÉ Station at 11AM relieved to ones to be town.	

Staats Cer

Army Form C. 2118.

WAR DIARY
or
INTELLIGENCE SUMMARY.
(Erase heading not required.)

6th Cavalry Bde
Jan 1918.

Place	Date	Hour	Summary of Events and Information	Remarks and references to Appendices
LONGPRÉ	16		On relief of 6th Dismounted Brigade 4 Pioneer Regt remained in reinfs of Tendiers known as 3rd Cavalry Pioneer Regt. This Bgde from 16/1/18 – Established being composed of 1 Captain & subalterns 6 sgts 6 cpls 188 O.R. The Pioneer Regt in strength were by night under the orders of 6th Dismounted Brigade.	62 & 1/40000
	21		At 6.15 6 3rd Cav. Pioneer Regt was sent up to form firing line no. 17 on 24th inst. By counter-orders indicated for her ice attack 1 Lieutenant & troops to former 13 O.R. installed 73 O.R. 3rd D.C. in A Sqn cond 1st/4th Hussars — 73 O.R. Rgn L & A R cavalry another Pioneer Regt strength 2 O.R. N.C.O 2 Instn ??? 73 O.R.	
	23		Relieved by G.O.C. 3rd Cav. Pioneer Regt returned to their ares 13th Australian Light Horse arrived to the Brigade ready to attachment & following purpose, they were killeted in LONGPRÉ + LOWDE	

J. Short Capt.

Army Form C. 2118.

WAR DIARY
or
INTELLIGENCE SUMMARY.
(Erase heading not required.)

6th Cav[alry] Bde Brigade
Jan 1918

Place	Date	Hour	Summary of Events and Information	Remarks and references to Appendices
LONGUET 15			Owing the chief of 6 Dragoons Lt Col Shaw continuing his 3rd Do in hospital - Major Lynt Rgt now O.C. the Bde & confers returned returns to station to the close of	
			S.S.M Holliday } 3rd D.G.	
			2/Corpl R Mills	
			16/11/en Lt Hesmer 14 CR being injured	
			The Brigade marched to enforced to Hills to St Clair	
LONGUET 28			B/HQ } BERRAY SUR SOMME 3DG } LACHYUSEE RAYNL. AILLY SUR SOMME	
			13 HA } { FRANQUAY BRADLY	
			ST JUSTIN M17 PICQUIGNY	
			6th Bde ARGOEUVES	
	29		The Brigade marched to Hills to	
			B.H.Q } Royals } HANGORNIERS 7/ST BAYON BILLETS	
			13 HR } MARLEZUATE { GRESBY WIENBURY	
			3 DG	
			ECPA BULLAVCOURT	

J.S. Ahenstoepl

Army Form C. 2118.

6th Cavalry Brigade
Jan 1918

WAR DIARY
or
INTELLIGENCE SUMMARY.
(Erase heading not required.)

Place	Date	Hour	Summary of Events and Information	Remarks and references to Appendices
MARICOPA	Jan 30		The Brigade marched to TERTRY area. Route from MIRAUMONT via BEAULENCOURT Bois. B.H.Q. } TERTRY N19. Q33a 1 BMS } Q33d 3 BMS } NEUVILLETTE 1 Cav Bde CAULAIGNY FARM Q32c 6 C.F.A. TRESCON. Many men were evacuated to hospital with flu & trench fever, & mumps also.	Ref. 6CB 1/40000

N. Horsburgh, Major
Brigade Major 6th Cav Brigade

Army Form C. 2118.

WAR DIARY
or
INTELLIGENCE SUMMARY.
(Erase heading not required.)

5th Cavalry Brigade
JANUARY 1918

APPENDIX I. CASUALTIES.

UNIT.	OFFICERS NAME	CASUALTY	O.R. KILLED	WOUNDED	
3rd Dragoon Gds	2/Lt N.J. Massey-Lynch	Wounded		3	Shell Shock
	Mjr. M.H. Stork	D. of Wounds	1		
Royal Dragoons	—	—	—	3×	× 1 accidental
N. Somerset Yeo.	—	—	1	1²	² Self Inflicted
1st M.Gun Sq.	—	—	2	1	

Army Form C. 2118.

WAR DIARY
INTELLIGENCE SUMMARY
(Erase heading not required.)

HQ 1st Canby Brigade 9th Feby 39

Place	Date	Hour	Summary of Events and Information	Remarks and references to Appendices
FORTRIE	1.		The Brigade remained at RLU G FORTRIE informing position [illegible] the 3rd Canby Power Regt remained at 1 HEUDECOURT A reconnaissance of Coy Pos? the N57 13a [illegible] B/c commences from Hoby on the Rea line to Drenning 17 UTHEHENCOURT Q35.C. The advanced party was on Brigade were today work on flea line to Tides was to drag but she started to work to inches Copi reviews Rock 3 to intown 160 P at ZEnzures AZILLECOUR 2 U&R AT HENDECOURT The GOC parts wrote [illegible] T & Rom line toning & shifting Fremicles to T Rome line control not	Ref. Maps 60.6 1/40,000
		6-8	Kicking Partie at FLACQ & Rf Brown line to ENGINEES on STH 12th 13th 20th 3rd LT's held the let front to engineers FLEZ	

J.M. Webb Capt

WAR DIARY
INTELLIGENCE SUMMARY.

(Erase heading not required.)

Army Form C. 2118.

6th Cavalry Brigade

January 1918

Place	Date	Hour	Summary of Events and Information	Remarks and references to Appendices
TEUCRY	1/1		Working parties were ready for 6 battns. R Engineers. Ref. map 62 c 1/40000 3rd Cavalry Pioneer Regt rejoining the Brigade from VENDELLES. Working parties returned to 7th Cavalry Bde. Parties proceeded to huts more East. Lt. H.W. Lee 3rd Car. Sur. Detachment on Siren line N.E. of CAULAINCOURT. 2 Officers 100 O.R. per Regt. Capt A.W. Pope M.C. in command. Working parties to Brown Line nr TEMPCOURT. 2 Officers 3 N.C.Os 1 MT Smith for Royal Arty. 50 O.R. from each Regt. Capt Allen 3rd D.G. in command. Working party on aerodrome nr PREZ. 1 Officer 6 N.C.Os 20 O.R.	

A Morris Col.

Army Form C. 2118.

WAR DIARY
INTELLIGENCE SUMMARY.
(Erase heading not required.)

Instructions regarding War Diaries and Intelligence Summaries are contained in F. S. Regs., Part II. and the Staff Manual respectively. Title pages will be prepared in manuscript.

Lt Carr by Bryant
Oct 14/18.

Place	Date	Hour	Summary of Events and Information	Remarks and references to Appendices
TERTRY	10th – 11th		Working parties from the Bn's continued work on Brown & Green line's in PREZ.	
	12th		Major G.T. CLIFF 3rd Dragoon Guards sick in No 5 Stationary Hospital TINCOURT, having fractured his thumb from effects of a toss from his horse.	
	13th		Working parties on outskirts of 30 mm less from Bn's & 10 more sick from Royal N.S.D. to Division. Major G.T. CLIFF 3rd D'gs. transferred to No 5 Stationary Hospital TINCOURT.	
	13–14th		Working parties on Green Line & Brown line as overlay.	
	15th		[illegible]	

J.S. Howard Capt.

Army Form C. 2118.

WAR DIARY
INTELLIGENCE SUMMARY

Sheet 4

Place	Date	Hour	Summary of Events and Information	Remarks and references to Appendices
TERRY	21st		8 Guns of 6th M.G. Sqdn. went into the line under Dismounted Divisions, as garrison for M.G. emplacements in BROWN LINE (3 officers 39 O.R.) Lt. J.B. BICKERSTETH 1st Royal Dragoons, assumed duties of Bde Intelligence officer, vice Maj RYCROFT (to Tank Corps) Readjustment of working parties as follows:-	See 62a.
	22nd		3rd Dragoon Gds 3 offs 111 OR working in Battle Zone, living at JEANCOURT. Capt. J.T. GIBBS i/c Party, including details of 8th Cav Bde.	
			Royals 3 offs 120 OR } working daily on GREEN N.S.Y. 3 offs 120 OR } line, under Capt H.W. POPE M.C. N.S.Y.	
			Royals 1 off 28 OR working daily in Battle Zone, riding to and from JEANCOURT.	
			N.S.Y. 1 off 20 OR working on Aerodrome near FLEZ.	

Bonaker Capt

Army Form C. 2118.

WAR DIARY
INTELLIGENCE SUMMARY.
(Erase heading not required.)

6th Cav Bde
7 Feb 1918

Instructions regarding War Diaries and Intelligence Summaries are contained in F. S. Regs., Part II. and the Staff Manual respectively. Title pages will be prepared in manuscript.

Place	Date	Hour	Summary of Events and Information	Remarks and references to Appendices
TERRY	24th		2/Lt S.L. JEFFREY, Royals, with 9 OR and 24 horses proceeded by road to I Corps School at VAUCHELLES-les-AUTHIE, to instruct Officers attending Fax School in Equitation.	See 62c
	26th		Working party on GREEN line (30th 120 ORs and from Royals & NSY) ceased work.	
	28th		Remainder of working parties, except party living at JEANCOURT (3 offs 114 OR, 3rd DGs), ceased work. In accordance with previously prepared Scheme, the Bde closed up so as to hand over hutts & stables for the 2 Sqdns N of TERRY to 8th Cav Bde.	

Brawler Capt
for Brigade Major
6th Cav Bde

Army Form C. 2118.

WAR DIARY
or
INTELLIGENCE SUMMARY.

(Erase heading not required.)

6th Cavalry Brigade
March 1918.

Place	Date	Hour	Summary of Events and Information	Remarks and references to Appendices
TERTRY	1		The Brigade remained in their camps around TERTRY with a portion of 1 Regt in the CAPECO area. Huts in the 6th Cav Bde area & 7th & 20th M.Gs were handed up to the 6th Cav Bde area owing to 5th Cav Div. taking over the Western End of 3rd Cav Div. area.	
	2		Reconnaissance carried out of new Bde concentration formed to be done by night near SOYECOURT.	Appendices &c.
	3		6th Cav Bde came on orders as an Infy Bde of 3 Brit Regs. Regtl. Dragoons were sent up to 1 Dragoon Gds. Reconnoitres of TAHURE Bde photographed. Present & M Schorley.	
	4		B.O.C. & M.G. Commander reconnoitred LE VERGUIER Inf & New trom system & VERMAND MEN.	
	5		Route continues with ROUEZ 3rd Bde roberts.	
	6		6 O.C. 1st & C.O. reconnoitres MOUCOURT Posen Post & the trenches of MASSIFER & ...with a view to counterattack.	N/Hants Coy

Army Form C. 2118.

6th Cavalry Bde
March 1918.

WAR DIARY
or
INTELLIGENCE SUMMARY.
(Erase heading not required.)

Place	Date	Hour	Summary of Events and Information	Remarks and references to Appendices
TERTRY	8		Owing to 7th Cav Bde being dismounted & being formed into 3 Machine Gun Battalions Officers & horses were taken from them to form the Bde.	
	9	11am	Summer time commenced.	
	12	9am	The whole remainder Tos were transferred from Bde to fifth Cavalry Bde. and 10.a P.W.O. Royal Hussars were transferred from 8th to 6th Cavalry Bde. The G.O.C Brigade Genl A.E.W. Harman D.S.O. addressed the No.th Somerset Yeo. & a farewell order (C. to fr. nt.a) The day was to hot.	
	13	At 2.30 pm	the Brigade marched to the DEMISE area. Their camps as follows. Bde HQ. Camp No. 4. r9a & DEMISE. 13 Hrs. " " 5. v9b Royal " No. 1. v26 v3a 3rd Dragoon Guards " " 2. v3a & c (no signal camp No. 6 v4c 6th Cav Bde amb SECRETs.	J.V. Hossop Bm

Army Form C. 2118.

6th Cavalry Bde
March 1918

WAR DIARY
or
INTELLIGENCE SUMMARY.
(Erase heading not required.)

Place	Date	Hour	Summary of Events and Information	Remarks and references to Appendices
DEVISE	14		Brig Gen A.G. SEYMOUR D.S.O. took over temporary command of 6th Cavalry Bde vice Brig Gen A.E.W. Harman D.S.O. temporarily in command of 3rd Cavalry Div.	
	15		Capt A.G.H.F HOWARD Duke of Wellingtons promoted to be A.D.C. to O.C. 6th Cav Bde temporarily vice Lt R Lawn O.O.O to return to 3rd Car Div temporarily.	
	16		Major H.A. TOMKINSON D.S.O. Royal Dragoons to be act Lt Col in command of 10th Hussars vice 9/11/Col W.O. GIBBS.	
	16		Capt T.C. HUMFREY from 11th M.G. Sdn to command 6th M.G. Sdn vice Capt C.D. Leyland to 1st Life Guards	
	18		The 6th Cav. Bde were ordered to find a working party of 350 O.R. with 7 Officers on Rear zone defences at P18c	Sheet 62c 1/40,000

J. Northcote

Army Form C. 2118.

6th Army B.de
March 1918.

WAR DIARY
or
INTELLIGENCE SUMMARY.
(Erase heading not required.)

Instructions regarding War Diaries and Intelligence Summaries are contained in F. S. Regs., Part II. and the Staff Manual respectively. Title pages will be prepared in manuscript.

Place	Date	Hour	Summary of Events and Information	Remarks and references to Appendices
DEFISE	18		The working parts of Crew 6th Cav B.de Pioneer Battalion under command of Capt H.E. de Trafford Royals. Strength 3 subalterns 5 days 192 O.R. Royals. 3 subalterns 5 days 125 O.R. 10th Hussars. 1 subaltern 1 days 19 O.R. 6 Sqn. C. Sqn. The 3rd Dragoon Guards were left with the training of horses & I.Sqn. The B.de Intelligence Officer commenced course of instruction during the week of training 8 out of 24 Regt. scouts in training & Intelligence duties. A deputation of officers in the 2 Regt. today were sent to a Photo Section, Cavalry for lecture & demonstration of aerial photographs & interpretation of aerial photographs.	
	19		Working parts continued as of 18th. Working parties & training continued. H.R.H. inspected troops of 10th Royals in the afternoon.	J Moore Capt. Bde. Int. Off. R.G.

Army Form C. 2118.

6th Cavalry Bde
March 1918

WAR DIARY
or
INTELLIGENCE SUMMARY.
(Erase heading not required.)

Place	Date	Hour	Summary of Events and Information	Remarks and references to Appendices
BERTSE	21		Heavy German bombardment commenced on whole of 1st 3rd 5th Army fronts. 3rd Army front at 5 am. 6.15am 3rd Cavalry Bde received orders to be in readiness to move forth can collect. The Bde ordered to stand to ready to move at 3.30 pm. Bde marched via CROIX MOLIGNAUX — ESMERY HALLON VILLESELVE — to bivouac nr BEAUMONT arriving about 1 am to bivouac. At 10 pm 6th Dr Bde ordered to embus at OGNY & proceed to OGNES to take under orders of 3rd Corps to be attached to 58th Div. 6th Dr Bde moved nominatim to OGNY embussed about 1 am 22nd under Lt. Col. A. Burt DSO STO. For ding of movement of 6th Dr Bde attd.	Maps 66c APPENDIX A [attached]

J. Harris Gen.

Army Form C. 2118.

C. M. Curthy Bole
intelligence
Nov 1918

WAR DIARY
or
INTELLIGENCE SUMMARY.
(Erase heading not required.)

Instructions regarding War Diaries and Intelligence Summaries are contained in F. S. Regs., Part II. and the Staff Manual respectively. Title pages will be prepared in manuscript.

Place	Date	Hour	Summary of Events and Information	Remarks and references to Appendices
BERMONT	22		At 5.30 A.M. B.H.Q. & Sgnl Sect marched to TULLOYER-AUMONT taking up H.Q. of 5th Dismounted Div. which found at 6th Cav Bde.	APPENDIX B [attached]
			Remainder of Personnel horse & transport of 6th Cav Bde marched at 7 A.M. under command of Major Stoughton Royal Scots to PONTOISE.	Major Stoughton
PONTOISE	23		Bivouaked in PONTOISE. About 12 noon the Bde at PONTOISE & 4 O/b & 50 of Reg'l Hdqrs under command of Major Hooker Wiltshires 10th Hussars left PONTOISE mounted & formed temporary detachment between PONTOISE & CAPPY PONT.	appendix C
			Remainder of Bde moved back to CAPPY PONT.	
CAPPY PONT	25		Remainder of Bde moved at 9 A.M. moved to CRECENCOURT. Horses remaining back at CAPPY PONT formed up to join Bde 12 noon at [?] at 10 A.M.	
	26		An aircraft moved men at CRECENCOURT here returned to join final Pickt detachment at 5.0 A.M.	

J. K. M. Cole

Army Form C. 2118.

WAR DIARY
or
INTELLIGENCE SUMMARY.
(Erase heading not required.)

6th Cavalry Bde
March 1915

Place	Date	Hour	Summary of Events and Information	Remarks and references to Appendices
CARLEPONT	26		The two horses of B Sqn with B de at CARLEPONT who moved to CHOISY the B de hoisted to move men and horses posted to sleep of infantry to the Regts. Stood horse.	
CHOISY AU BAC	27		6th Div and Bde united therewith at CHOISY AU BAC and sent 28th where gen Bridges there marched on for CHOISY at 11am 29th for the Inniskillings. The 6th Bde of big than & CHOISY marched early of for Butts detachments reported in front of CHOISY thou	
CHOISY	28		Each morning the Brigade camp was bombarded by the aircraft. Several casualties resulting. Reinforce.	
CHOISY	29		The Brigade marched via CARLEPONE & CLERMONT & ARRON & bivouacs for the night. Capt TURNER joined with 15 NCO's & 3 Reft from 5th Hussars. Detachment rejoined the Bde at ARRON.	
ARRON	30		The Brigade marched accompanied only by A Sch B de at 6am to AMIENS. 30 miles. Billeted in town.	
AMIENS	31		AMIENS — A/2nd Nicholson RAMC joined Bde to taking place of Dr. 3.30pm Bde did not move.	

J.S.[signature]

SPECIAL ORDER
BY
BRIGADIER GENERAL A.E.W. HARMAN. D.S.O.
Commanding 6th Cavalry Brigade.

12th March 1918.

After bidding farewell to the Officers, Non-commissioned Officers, and Men of the 1/1st North Somerset Yeomanry, I wish to put on record the feelings of regret with which all ranks remaining with the 6th Cavalry Brigade part with the North Somerset Yeomanry today.

Since November 13th, 1914, when they joined the 6th Cavalry Brigade, the North Somerset Yeomanry, by their high sense of duty, keenness, and loyalty, by their efficiency in the fighting round YPRES in November 1914, February 1915, April 1915, on May 13th 1915, at LOOS in September 1915, at the HOHENZOLLERN REDOUBT January 1916, and at MONCHY-le-PREUX April 1917, have equally maintained the highest traditions of the Brigade.

In saying goodbye and wishing them God-speed today, I feel I am voicing the sentiments of all ranks of the Brigade, who though losing their comrades-in-arms, will ever retain the true spirit of friendship in which they have fought and played together as members of the 6th Cavalry Brigade.

Army Form C. 2118.

APPENDIX C.

WAR DIARY
or
INTELLIGENCE SUMMARY.

6th Cavalry Brigade.
March, 1918.

(Erase heading not required.)

Place	Date	Hour	Summary of Events and Information	Remarks and references to Appendices
			CASUALTIES O.R.	

Date.	Regiment.	Killed.	Wounded	Missing	
21st.	6th Signal Troop.		2		
"	Royals	1	1		
22nd	10th Hussars.		2*		*at duty
23rd	3rd D.Gds.	7	7		
"	Royals.	7	11		
"	10th Hussars	4	15	3	
24th	3rd D.Gds.	4	25	8	
"	Royals	2	21	3	
"	10th Hussars	-	3	3	
"	6th M.G.Sqn.	2	6	3	
25th	3rd D.Gds.	5	10	1	
"	Royals	4	11	-	
"	10th Hussars	1	*22*	5	*3 at duty
26th	Royals.			1	
"	6th M.G.Sqn.		2		
27th	3rd D.Gds.	6	13	1	
"	10th Hussars		1		
28th	3rd D.Gds.		1		
"	Royals.		3		
"	6th M.G.Sqn.		4		
"	6th C.F.A.		1		

[signature] Capt.
Brigade Major 6th Cavalry Bde.

Army Form C. 2118.

WAR DIARY
INTELLIGENCE SUMMARY

APPENDIX 'C'

6th Cavalry Brigade.

March, 1918.

(Erase heading not required.)

Summary of Events and Information

CASUALTIES March, 1918.

Officers.

Date	Regiment	KILLED	WOUNDED
22nd	3rd D.Gds.	Lt. N.T.KING	
23rd	3rd D.Gds.		Lt. F.B.KATINAKIS (D. of W. 27/3/18)
"	10th Hussars		Capt. E.W.E.PALMES, M.C.
"	10th Hussars		Lt. W.J.BRISLEY
24th	3rd D.Gds.		Lt. T.KOHLER
"	Capt.& 3rd D.Gds.		Capt. R.B.ALLEN
"	3rd D.Gds.		Lt. R.D.YOUNGER
"	Royals		Lt. Hon.W.H.CUBITT (D. of W. 24/3/18)
"	Royals		Lt. A.R.COOPER
"	Royals		Lt. D.A.F.HARRIS
"	10th Hussars		Lt. F.R.GASKELL
25th	3rd D.Gds.		Lt. M.J.CLERY.
"	Royals		Lt. E.St.G.STEDALL (at duty)
24th	6th M.G.Sqn.		Capt. F.B.RATCLIFFE
"	6th M.G.Sqn.		Lt. A.COLE
"	6th M.G.Sqn.		Lt. J.A.WILKES (& missing)
25th	6th M.G.Sqn.	Lt. G.H.EATON	
26th	R.A.M.C.att. Royals		Capt. A.W.FORREST (at duty)

[signature] Capt.

3rd Cav.Div.

WAR DIARY

Headquarters,

6th CAVALRY BRIGADE.

A P R I L

1 9 1 8

Attached:
Appendices "A" and "B".

WAR DIARY
INTELLIGENCE SUMMARY

Instructions regarding War Diaries and Intelligence Summaries are contained in F.S. Regs., Part II. and the Staff Manual respectively. Title pages will be prepared in manuscript.

(Erase heading not required.)

6th Cavalry Brigade
April, 1918.

Place	Date	Hour	Summary of Events and Information	Remarks and references to Appendices
SAINS-EN-AMIENOIS.	1st.	6 A.M.	The Brigade proceeded via BOVES Wood to St.HUBE - BOVES to BOIS de GENTELLES. Brigade H.Q. at X tracks N.N.W. of Wood.	Map 1/40,000 62 D
		12 noon	3rd Dragoon Gds. sent out patrol of 1 officer 6 men to reconnoitre Wood U.18.b. and c. (East of Bois de HANGARD) to find out if occupied and to ascertain position of our front line, and another patrol 1 officer and 6 men towards MARCELCAVE to discover by whom held and position our own line.	
		1 P.M.	Royals and 10th Hussars sent patrols to reconnoitre tracks running North of the main AMIENS - NOYON Road from Bois de GENTELLES as far as River LA LUCE East of DOMART.	
		6.45 P.M.	The Brigade moved to Wood in N.34.c. (1000 yards N.N.W. of Bois de GENTELLES) and bivouaced there for night.	
N.34.c.	2nd.		The Brigade remained in bivouac in wood in N.34.c. all day. Bde. H.Q. moved to old prisoner of War Camp N.28.d.1.5. During the morning a patrol was sent to get in touch with 41st Infantry Brigade, at U.25.a., and found that Infantry were in touch with French on River LUCE. A second patrol was sent out to find information in and round Woods U.18.b.	
		11 A.M.	Warning received that Brigade would probably be required to be in Reserve to the 1st Cavalry Divn. tonight.	
		6 P.M.	Orders received that 6th Cavalry Brigade was placed under orders of 1st Cavalry Divn. from 9.30 P.M.	
		8 P.M.	Royals marched under orders of 1st Cavalry Divn. to concealed Rendezvous position about 0.22.a. and then went on foot to dig strong point in P.25. P.19.d., P.20.a. (i.e. in S.W. direction from Bois de VAIRE towards VILLERS BRETONNEUX). The remainder of the Brigade remained in the same bivouac as for night April 1st/2nd.	
N.28.d.1.5.	3rd.	4.30 A.M.	10th Hussars and 1 Section 6th M.G.Sqn. marched to FOUILLOY, where they went into billets	
		7.30 A.M.	3rd Dragoon Guards marched to the Northern parts of Bois L'ABBÉ. Royals on completion of digging had also concentrated there.	
		8 A.M.	6th Machine Gun Sqn. (less 1 Section) also marched to Bois L'ABBÉ, and bivouaced near 3rd Dragoon Guards.	
		8.30 A.M.	Brigade H.Q. and 6th Signal Troop marched to FOUILLOY, where Brigade Report Centre was established.	
			6th Cavalry Field Ambulance was at BLANGY TRONVILLE	

Instructions regarding War Diaries and Intelligence
Summaries are contained in F.S. Regs., Part II.
and the Staff Manual respectively. Title Pages
will be prepared in manuscript.

INTELLIGENCE SUMMARY
(Erase heading not required.)

6th Cavalry Brigade.
April, 1918.

Place	Date	Hour	Summary of Events and Information	Remarks and references to Appendices
FOUILLOY.	3rd.		During the morning 3rd Dragoon Guards and 10th R.Hussars sent 2 officers each to reconnoitre the posts that had been dug by the Royals the previous night.	Map 1:40 1/40,000 Sheet 62D
		8.30 P.M.	Royals ordered to continue digging on the same posts as last night. During the night 3rd/4th 14th Infantry Division relieved 1st Cavalry Division and part of the 16th Division in the Sector River SOMME - HAMEL - Bois de TAILLOUX - WARFUSEE - ABANCOURT. 6th Cavalry Brigade was ordered to remain in reserve to the 14th Infantry Division and to remain in present position night 3rd/4th.	
FOUILLOY	4th. 5.30 A.M.	Enemy began heavy bombardment of front held by 14th Division, i.e. from River SOMME to Point West of WARFUSEE on VILLIERS BRETONNEUX--WARFUSEE Road.	
		6.25 A.M.	G.O.C. 14th Division moved his Headquarters to large yellow orphanage in O.10.c.6.3 6th Cavalry Brigade moved its H.Q. there at the same time.	
		7 A.M.	Owing to our Infantry being forced back from front line posts, 43rd Infantry Brigade were ordered to move up into position on the high ground about P.13 - 0.24. G.O.C. 6th Cavalry Brigade received verbal instructions (later confirmed in writing) to send 10th Hussars from FOUILLOY, with 1 Section of Machine Guns) to operate on the left flank of the 43rd Bde. North of FOUILLOY - WARFUSEE Road, and the 3rd Dragoon Guards and Royals with 2 Sections 6th M.G. Sqn. to operate on the right flank of 43rd Brigade North of VILLIERS BRETONNEUX - WARFUSEE Road. If the 43rd Brigade were found already in position the Cavalry were to operate on their flanks, but in the event of the Infantry not yet having arrived on this high ground, it was to be held by the Cavalry.	
		7.50 A.M.	Message received that Royals and M.Gun Sqn. bivouac in Bois L'ABBE was being heavily shelled, and that they had moved into the Valley between the Wood and FOUILLOY.	
		9.5 A.M.	10th Hussars ordered to reconnoitre between HAMEL and Bois de VAIRE and fill in any gaps there might be between 41st and 42nd Infantry Brigades.	
		9.15 A.M.	Lieut.Colonel BURT,3rd Dragoon Gds. ordered to reconnoitre left of Australian Brigade and right of 41st Brigade, and to fill in any gaps that might have occurred.	
		9.30 A.M.	10th Hussars reported that their Regimental H.Q. was at 0.13.b.4.9. that 1 Sqn. was at P.13.a. in touch with 7th Battn. K.R.R. 43rd Infantry Bde., and that patrols had been sent out to get in touch with 3rd Dragoon Guards and Royals.	
		9.40 A.M.	Message received from 3rd Cavalry Division that 7th Cavalry Brigade had been ordered to move up to about 0.22. in readiness.	
		9.45 a.m.	3rd Dragoon Guards reported that H.Q. of 3rd D. Gds. and Royals was at 0.24.a.3.3., both Regiments under command of Lieut.Colonel A.BURT,3rd Dragoon Gds.	

Capt.

INTELLIGENCE SUMMARY.

(Erase heading not required.)

April, 1918.

Summaries are contained in F.S. Regs., Part II. and the Staff Manual respectively. Title pages will be prepared in manuscript.

Place	Date	Hour	Summary of Events and Information	Remarks and references to Appendices
FOUILLOY	4th	10.15 A.M.	Message received from Lieut.Col. BURT,3rd Dragoon Gds, that line ran East of Bois TAILLOUX to P.28., line further South not known. 1 Squadron 3rd Dragoon Gds in touch with Reserve Infantry P.19.c. 2nd Sqn. on right of First. 3rd Sqn. forming a defensive flank, south. Left Squadron was in touch with 10th Hussars. Sqn. of Royals and 1 sub-section 6th M.G.Sqn. had been sent to get in touch with Australians about WARFUSEE.	Map 1/40,000 62 D
		11.15 A.M.	7th Battn. K.R.R. were supposed to counter-attack from the Quarry in P.21. but this counter-attack never materialised.	
		11.30 A.M.	10th Hussars reported that they were holding a line from P.S.central (1000 yards west of HAMEL village) to P.13.b. (about 800 yards West of Bois de VAIRE). Enemy were on high ground on both sides of the HAMEL - WARFUSEE Road.	
		11.45 A.M.	Message received from Lt.Col. BURT,3rd D.Gds., that the enemy were massing in Bois TAILLOUX and requesting that a Regiment of the 7th Cavalry Brigade should be sent up as he had no reserves. He also reported that the Royals had filled the gap between the Infantry and the Australians just in time, and that the Australians were holding the line from the Railway to main AMIENS - ST.QUENTIN Road, 1000 yards East of VILLERS BRETONNEUX.	
O.23.d.		11.50 A.M.	Brigade H.Q. moved up to O.25.d. and 3rd Cavalry Divn. to Orphanage in FOUILLOY.	
		12 noon.	O.C. 10th Hussars reported enemy massing in the Bois de VAIRE and Bois de HAMEL, and advancing between the Bois de HAMEE and HAMEL, and that 10th Hussars were in touch with Infantry on the right and with Infantry M.Gs. who held a line on his left to the Canal well East of VAIRE - 3 sus CORBIE.	
		12.50 P.M.	Royals reported that they were in touch on their right with the Australians at cottages in P.25.c. Infantry echeloned on their left rear. Enemy appeared to be digging in P.22 and P.28 Australian right on Railway V.2.b. 1 Sqn. 17th Lancers had reinforced Royals, and were helping to consolidate.	
O.23.d.		1.45 P.M.	Message received from 10th Hussars that line now ran roughly along the road from P.20.a.0.8. to VAIRE-SUS-CORBIE, that they were in touch with the Infantry on their right, who had few men left, and those very tired, that there were Infantry on their left towards VAIRE-SOUS-CORBIE, and that they now had all their men in the line and no reserves saying that the enemy were advancing. At the same time another message was received saying that a heavy attack was developing between Bois de VAIRE and HAMEL, and asking for Artillery Support. This was communicated to the R.A. who acted on it immediately.	
		2.15 P.M.	Message received from 3rd Cav.Div. that one Regiment (7th Dragoon Guards) and 4 M.Gs. had been sent from 7th Cavalry Bde. to reinforce 10th Hussars.	
		3 P.M.	A Medical Officer with 1 motor ambulance was at O.23.c. and was arranging for evacuation of wounded to A.D.S. FOUILLOY. 6th C.F.A. were about Bois L'ABBE	

INTELLIGENCE SUMMARY.

(Erase heading not required.)

6 Cavalry Brigade
April 1918.

Place	Date	Hour	Summary of Events and Information	Remarks and references to Appendices
O.23.d.	4th	4.30 P.M.	10th Hussars reported that they were holding line along road from P.20.a. to P.2.c. Enemy still concentrated in road leading to from P.2.c. to E.N. of Bois de VAIRE.	Map. 1/40,000 62 D
		5.30 P.M.	O.C. Royals reported that Australians were falling back on their right flank. Colonel MELVILLE, 17th Lancers, with 1 Sqn. and 2 M.Gs. was sent to clear up the situation and form a defensive flank F necessary. 17th Lancers at once sent patrols to VILLERS BRETONNEUX to the South.	
		6 P.M.	Staff Officer of 6th Cavalry Brigade sent to gain touch with the O.C. 33rd Australian Battn. which was falling back, and orders were issued for this Battalion with 2 companies of the 34th Battalion to resume its former position.	
		6.45 P.M.	Message received from 3rd Cavalry Divn. that 1 Sqn Inniskilling Dragoons had been ordered to report at once to 6th Cavalry Brigade, in support.	
		7 P.M.	The situation was again normal and there was no further fear of any gap in our line. Heavy rain fell during the whole day.	
		8.30 P.M.	Orders were received for 3rd Cavalry Divn. with the 15th Australian Bde. would relieve the 14th Divn. during the night 4th/5th. The 6th Cavalry Brigade,totake over the right sector (plus 17th Lancers,Inniskillings, and 8th M.G.Sqn. (i.e. from FOUILLOY - WARFUSEE Road about P.20.a.0.9. to VILLERS BRETONNEUX - WARFUSEE Rd. about P.25.c.a.2.). The 15th Australian Bde. to take over the left Sector(i.e. from the Somme River to FOUILLOY - WARFUSEE Road about P.20.a.0.9.) from the 43rd Infantry Bde., 10th Hussars, and 7th Dragoon Guards. The 17th D.Gds. not being relieved till nearly dawn were kept in Brigade Reserve in the Right Sector. All machine guns remained in their present position pending further orders. Artillery covering 14th Divl. front to cover the front of the 3rd Cavalry Divn. During the night 4/5th, these reliefs took place, though it was almost dawn.before the 15th Australian Bde. relieved the 10th Hussars and 7th D.Gds. and enabled them to join the 6th Cavalry Brigade. All horses of Regiments and M.G.Sqns. were sent back during the night to Wood in N.34.c. under orders of 7th Cavalry Brigade. The Sector held by the 6th Cavalry Brigade was divided into 2 Sub-sectors, with dividing line about X tracks at P.25.b.2.8. Lieut.Col.MELVILLE (17th Lancers) with Inniskillings and 17th Lancers took over the right Sector. Lieut.Colonel BURT, with 3rd D.Gds. Royals and 10th Hussars taking over the left Sub-sector. During the night the 11th Kings Liverpools, under 43rd Infantry Bde. dug in a line of posts	

INTELLIGENCE SUMMARY.

(Erase heading not required.)

6th Cavalry Brigade.
April 1918.

Place	Date	Hour	Summary of Events and Information	Remarks and references to Appendices
O.23.d.	4th		from O.30.central to O.24.d.central and O.18.d.central, and occupied them. 43rd Infantry Brigade on relief remained under orders of 3rd Cavalry Divn. and concentrated about O.24.a.	Map 1/40,000 62D
	5th	5.25 A.M.	Message received from 3rd Dragoon Gds.(left Subsector) that they had taken up their new position, that the Royals were digging posts, and the 10th Hussars had just reported.	
		5.35 P.M.	7th Dragoon Guards arrived at Brigade H.Q. on relief by Australians, and were kept in Brigade Reserve.	
		6.5 A.M.	Lieut.Colonel MELVILLE (Right Sub-sector) reported 17th Lancers and 1 Sqn. Inniskillings were in position in front line, remainder of Inniskillings in Reserve. Touch with 6th Cav.Bde. on left had been established.	
		7.30 A.M.	Lieut.Colonel MELVILLE reported that he was in touch with Australians on his right.	
		8.a.m.	Enemy shelled Valley where Brigade H.Q. were situated, killing 1 man and several horses.	
			Rain fell throughout the night and till midday. 10.0.a.m. Bde moved HQ. to O.7.c.4.9	
O.7.c.4.9.		10.45 A.M.	Enemy opened a heavy bombardment on the whole sector front. This continued for ¾ hour, and was accompanied by extremely accurate indirect M.G. barrage. Under cover of this bombardment the enemy attempted to attack, was but was stopped by our Artillery and M.G.fire. He appeared however in considerable force.on the skyline.about 900 to 1,200 yards from our posts and began to dig it. This excellent target was at once communicated to the artillery who dealt with it.	
		2 P.M.	Message received from 3rd Cavalry Division that Australian Battn. on our left reported enemy appeared to be massing along whole front. This attack never developed.	
		4.30 P.M.	Warning order received that 5th Australian Divn. would relieve troops of 3rd Cavalry Divnz and 14th Division.	
		10.30 P.M.	Relief of 6th and 7th Cavalry Brigades by 14th Australian Bde. began, and was completed by 2.30 A.M. The 6th and 8th Machine Gun Squadrons stayed in the line for another 24 hours.	
N.34.c. CAMON	6th	5 A.M. 9.30 A.M.	Regiments were back in wood in N.34.c Bde. less 6th M.G. Sqn. marched into billets at CAMON.	

INTELLIGENCE SUMMARY.

(Erase heading not required.)

Instructions regarding War Diaries and Intelligence Summaries are contained in F.S. Regs., Part II. and the Staff Manual respectively. Title pages will be prepared in manuscript.

Place	Date	Hour	Summary of Events and Information	Remarks and references to Appendices
CAMON.	6th.		North Somerset Yeomanry reinforcements (Officers and men) arrived and were allotted to the three regiments of the Brigade. (for detail see page 7)	
CAMON.	7th.		Brigade occupied in re-organising and refitting.	
CAMON.	8 & 9th.		Brigade remained at CAMON.	
CAMON.	10th.	10.30 a.m.	Brigade ordered to "stand to" at 1½ hours notice.	
BUIRE-AU-BOIS.	11th.	7.15 AM	1st and 2nd Cavalry Divisions moved North owing to German offensive S.W. of ARMENTIERES. Brigade marched via AMIENS - FLESSELLES - CANAPLES - BERNAVILLE - AUXI-le-CHATEAU to BUIRE-au-BOIS (distance about 30 miles) and went into billets.	
CONTEVILLE.	12th.	11.30 am.	Brigade ordered to "stand to" at ½ hour's notice.	
		2 pm.	Brigade assembled at CONCHY-sur-CANCHE and marched to southern exit of HUMIERES.	
		6.30 pm.	Continued march into billets CONTEVILLE - HESTRUS - EPS. While watering at WAVRANS, hostile aircraft dropped several bombs at less than 100 yards from horses.	
FERFAY.	13th.	2 a.m.	Orders received to concentrate N.W. of AUMERVAL - FERFAY road by 8 a.m.	
		6.30 a.m.	Brigade marched via TANGRY and SACHIN to BAILLEUL-les-PERNES and halted there till 12.30 pm. Brigade H.Q. then moved intombillets at FERFAY, 3rd Dragoon Guards BAILLEUL-les-PERNES, 10th Hussars and 6th M/Gun Squadron AUMERVAL, 1st Royals, 6th C.F.A. and 13th M.V.S. FERFAY. Brigade saddled up at 6.30 a.m. and remained at 1½ hours notice to move throughout the day.	
FERFAY.	14th.		Brigade remained at 1½ hours notice to move.	
FERFAY.	15th.		Lt.Col. A.BURT, D.S.O. left the Brigade to assume the command of 7th Cavalry Brigade, vice Brig.Genl. PORTAL. Lt.Col. G.L.ROME assumed command of 3rd Dragoon Guards.	
FERFAY.	16th.			
FERFAY.	17th.		Brigade "stood to" at 1½ hours notice.	
FERFAY.	18th.		2 Officers per Regiment and 1 M/Gun Officer reconnoitred reserve line E, of ST. VENANT running approximately from LA MALADERIE (J.34) to LES AMUSOIRES (P.17) in the event of the Brigade being required to move forward in support of the XI Corps.	Sheet 36A 1/40,000.
FERFAY.	19 - 23rd.		Brigade remained in billets at FERFAY on ½ hour's notice from 6 a.m. to 8 a.m. and on 3¾ hours notice for the remainder of the day.	
FONTAINE-LEZ-HERMANS.	24th.		Brigade Headquarters, Royals, 6th C.F.A. and 13th M.V.S. moved into billets. Brigade H.Q., 6th C.F.A. and 13th M.V.S. FONTAINE-LEZ-HERMANS; 1st Royals NEDD NCHELLE. The remainder of the Brigade remained in billets as before.	
	25th.		Brigade "stood to" from 6 a.m. to 8 a.m. at ½ hour's notice and at 3¾ hours notice for remainder of the day.	
	26th.	6 pm.	Brigade "stood to" as for yesterday. Bridges over the Canal DE LA LYS immediately N.W. of ST. VENANT reconnoitred. Orders in the event of Brigade moving up to support XI Corps changed. Brigade will now	

Place	Date	Hour	Summary of Events and Information	Remarks and references to Appendices
FONTAINE-LEZ-HERMANS.	26th.	6pm.	hold all bridges along the Canal D'AIRE from P.29.c. - P.20.central and will also be responsible for providing nucleus garrisons for the BUSNES - STEENBECQUE Line from Corps Boundary at P.32.central, to DRawbridge P.20.central.	
	27th.		Reconnaissances carried out by G.O.C. 6th Cavalry Brigade and Officers commanding regiments in conjunction with 7th Cavalry Brigade of new area where Brigade might be required to support XI Corps.	
	28 - 30th.		Brigade remained in billets "standing to" at ¾ hour's notice from 6 a.m. to 8 a.m. and at 3½ hours notice for the remainder of the day.	

Brigade Major, 6th Cavalry Brigade.

Captain,
Brigade Major, 6th Cavalry Brigade.

Reinforcements received from Yeomanry Regiments on 6th April, 1918.

3rd Dragoon Guards.
Capt. A.B.MITCHELL, N.S.Y.   Lieut. L.J.HANNAN,N.S.Y.   2/Lt.G.N.EVANS, N.S.Y.
Lieut. F.LUFF,   N.S.Y.   Lieut. W.B.STARKEY, "   2/Lt.A.W.HOLMES, N.S.Y.
Lieut. H.L.HILL,   N.S.Y.   Lieut. W.H.L.SHEPPARD "   2/Lt.C.R.MASTERS, N.S.Y.
2/Lt. C.PATES,   N.S.Y.   2/Lt. A.S.HARLEY, N.S.Y.
and 85 Other Ranks.

1st Royal Dragoons.
Lieut. R.E.F.COURAGE and 77 other ranks N.S.Y.

10th Royal Hussars.
Capt. A.W.PHIPPS, Lieut.C.S.CAMPBELL, Lieut.W.SHAKESPEARE, 2/Lt.C.M.HAKEMAN and 109 other ranks N.S.Y.
Lt.Col.F.H.D.C.WHITMORE,CMG,DSO., and 2 Other Ranks ESSEX YEOMANRY.

APPENDICES

"A" and "B".

Summary of Events and Information

CASUALTIES. April, 1918.

Officers.
KILLED.
2/Lt. R.C.HOLLIS.

WOUNDED.
Lieut. A.W.G.WINDHAM.

Men.

Date	Regiment	Killed	Wounded	Wounded (at duty)	Missing	Remarks
4th.	6th M.G.Sqdn.	3	8	-	3	
5th.	6th M.G.Sqdn.	4	10	2	2	∅ 1 Gassed.

Date	Regiment	Killed	Wounded	Wounded (at duty)	Missing	Remarks
4th.	3rd D.Gds.	4	18	-	4	∅ 3 believed killed.
"	1st R.Dns.	-	1	-	-	
"	X.R.H.	-	4	-	1	
"	(Essex Yeo.attd.	-	-	-	-	
"	(A.V.C. attd.	-	-	-	-	
"	6th M.G.Sqdn.	1	4	7	-	
"	6th C.F.A.	-	1	-	-	
5th.	X.R.H.	-	∅ 10	-	-	∅ self-inflicted.
"	6th M.G.Sqdn.	1	-	-	-	∅ 1 accidentally.
"	Brigade H.Q.	-	-	-	-	

Place	Date	Hour	Summary of Events and Information	Remarks and references to Appendices
			HONOURS AND REWARDS. (Immediate Rewards)	

3rd Dragoon Guards.
Lt.Col. A.BURT, D.S.O.   Bar to D.S.O.
Lieut. A.B.PL.VINCENT.   Bar to M.C.
Capt. G.P.R.ALSOP,R.of O.   Military Cross.
Lieut. M.J.CLERY.   Military Cross.
D/19899 S.S.M.WOOLGAR.S.   D.C.M.
6659   Cpl. E.BROWN.   Military Medal.
16571 Cpl. F.NEASHAM.   Military Medal.
4362   Pte. S.PORTER.   Military Medal.
5489   Pte. F.D.JONES.   Military Medal.
14666 Pte. T.G.ASHBY.   Military Medal.
D/6982 L/c. W.GROOM.   Military Medal.
3202   Sgt. J.GARDINER.   Military Medal.
5306   Sgt. G.COX.   Military Medal.
5340   Sgt. J.McKNIGHT&   Military Medal.
10520 Sgt. C.S.MARTIN.   Military Medal.
D2115 L/Cpl. R.REDMOND,DCM.   Military Medal.
19927 L/Cpl. R.SEALE.   Military Medal.
5539   L/Cpl. G.WOOD.   Military Medal.
3285   Cpl. A.WATSON.   Military Medal.
2877   Pte. F.W.HAWKINS.   Military Medal.
4013   L/Cpl. B.ANTHONY.   Military Medal.

1st Royal Dragoons.
Major (A/Lt.Col) H.A.TOMKINSON,D.S.O.   Bar to D.S.O.
Capt. C.W.TURNER.   The Military Cross.
Capt. W.P.BROWNE.   The Military Cross.
Capt. E.W.T.MILES.   The Military Cross.
Lieut. D'A.F.H.HARRIS.   The Military Cross.
Lieut. E.St.G.STEDALL.   The Military Cross.
D13871 Pte. T.O.COCKBURN.   D.C.M.
D/8311 Pte. W.J.SMART.   D.C.M.
D/4219 Cpl. H.T.NEALE.   Military Medal.
D/5961 Pte. A.McKENZIE.   Military Medal.
D/4228 Sgt. C.A.BOLES.   Military Medal.
D/20691 Sgt. J.RICKEARD.   Military Medal.
D/12827 L/c. T.GUY.   Military Medal.
D/9564 L/c. W.C.RITCHIE.   Military Medal.
D/4234 Pte. S.FAUTLEY.   Military Medal.

10th Royal Hussars.
Major E.H.W.WILLIAMS.   D.S.O.
Capt. G.E.GOSLING.   Military Cross.
Lieut. D.H.GOUGH.   Military Cross.
913   Sgt. G.W.HAWKINS.   Military Medal.
200047 Pte. T.P.MORGAN.   Military Medal.
28603 Pte. E.A.COOKE.   Military Medal.
Lieut. A.N.LOCKETT.   Croix de Guerre.
2692   Sgt. S.J.NELSON.   Military Medal.
977   Cpl. S.ECKERS.   Military Medal.
2947   Pte. B.MALTSON.   Military Medal.
5905   Cpl. B.BAXTER.   Military Medal.
3609   Pte. G.H.KNIGHT.   Military Medal.
4871   Sgt. H.DUNK.   Croix de Guerre.

INTELLIGENCE SUMMARY.

(Erase heading not required.)

Place	Date	Hour	Summary of Events and Information	Remarks and references to Appendices
			HONOURS AND REWARDS (Continued).	
			6th Machine Gun Squadron.	
			Lieut. A.W.G.WINDHAM (6th Dragoons attd.) The Military Cross.	
			2/Lt. H.N.ELLIS. The Military Cross.	
			51041 Sgt. A.ARCHER. The D.C.M. 50613 Pte. H.LAMB. Military Medal.	
			39929 Cpl.(A/Sgt) J.SANDILANDS. The D.C.M. 50195 Cpl. C.TURNBULL. Military Medal.	
			50619 L/c. A.McKENZIE. Military Medal. 105499 L/c. G.CHAPMAN. Military Medal.	
			6th Cavalry Field Ambulance:	
			Capt. (A/Lt.Col) C.H.STRINGER, RAMC. The D.S.O.	
			339024 Sgt. G.L.McARTHUR, RAMC. Military Medal.	
			368088 Cpl. R.M.WATCHORN, D.CM. RAMC. Military Medal.	
			T/20690 Dvr.(A/Sgt) R.HALLAM, ASC. Bar to Military Medal.	
			32668 Cpl. L.E.SMITH, RAMC. Military Medal.	
			6th Signal Troop, R.E.	
			29678 Cpl. J.MITCHINSON. Military Medal.	
			161431 Spr. A. E. WALL. Military Medal.	

Army Form C. 2118.

WAR DIARY
of
INTELLIGENCE SUMMARY.
(Erase heading not required.)

6th Cavalry Brigade.

May, 1918.

Instructions regarding War Diaries and Intelligence Summaries are contained in F.S. Regs., Part II. and the Staff Manual, respectively. Title pages will be prepared in manuscript.

Place	Date	Hour	Summary of Events and Information	Remarks and references to Appendices
FONTAINE-LEZ-HERMAN.	1st.		Brigade remained in billets, and continued mounted and dismounted Training.	
VACQUERIE-le BOUCQ	4th		Brigade marched via PERNES - VALHUON - St.POL - FLERS to billeting area as under: Brigade H.Q.) 6th Cav.Fld.Amb.) VACQUERIE-le-BOUCQ. 13th Mob.Vet.Sect.) 3rd Dragoon Gds.) BOUBERS-SUR-CANCHE, MONCHEL. 1st, R, Dragoons) 10th Hussars) 'C' Battery R.H.A.) CONCHY-SUR-CANCHE, ROUGEFAY. 6th M.G.Sqn.)	
FROHEN-LE-GRAND.	5th		During the afternoon, the Brigade moved about 3 or 4 miles into the following billeting area: Brigade H.Q., 13th M.V.S., 6th C.F.A. - FROHEN-LE-GRAND. 3rd Dragoon Gds., 10th Hussars. - VILLERS L'HOPITAL. 1st, R, Dragoon. .... - NOEUX. 'C' Battery R.H.A. .... - WAVANS. 6th M.Gun Sqn. .... - BOFFLES.	
CONTAY	6th		Brigade, marching via DOULLENS - BEAUQUESNE - TOUTENCOURT, moved into bivouac area at CONTAY, and came into Fourth Army Reserve in III Corps Area. The horses were in the fields along the HALLUE River, and the majority of the men in bivouacs. Bde.H.Q. in the village.	
CONTAY	7th		Brigade "stood to" at 2 hours notice from 6 A.M. Brigade found Working Party to work on line East of HENENCOURT, at 9 P.M. Strength:120 men per Regiment.	
CONTAY	8th		The brigade was saddled up ready to move at 5 a.m., and at 5.30 a.m. came on 2 hours notice.	
CONTAY	9th		Brigade saddled up at 5 a.m. and remained on same notice as yesterday. Reconnaissances were carried out by Regiments, C.Os reconnoitring the spurs about HENENCOURT and LAVIEVILLE with a view to having to move up in support of III Corps.	

In Fuller Captain.

Army Form C. 2118.

Sheet 2.

WAR DIARY
INTELLIGENCE SUMMARY.

(Erase heading not required.)

6th CAVALRY BRIGADE.
May, 1918.

Instructions regarding War Diaries and Intelligence Summaries are contained in F. S. Regs., Part II. and the Staff Manual respectively. Title pages will be prepared in manuscript.

Place	Date	Hour	Summary of Events and Information	Remarks and references to Appendices
CONTAY	10th.	9 p.m.	Brigade found a digging party to work on line East of HENENCOURT, strength 150 per Regiment. Ground reconnoitred by Commanding officers, with a view to holding a line from LAVIEVILLE to V.22.central.	
CONTAY	11th.		G.O.C. and Commanding Officers studied ground in forward area in order to formulate plans for the re-taking of (a) HENENCOURT (b) LAVIEVILLE, if necessity arose.	
CONTAY	12th.	10.30 a.m.	Brigade found Working Party (strength 200) to work on line East of HENENCOURT. Captain S.G.HOWES,M.C. was appointed G.S.O.2 3rd Cavalry Divn. and left the Brigade. Captain E.A.FIELDEN,10th Hussars, assumed duties of Brigade Major,vice Captain S.G.HOWES,M.C. 21st Lancers, appointed G.S.O.2. 3rd Cavalry Division.	
CONTAY	13th	9.30 P.M.	Brigade found Working Party to work East of HENENCOURT,strength 450. Conference of C.Os at Brigade Headquarters.	
CONTAY	14th		Staff Ride for Officers Commanding Regiments.	
CONTAY	15th.	10.30 a.m.	Brigade found Working Party (strength 298) for work East of HENENCOURT. Tracks reconnoitred for by Brigade for 18th Divisional Artillery from BAIZIEUX into LAVIEVILLE.	
CONTAY	17th.		Brigade marched at 5 a.m. via RAINNEVILLE,COISY,BERTANGLES,ST.SAUVEUR, to BELLOY-SUR-SOMME. Brigade Headquarters in the Chateau D'en HAUT, with the 13th M.V.S. 3 Regiments and 6th Machine Gun Squadron in the BOIS de BELLOY. 6th Cav.Fld.Ambulance and 'C' Battery R.H.A. were in the lower part of the village.	
BELLOY.	19th	11.15 a.m.	Brigade paraded at full strength,dismounted; after a short service, the Corps Commander presented to Officers and men decorations won by them during the recent operations since March 21st. The Australian Band was present, and after the ceremony, the Brigade marched past the Corps and Divisional Commanders.	
BELLOY	20th 30th		Brigade remained at BELLOY, and carried out mounted and dismounted training. The weather remained remarkably fine throughout this period.	
BEHENCOURT	31.		Brigade, plus 1 Troop,3rd Field Sqn.R.E. and 1 Section D.A.C., marched via BERTANGLES - VILLERS BOCAGE and MOLLIENS-AU-BOIS to BEHENCOURT, in relief of the 7th Cavalry Brigade. Brigade H.Q. were in the Chateau at BEHENCOURT; the 3 Regiments were bivouaced in the Wood in B.23.central; "C" Battery R.H.A. and 6th M.G.Sqn. were camped along Western side of R.HALLUE, 6th C.F.A. and 13th M.V.S. were in MONTIGNY. On arrival in this area, the Bde. came on 1½ hours notice.	

Th Fielden
Captain
Brigade Major 6 Cavalry Brigade

Sheet 1

Army Form C. 2118.

WAR DIARY

~~INTELLIGENCE~~ SUMMARY.

(Erase heading not required.)

6ᵗʰ Cav Bde

June, 1918.

No 43

Instructions regarding War Diaries and Intelligence Summaries are contained in F. S. Regs., Part II. and the Staff Manual respectively. Title pages will be prepared in manuscript.

Place	Date	Hour	Summary of Events and Information	Remarks and references to Appendices
BEHENCOURT	1st		Concentration area East of BEHENCOURT reconnoitred by all units. Patrol of 1 Officer and 10 O.R. "stood to" at 6.a.m. Regiments found this patrol every morning, in turn.	
		9.15 pm.	3rd Dragoon Guards found a Digging Party of 3 Officers and 150 O.R. for work on general defences of HENENCOURT.	
	2nd.		2 Officers from each unit reconnoitred tracks forward. This work went on for several days until tracks to every part of the III Corps Sector were thoroughly known.	
	3rd.		G.O.C. inspected "C" Battery R.H.A. in Marching Order.	
	4th.		G.O.C. inspected the Royal Dragoons in Marching Order. Working Parties were found every night by one of the Regiments (strength same as 1st June) for work N.E. of HENENCOURT and between that village and LAVIEVILLE.	
	5th.		G.O.C. inspected 10th Hussars in Marching Order.	
	6th.		G.O.C. inspected 3rd Dragoon Guards in Marching Order.	
		4.30 p.m.	Telegram received from III Corps saying that G.H.Q. considered it probable that enemy would attack between MONTDIDIER and the OISE tomorrow morning, and that a simultaneous attack on this front was possible. Brigade was ordered to "stand to" the following morning.	
	7th.		Brigade "stood to" but front remained quiet. Orders received that Brigade might have to support the XXXI French Corps holding the line South of the Australian Corps. Officers from each Regiment sent to reconnoitre bridges between VECQUEMENT and CAMON, in the event of Brigade moving South in support of French.	
	8th.		The Corps Commander visited the Brigade and inspected the horse lines.	
	9th.		The Germans attacked between MONTDIDIER and the OISE, but everything quiet on this front.	
	11th.		No digging Parties tonight in view of possible operations by III and Vth Corps.	

Army Form C. 2118.

6 Cavalry Brigade Sheet 2.

WAR DIARY
INTELLIGENCE SUMMARY
JUNE, 1918.

(Erase heading not required.)

Instructions regarding War Diaries and Intelligence Summaries are contained in F. S. Regs., Part II. and the Staff Manual respectively. Title pages will be prepared in manuscript.

Place	Date	Hour	Summary of Events and Information	Remarks and references to Appendices
BEHENCOURT	12th		G.O.C. held a Staff Ride with Commanding Officers.	
BELLOY-SUR-SOMME.	14th		Brigade moved back to BELLOY-SUR-SOMME, being relieved by 7th Cavalry Brigade.	
	15th		G.O.C. with Brigade Major, and O.C. 10th Hussars, went down to BOVES and BOIS de GENTELLES to reconnoitre ground in the event of Brigade moving from here to support the French	
	14th-25th.		Brigade remained in bivouac in BELLOY Wood. During the latter part of this period an epidemic of influenza started, so called "P.U.O." On June 24th there were nearly 200 cases in the Brigade. The 6th Cavalry Field Ambulance formed a special hospital under Canvas at BELLOY for dealing with the epidemic. In most cases the attack lasted about 3 days, and is accompanied by high fever, which leaves the man unfit for full duty for atbleast a week after he has got rid of the fever.	
LE MESGE.	25th		Brigade moved into a new billeting area. Brigade H.Q. Royals. SOUES. 13th M.V.S. } LE MESGE. 10th Hussars. 3rd Dragoon Gds. } 'C' Battery R.H.A. } RIENCOURT. 6th M.Gun Sqn.	
	29th.		"P.U.O." has now reached the total of 340 in the Brigade. A large percentage of Officers have got the disease. Captain E.A.FIELDEN,M.C.,Brigade Major 6th Cavalry Brigade, left for England to attend the Staff College at CAMBRIDGE. "C" Battery R.H.A. moved into the Australian Corps Area - Wagon lines just South of PONT NOYELLES. (Map reference H.24.a.6.8.	

[signature] Captain,
a/Brigade Major 6th Cavalry Brigade.

Army Form C. 2118.

WAR DIARY
INTELLIGENCE SUMMARY.
(Erase heading not required.)

6th Cavalry Brigade.

July, 1918.

Instructions regarding War Diaries and Intelligence Summaries are contained in F. S. Regs., Part II. and the Staff Manual respectively. Title pages will be prepared in manuscript.

Place	Date	Hour	Summary of Events and Information	Remarks and references to Appendices
LE MESGE.	1st to 31st		Throughout the month the Brigade remained in the LE MESGE - SOUES - RIENCOURT Area, and continued training. The epidemic of "P.U.O." was finished by the middle of the month.	Ref. Map AMIENS 1/100,000
	4th.		Captain D.E.WALLACE, M.C., 2nd Life Guards, rejoined the Brigade from CAMBRIDGE, and assumed the duties of Brigade Major, during temporary absence of Captain E.A.FIELDEN, M.C. 10th Hussars.	
	15th.		The Rev. A.R.GRANT joined the Brigade as Brigade Chaplain.	
	18th.		Commanding Officers and Brigade Major reconnoitred Vth Corps area from high ground by HEDAUVILLE, in readiness, if called on, to support that Corps.	

Captain,

Brigade Major 6th Cavalry Brigade.

Army Form C. 2118.

WAR DIARY
or
INTELLIGENCE SUMMARY.
(Erase heading not required.)

6th Cavalry Brigade.
5/8/18 to 12/8/18.

Instructions regarding War Diaries and Intelligence Summaries are contained in F.S. Regs., Part II. and the Staff Manual respectively. Title pages will be prepared in manuscript.

Place	Date	Hour	Summary of Events and Information	Remarks and references to Appendices
LE MESGE	5th	10pm	The Brigade closed up into the Southern portion of the area (LE MESGE and RIENCOURT).	
RIENCOURT N.31.D.	6th	10.30pm	Brigade marched into forward Concentration Area S.W. of AMIENS (RENANCOURT & Pt.St.JEAN).	
	7th	9.30pm	Brigade (less A.2 Echelon) marched to Assembly Area in (62D) N.31, arriving about 2 a.m. on 8th.	
	8th	4.20am	ZERO.	
		5.40am	Brigade followed 7th Cavalry Brigade up Cavalry Track, in accordance with O.O.14.	
		7.15am	Brigade arrived West of CACHY (U.2.c.5.9).	
		9.30am	Brigade moved on to a point East of MORGEMONT Wood, crossing front line trenches at 9.50 a.m.	
		10.25am	Message received from Liaison Officer with 7th Cavalry Brigade as follows "Situation at 10.25 a.m. Infantry and Tanks in D.3.central making towards Hill 102. Canadian Cavalry Bde. at IGNAUCOURT. 7th Cavalry Bde. following in close support. Enemy appears to be retiring in direction of BEAUCOURT".	
D.16.a.		10.50am	Brigade moved off towards DEMUIN crossed the River LUCE there and halted in D.16.a. The Canadian Cavalry Brigade was operating in and about BEAUCOURT, the enemy offering considerable resistance from Woods in D.24. The 7th Cavalry Brigade were working round to the left flank and made good CAYEUX WOOD, but was held up by heavy machine gun fire from the South.	
		1 pm	The Royals, with 1 Section 6th M.G. Sqn. were ordered to support 7th Cavalry Bde.	
		1.45 pm	It was decided that the 6th Cavalry Brigade should push on towards LE QUESNEL. 10th Hussars were ordered to advance on the left of the Canadians, and the following message was sent to Lieut.Colonel PATERSON Commanding 7th Cavalry Bde. "G.O.C. 3rd Cavalry Divn has ordered me to withdraw Royals into support of my own Brigade as soon as you can spare them AAA They should concentrate about D.10.c. and send forward a Patrol to obtain touch with 6th Cavalry Brigade.	
D.16.a.		2.15 pm	Received verbal orders to support 7th Cavalry Brigade on left front.	
E.7.A.0.c.		2.45 pm	The Brigade, less Royals, moved to the left flank and passed through CAYEUX Wood.	
	(about)3.15pm		The 10th Hussars were immediately sent forward to support Royals who had received orders from Lt.Colonel PATERSON to push forward to the VRELY - WARVILLERS Line.	
		3.30 pm	Message received from 3rd Cavalry Division "1st Cavalry Division has penetrated beyond BLUE Line in direction of FRAMERVILLE AAA 2nd Cavalry Division,less 1 Brigade in Corps Reserve, will move in the direction of CAIX and make good the high ground in E.10. - 16. - 22 AAA 3rd Cavalry Division will conform and join up with 2nd Cavalry Division AAA Dividing Line between 6th and 7th Cavalry Brigades K.3.B.1.4. AAA 6th Cavalry Brigade will join up with Motor Machine Gun Battery on ROYE Road AAA." This message was subsequently cancelled and as a consequence 10th Hussars and Royals were not recalled from the left flank. The remainder of	
	(about 4 pm		the Brigade moving up to E.9.c.	

Sheet 2.

WAR DIARY
or
INTELLIGENCE SUMMARY.
(Erase heading not required.)

Army Form C. 2118.

6th Cavalry Brigade.

AUGUST 1918.

Place	Date	Hour	Summary of Events and Information	Remarks and references to Appendices
	8th (about)	4 pm	Royals and 10th Hussars however had been unable to advance beyond the Wood in E.15 owing to high ground East of LE QUESNEL being strongly held by M.G. Royal were holding a series of posts from E.15.b.9.0. to E.21.b.9.a. with 1 Squadron and Machine Guns holding Southern edge of WOOD in E.15. Patrols tried to push forward and 10th Hussars were ordered to work round the left flank through E.22.b. and E.23.c.	Ref MAP. 1/40,000 G.S.G.S.
		5.30 pm	Orders were received from 3rd Cavalry Divn. that the Brigade was to remain in the line it then held, and the following order was issued :- " BM.10 8th AAA 2 Cav.Div. have been ordered to advance in direction of ROYE leaving 3 Cav.Div. to hold AMIENS OUTER DEFENCES AAA 6 Cav.Bde. have been allotted Sector K.3.a.1.4. to E.16.d.8.6 both inclusive AAA 10 Hussars will hold Right Sub-sector and Royals Left Sub-Sector AAA point of junction E.21.d.7.7. inclusive to Royals AAA 1 Section 6 M.G.Sqn. is allotted to each of above Regiments AAA Remainder of 6 M.G.Sqn. will be disposed under orders of O.C. to hold the line held by the Brigade AAA 'C' Battery will cover the exits of BEAUFORT and the Wood West of it AAA 3 D.G will be in Bde.Reserve West of the Wood in E.15. AAA 10 Hussars will get touch with 7th Cav.Bde. and Royals with 1 Cav.Div. AAA Units willreport what portions of their line are occupied by Infantry but will not vacate them without further orders AAA Brigade H.Q. will be established about E.15.c.2.6.at 6.15 p.m. AAA addedAdded.all units 6 Cav.Bde.reptd.7 Cav.Bde Right Bde.1 Cav.Div. 3rd Cav.Div. 6 Cav.Bde. E.10.b.1.9 5.45 p.m." Brig.General A.G.SEYMOUR was obliged by illness to hand over his command to Lt.Col. F.H.D.C.WHITMORE, Commanding 10th Hussars ; Captain GORDON CANNING assumed Command of 10th Hussars.	

		6 pm.	Following message sent to 3 Cav.Div.
			  AAA
			"Situation on Right flank of Bde. 5.50 p.m. AAA 12 Canadian Inf.Bde. in touch with RoyalsAAA Line prolonged by 8 Hussars North of CAIX - ROSIERES Road AAA 4 D.G. and 1 Canadian Battn. in Reserve in E.9.b. AAA
			  6 Cav.Bde. 6 p.m.	

		6.30 pm	B.H.Q. moved to E.14.d.8.7.	
		6.40 pm	Royals reported enemy dribbling in small parties into Wood in E.23.c. 'C' and 'K' Batteries fired on this Wood	

Army Form C. 2118.

SHEET 3.

WAR DIARY
INTELLIGENCE SUMMARY

6th Cavalry Brigade.

AUGUST 1918.

(Erase heading not required.)

Instructions regarding War Diaries and Intelligence Summaries are contained in F.S. Regs., Part II. and the Staff Manual respectively. Title pages will be prepared in manuscript.

Place	Date	Hour	Summary of Events and Information	Remarks and references to Appendices
E.14.d.8.7.	8th	7 pm	Following message sent to 3 Cav.Div. BM.13. 8 AAA " Situation first flank AAA 10 Hussars report Canadian Infantry hold line E.21.b.3.8. to E.26.d.3.7. unable advance to BLUE Line owing to M.G.fire from high ground between LE QUESNEL and BEAUFORT AAA 10 Hussars are stiffening up this line. 6 Cav.Bde. 7 pm. "	REF. MAP 1/40,000 1 : 5 : 66E
		8.25 pm	Following from 7 Cav.Bde. G.G.10. 8. AAA "S.O.S. has gone up from S.E. corner of Wood AAA Please be ready to reinforce dismounted E.15.d. AAA Enemy massing S.E. of Wood. 7 Cav.Bde. 8.20 p.m. " In consequence, Royals were ordered to be prepared to reinforce with 2 Squadrons which were already dismounted	
		9. pm	Led horses were moved on to slope West of the Valley in E.15. owing to the great congestion there, and following message sent to 3 Cav.Div. BM.19. 8 AAA "Situation 9 pm AAA Royals Squadron in S.E. corner of Wood in E.15. were fairly heavily shelled about 8.30 p.m. AAA Infantry have sent up S.O.S. in E.22.b.AAA Certain amount M.G.fire from direction BEAUFORT AAA A counter-attack from BEAUFORT down valley N.W. seems likely AAA 6 Cav.Bde. 9.10 p.m."	
		10.45 pm	Galloper from 3 Cav.Div. arrived with request for details of dispositions, and following was dispatched B.M.20 8 GC.16. "The state of the defences of 3rd Cavalry Divn Sector are approximately as followsAAA E.26.central E.20.d.9.0. E.21.central E.22.a.5.5. E.16.d.7.7. AAA A few forward positions are in front of the line from E.26.central to E.21.central AAA Many machine guns and Hotchkiss are employed in this Section of the line commanding the high ground East of LE QUESNEL and BEAUFORT AAA Distribution of Troops as follows AAA	

Army Form C. 2118.

SHEET 4.
WAR DIARY
—of—
INTELLIGENCE SUMMARY.
(Erase heading not required.)

6th Cavalry Brigade.

AUGUST 1918

Instructions regarding War Diaries and Intelligence Summaries are contained in F. S. Regs., Part II. and the Staff Manual respectively. Title pages will be prepared in manuscript.

Place	Date	Hour	Summary of Events and Information	Remarks and references to Appendices
E.14.d.8.7.8th			7 D.G. on right flank guarding flank Inniskillings E.27.a. * 17 Lrs. and 10 Hrs. South edge of Wood E.21.a.and b. Royals from that point to E.16.b.7.7. AAA 12 and 11 Canadian Bdes. are holding a line in conjunction with 3 Cav.Div. AAA Intermittent M.G.fire continues from LE QUESNEL and BEAUFORT AAA A large concentration of enemy troops at and about BEAUFORT AAA Preparations for enemy counter-attack in morning as follows AAA All troops in line in Battle positions at 4 a.m. AAA 3 D.G. intact in hand in Valley Masters E.15.AAA Led horses 6 Cav.Bde. 1 man to 4.E.14.central Led horses 7 Cav.Bde. in valley E.15. AAA 'O' and 'K' Battys. in action E.15.b. and E.14.d.respectively AAA 11 Canadian Bde. on our right and Scottish Canadian Battn. on the left AAA Ammn. O.K. AAA Watercarts badly wanted AAA By request of Col.PATERSON I have taken over command of Divl.Sector for the night. 11.25 p.m. * 6 Cav.Bde.	REF.MAP 1/40,000 666
			The Counter-attack did not materialise, and the situation remained quiet throughout the night.	
	9th	4.50 am	Message received from 78 Canadian Battn.that 11 Canadian Bde. had been ordered to advance to the BLUE Dotted Line.	
		7.45 am	Orders received for the Divn. to concentrate on the River between CAIX and CAYEUX.	
		8.15 am	Brigade ordered to arrange relief with 12 Canadian Bde. and withdraw to W.26.c. BM.25. @ 9 AAA * Royals and 10 Hrs. will withdraw from positions now held as soon as relieved by Infantry AAA The Bde. will concentrate in area CAYEUX - CAIX and water on South side of River AAA 1 Officer and 2 O.R. per unit will meet Staff Captain at 9.30 a.m. at Y Rds in E.2.d. AAA 3 D.G. and 'C' Battery will march independently so as to arrive at E.2.d. at 9.45 and 10 a.m respectively AAA Royals 10 Hrs. and 6 M.G.S. independently as soon as relieved AAA Guides will meet all units in E.2.d. AAA OsC.Royals 10 Hrs. and 6 M.G.S. to report at B.H.Q. forthwith to arrange details of relief AAA B.H.Q. will march to new area as soon as relief is complete AAA Ack AAA 6 Cav.Bde. 8.40 a.m.	
		9.15 am	O.C.85 Canadian Battn. asked that Royals should remain in support of his Battn. until he was satisfied with the progress of our attack which was due to start at 10 a.m. 6 M.G.Sqn. were also left in position.	

SHEET 5.

WAR DIARY
or
INTELLIGENCE SUMMARY.
(Erase heading not required.)

Army Form C. 2118.

6th Cavalry Brigade.

5/11 August 1918

Place	Date	Hour	Summary of Events and Information	Remarks and references to Appendices
W.26.c.	9th	12 noon.	Brigade less Royals and 6 M.G.S. concentrated W.26.c. and off-saddled.	Ref. MAP 1/40,000 62D.
		1.30 pm.	Royals and 6 M.G.S. rejoined.	
		3 p.m.	Bde. ordered to saddle up and G.O.C. to go to Divl.H.Q.	
		8.30 p.m.	Orders for Bde. to off-saddle and be ready to move at 5 a.m. tomorrow	
	10th	3.40 am	G.O.C. 22 received from 3 Cav.Div. and following issued: BM.48. 10th. AAA "6th Cav.Bde. is to take over patrols now found by 2 Cav.Div. on front BOUCHOIR - ROUVROY both inclusive AAA 3 D.G. will take over Right Sector and Royals left Sector AAA These Regts. will each send 1 Sqn forward at 5 a.m. AAA Rest of Bde. will move 5.30 am AAA C.Os and all units and Leading Squadron Leaders of 3 D.G. and Royals meet Brigadier 4.45 am at present H.Q. Royals AAA 6th Cav.Bde. 4.10 a.m."	Ref. Map 1/40,000 66E
		5 am.	'C' Sqn. 3 D.G. (Capt.VINCENT) and 'A' Sqn.Royals (Capt.MILES) marched to 2 Cav.Div.H.Q in E.30.a. and took over patrols from 5 Cav.Bde and 3 Cav.Bde. respectively.	
		6.45 am	Advanced B.H.Q. established at E.30.a.	
		8.20 am	Remainder of Bde. concentrated in E.23. AAA BM.51. 10 AAA "Dispositions AAA Sqn. 3 D.G. at FOLIES with patrols at L.1.c.5.5. and K.18.c.4.5. AAA Infantry in considerable numbers are in front of patrol AAA Sqn.Royals, dismounted, in support of 5 Canadian Inf.Battn.holding L.8.c.9.5. - L.8.c.4.2. with led horses behind ROUVROY Cemetery AAA H.Q. 2 Canadian Inf.Bde. alongside us here report that Infantry are attacking through them at 8 a.m. AAA Bde.Report Centre established here AAA E.30.a.1.9. 8.25 am.	
		8.30 am	Following orders issued to Advanced Sqns BM.52. 10. AAA "In event of Infantry advance patrols will be sent to keep closest possible touch with	

Army Form C. 2118.

WAR DIARY
INTELLIGENCE SUMMARY

4th Cavalry Brigade.
August 1918

(Erase heading not required.)

Place	Date	Hour	Summary of Events and Information	Remarks and references to Appendices
E.30.a.1.9.	10th		"The situation and Sqns. will be supported by their own Regts. if necessary AAA Dividing line AAA 3 D.G. BOUCHOIR - LA GAMBUSE inclusive GOYENCOURT exclusive GRUNY inclusive to FOLIES PARVILLERS and CREMERY all inclusive, Royals thence to ROUVROY inclusive. FOUQUESCOURT exclusive FRANSART and HATTENCOURT both exclusive AAA. Situation reports to be sent to 6 Cav.Bde.direct every hour AAA B.H.Q. remaining at old 2 Cav.Div.H.Q. at E.30 a.1.9. E.30.a.1.9. 8.30 a.m.	Ref.Map 1/40,000 66E.
		10.30 am	Reports received that Infy.attack was making progress. Verbal orders issued to OsC 3 D.G. and Royals to move up in support of their advanced Sqn. and to remainder of Bde. to move forward. BM.53. 10th. AAA "Royals will move forward forthwith to neighbourhood of BEAUFORT and 3 D.G. to about BOUCHOIR AAA 'C' Battery 6 M.G.S. less sub-sections attached to Regts. and 10 Hrs. to about 2nd L of LE QUESNEL AAA B.H.Q. will close here at 11.15 a.m. and open about 800X North of FOLIES Church AAA. 4th Cav.Bde. E.20.a.1.9. 10.45 a.m	
K.11.c.8.5.		11.30 am	G.O.C. 32nd Div. and G.O.C. 97th Inf.Bde. interviewed. Both gave very good reports of Infantry advance, which were sent on to 3rd Cavalry Divn. This information subsequently proved to be very misleading.	
K.12.c.5.0.		11.56 am	Brigade Report Centre moved forward to K.12.c.5.0. Message received from Advanced Sqn.3 D.G. V.4. 10th AAA Enemy holding line running N. and S. in front of PARVILLERS and DAMERY AAA Line reported to be strongly wired AAA HEROX FOLIES 11.40 a.m.	
		11.57.am	Message received from 3 D.G. AAA A.215/1 10th AAA " Just heard that PARVILLERS has fallen and sending leading Sqn. on to LE QUESNOY and going on myself with it to reconnoitre" X Rds.just E. of FOLIES Church 11.50 am.	
		11.58 am	Royals reported that G.O.C. 97 Inf.Bde.stated his Bde.had reached line FRANSART - LA CHAVETTE and enemy were on the run.	

Army Form C. 2118.

SHEET 7.
WAR DIARY
INTELLIGENCE/SUMMARY.

(Erase heading not required.)

6th Cavalry Brigade.
— AUGUST 1918

Instructions regarding War Diaries and Intelligence Summaries are contained in F.S. Regs., Part II. and the Staff Manual respectively. Title pages will be prepared in manuscript.

Place	Date	Hour	Summary of Events and Information	Remarks and references to Appendices
K.12.c.5.0.	10th	1 pm.	1 Section 'C' Battery sent to join 3 D.G. 2 Officers patrols 10 Hrs. sent to report on suitability of ground on our front for movement of large bodies of Cavalry.	Ref Map 1/40,000 66E
		1.10 pm	Message from 3rd Cav.Div. that 18 Whippet Tanks were being sent to join the Bde. Message from Royals that PARVILLERS still held by enemy, and leading Squadron unable to advance.	
		1.30 pm.	3r d D.G. reported that PARVILLERS was strongly held by cross fire from M.G. and our Infantry on a line 500x N.W. of it. Whippet Tanks arrived	
		1.45 pm	Message to 3 D.G. and Royals BM.59. 10th AAA 14 Whippet Tanks will start about 2 p.m. from N.exit of WARVILLERS and advance on PARVILLERS AAA When near that place they will divide and go round either side AAA 3 D.G. and Royals will keep close touch with Royals and exploit any success. 1.45 p.m. 6 Cav.Bde.	
		1.50 pm.	Royals reported that it was out of the question for Sqns. to advance at present. Country East of ROUVROY much wired and entrenched. 2 Officers patrols sent towards LA CHAVETTE and South of ROUVROY – ROYE Road.	
		2.20 pm	10th Hussars Officers patrols returned with report on ground BM.60. 10th AAA (to 3 Cav.Div) " 2 Officers patrols were sent out from here o report on ground on Bde.front especially towards PARVILLERS AAA They report that there is an old trench system about the line ROUVROY – LE QUESNOY and that the movement of large bodies of Cavalry at any pace would be quite impossible AAA Both Advanced Regts.have made similar reports and state that any further advance on present front must be made dismounted K.12.c.5.0. 6 Cav.Bde. 2.35 p.m. Tank Commander said ground would be impossible for Whippets. Plan given in B.M.59 cancelled. Arranged for Tanks to advance up ROUVROY – PARVILLERS – PARVILLERS Road supported by Royals and 3 D.G.	
		2.35 pm.	Message from 3 Cav.Div. that Canadian Cav.Bde. had been ordered to pass through and seize	

Army Form C. 2118.

WAR DIARY
INTELLIGENCE SUMMARY

(Erase heading not required.)

6th Cavalry Brigade.
AUGUST 1918

Instructions regarding War Diaries and Intelligence Summaries are contained in F.S. Regs., Part II. and the Staff Manual respectively. Title pages will be prepared in manuscript.

Place	Date	Hour	Summary of Events and Information	Remarks and references to Appendices
K.12.c.5.0.	10th.		high ground N. and E. of ROYE and 6th Cav.Bde were to support them.	Ref Map 1/40,000 6oE
		2.45 pm	G.OsC. 3 Cav.Div. and Canadian Cav.Bde. came up to Bde.Report Centre.	
		2.55 pm.	Following message from 3 D.G.(Col.ROME) R.l. 10th AAA "My patrol along ROYE - AMIENS Road reports at 1.45 p.m. 1/ Enemy still holds ANDECHY - 2/ Our troops in La CAMBUSE and W.edge of DAMERY. I am sending a Sqn. down the AMIENS - Roye Road, with orders to assist if possible in the attack on DAMERY. FOLIES 2.45 p.m."	
		3 p.m.	Report timed 1.58 p.m. from Lt.DIGBY,Royals, who had gone to Infantry front line that left flank of 32nd Div. was out of touch with Canadians and attack on PARVILLERS held up by M.Gs and snipers.	
		3.30 pm.	3 D.G. confirmed that enemy still held PARVILLERS	
		4.10 pm	Necessity of supporting Canadians on right flank and unsuitability of ground caused Tank attack to be abandoned. Tanks attacking from ROUVROY had already started but Lt.BIRCH 1 R.D. went forward and got them back. Royals withdrawn to K.12.a. so as to be ready to move south.	
		5.48 p.m.	Message from 3 Cav.Div. GC.58 10th AAA "Canadian Cav.Bde. have galloped Hill 100 with 1 Regt. and are now there AAA You must support them closely and keep in touch with them AAA 5.43 p.m." Ordered 10th Hussars to advance to support Fort Garry Horse, under orders of Canadian Cavalry Bde. Royals to move to FOLIES.	
		6.15 pm	Bde.H.Q. moved to L.25.b.5.0. S.W. of LE QUESNOY. Royals closed up on 10th Hussars in K.36.b. Battery and M.G.S. to L.19.a.	

Army Form C. 2118.

WAR DIARY

Sheet 9.

~~INTELLIGENCE SUMMARY~~XXXXXXX

6th CAVALRY BRIGADE
August, 1918.

Instructions regarding War Diaries and Intelligence Summaries are contained in F. S. Regs., Part II. and the Staff Manual respectively. Title pages will be prepared in manuscript.

(Erase heading not required.)

Place	Date	Hour	Summary of Events and Information	Remarks and references to Appendices
L.25.b.5.0.	10th		Message received from Liaison Officer that Fort Garry Horse had been unable to capture HILL 100. LA CAMBUSE and DAMERY were still held by the enemy.	Ref.Map 1/40,000 66E.
		7.40 pm	Situation as follows:- 10th Hussars, Royals, 'C' Battery, and 6th M.Gun Sqn. as at 6.15 p.m. 3rd Dragoon Gds. 2 Sqns. at LE QUESNOY, 1 at FOLIES.	
		8.pm	Brigade H.Q. was heavily shelled, with loss of 2 O.R. (wounded) and 7 chargers.	
		8.30 pm	Brigade H.Q. moved back to K.17.c.5.6.	
		9.30 pm	Brigade concentrated West of FOLIES (Approx. in squares K.16.a., b., and d.) for the night.	
	11th.	12.40 am	Orders issued to units to be ready to move at 1 hours notice from 5 a.m. The Brigade remained in bivouac throughout the day.	
		5.30 p.m.	Brigade moved westwards keeping South of ROYE - AMIENS Road and arrived in BOVES - FOUENCAMPS area shortly before midnight.	
FOUENCAMPS	13th.		Commander-in-Chief visited all units in the Brigade.	
	15th		Lieut.Colonel EWING PATERSON, D.S.O., Inniskilling Dragoons, assumed command of the Brigade.	
		8 p.m.	Brigade marched via RUMIGNY - VERS - CLAIRY SAULCHOIX - PISSY - FLUY - BRIQUE-MESNIL - CAVILLON to the LE MESGE - SOUES - RIENCOURT area., arriving about 4 a.m. Brigade H.Q. LE MESGE	Ref.Map 1/100,000 AMIENS.
LE MESGE	16th		Brigade ordered to move to area St.LEGER-les-DOMART tonight - orders subsequently cancelled owing to there being no accomodation in that area.	
	19th) 20th)		Training recommenced.	
	21st	5 am	Brigade on three hours notice to move.	
		7.15 pm	Orders received for Brigade to move to MONTRELET - FIEFFES area.	

Army Form C. 2118.

WAR DIARY
Sheet 10.

INTELLIGENCE SUMMARY

(Erase heading not required.)

6th CAVALRY BRIGADE.
August, 1918.

Place	Date	Hour	Summary of Events and Information	Remarks and references to Appendices
LE MESGE	21st	11.40 pm.	Brigade, less "B" Echelons, marched from SOUES - PICQUIGNY - CROUY - CAVILLON X Roads via LA CHAUSSEE - CANAPLES to MONTRELET - FIEFFES area. Brigade H.Q. established at FIEFFES at 3 a.m.	Ref. Map 1/100,000 LENS.
FIEFFES	22nd) 24th)		"B" Echelons marched to BETHENCOURT-St.OUEN, whence they were Divisionalized. Brigade remained on three hours notice.	
	25th	4 pm	Orders received for Brigade to move to AUTHIE Valley tonight.	
		9.30 pm.	Brigade, less "B" Echelons, marched via FIENVILLERS - BERNAVILLE - PROUVILLE - MAIZICOURT - AUXI-le-CHATEAU to the area GUESCHART - VILLEROY-sur_AUTHIE - LE PONCHEL - WILLENCOURT - VITZVILLEROY - CUMONVILLE. Brigade Headquarters established at GUESCHART on arrival (3 a.m.).	
GUESCHART.	26th	6 am.	"B" Echelons rejoined the Brigade from BETHENCOURT St.OUEN.	
		3.30 pm.	Telephone message received that Brigade was to move to the CANCHE Valley forthwith.	
		5.10 pm	Brigade, less "B" Echelons, marched via NEUILLY-le-DIEN - AUXI-le-CHATEAU - VACQUERIE-le-BOUCQ - LIGNY-sur-CANCHE to the area NUNCQ - SIBIVILLE - SERICOURT - GRAND & PETIT BOURET, arriving about 9 p.m. Brigade Headquarters, NUNCQ. "B" Echelons moved to WILLENCOURT, where they were Divisionalized.	
NUNCQ.	27th.	10 am	Brigade on 1 hours notice to move.	
		11.15 am	Brigade on 3 hours notice to move.	
	28th.		Brigade remained on 3 hours notice to move.	
		12.30 pm	Orders received for Brigade to move to WAILLY area tonight	
		3 pm.	Billeting parties started for new area.	
		4.55 pm.	Move to WAILLY cancelled. Billeting Parties recalled by motor Cyclist.	
	29th.		Brigade remained on 3 hours notice.	

Army Form C. 2118.

Sheet 1:

WAR DIARY

~~INTELLIGENCE~~ SUMMARY.

6th CAVALRY BRIGADE.
August, 1918.

(Erase heading not required.)

Instructions regarding War Diaries and Intelligence Summaries are contained in F. S. Regs., Part II. and the Staff Manual respectively. Title pages will be prepared in manuscript.

Place	Date	Hour	Summary of Events and Information	Remarks and references to Appendices
MUNCQ	30th	10 am	G.O.C. and Brigade Major attended Conference at Divisional H.Q. Brigade ordered to move to WAILLY area tonight.	Ref Map ENS 1/100,000
		1.20 pm	Move to WAILLY cancelled, and orders received for 10th Hussars only to move to WAILLY.	
		7 pm	10th Hussars, and 1 Section 6th Machine Gun Squadron, left the Brigade area for WAILLY.	
			Remainder of Brigade on six hours notice, and orders issued for training to be resumed.	
	31st.		3rd Dragoon Guards moved to FREVENT.	
		8 pm.	Brigade "B" Echelon rejoined from WILLENCOURT.	

signature

Captain,
Brigade Major 6th Cavalry Brigade.

Army Form C. 2118.

WAR DIARY

~~INTELLIGENCE SUMMARY.~~

(Erase heading not required.)

6th CAVALRY BRIGADE.
AUGUST, 1918.

Summary of Events and Information

APPENDIX A.
****

CASUALTIES.

	Officers.	Cas.	OTHER RANKS.		
			K.	W.	M.
3rd D.Gds.				7	
1st Royal Dragoons.				8	
10th Hussars.	Lt.G.H.PERRETT	K.	3	13*	2	*2 at duty.
	Lt.T.ROBINSON	W.			
'C' Battery R.H.A.				2*		*1 at duty.
6th M.G.Sqn.				1	
6th Cav.Bde.H.Q.	Lt.AWG.WINDHAM,MC.	W.		2	
6th Signal Troop.				1	
TOTAL.			3	34	2.

* *

HONOURS & REWARDS.

R.A.M.C.	T/Capt.A.NEILSON,MB.	Awarded Military Cross.	22/8/18	(Immediate Reward.)
1st,R,Dns.	Lieut.J.R.WINGFIELD-DIGBY	" "	22/8/18	(" ")
1st,R,Dns.	12834 Cpl.HEWSON,T.C.	" Military Medal	17/8/18	(" ")
A.S.C.(6th C.F.A)	T/32801 Dr.H.G.WEST	" "	17/8/18	(" ")
A.S.C.(6th C.F.A)	T4/250081 Dr.F.W.LARRETT :	" "	17/8/18	(" ")

Capt.

S E C R E T.
****

Copy No. 13

6th CAVALRY BRIGADE ORDER No.11

Ref.Map 1/100,000
AMIENS Sheet.

4th August, 1918.

1. The village of SOUES will be handed over to Canadian Cavalry Brigade at midnight August 5th/6th, and the 6th Cavalry Brigade will close up in the remainder of it's present area.

2. In consequence, the following readjustments of billeting areas will be made:-

   (i) 6th M.Gun Sqn. will move to LE MESGE
  (ii) 6th C.F.A.   " " " LE MESGE
 (iii) Royals   " " " RIENCOURT.

3. Movements will be carried out as in March Table on reverse.

   ALL moves to take place under cover of darkness.

4. "A" and "B" Echelons will march with units.

5. Billeting Officers will meet the Staff Captain as follows:-

  (i) 6th C.F.A.   )
      6th M.Gun Sqn.) at Brigade H.Q. at 9 a.m. 5th August.

  (ii) Royals   )
      10th Hussars   ) at H.Q. 10th Hussars at 10 a.m. 5th Aug.

6. ~~ACKNOWLEDGE~~

D.K.Wallace Captain,
Brigade Major 6th Cavalry Brigade.

Issued at 11 a.m.

Copies No. 1 3rd D.Gds.   Copy 8 6th Signal Troop.
        2 Royals   9. Camp Commandant.
        3 10th Hussars.   10. Supply Officer.
        4. 'C' Battery   11. Transport Officer
        5. 6th M.G.Sqn.   12. Staff Captain.
        6. 6th C.F.A.   13. 3rd Cavalry Divn.
        7. 13th M.V.S.

P. T. O

MARCH TABLE 5/8/1918.

Serial No.	Unit.	Starting Point.	Time.	Route.	Destination.	Remarks.
1.	6th M.Gun Sqn.	RIENCOURT Church.	10. p.m.	Main Road West of R.LANDON.	LE MESGE	To be clear of main SOUES - RIENCOURT Road by 10.35 p.m.
2.	6th C.F.A.	RIENCOURT Church	10.15 p.m.	Main Road West of R.LANDON.	LE MESGE	To be clear of main SOUES - RIENCOURT Road by 10.50 p.m.
3.	Royals.	N. Exit of LE MESGE	11. p.m.	Main Road West of R. LANDON	RIENCOURT	

SECRET.
****

GX700/21

Copy No. 13

6th CAVALRY BRIGADE ORDER No.12.

Ref.Map 1/40,000 Sheet 62E.   6th August, 1918

1. 6th Cavalry Brigade (less "B" Echelon, Heavy Section 6th C.F.A., and "C" Battery R.H.A.) will move tonight to a concentration area about RENANCOURT (R.8.central) in accordance with March Table "A" overleaf.

2. "A" Echelons will accompany units

3. Cyclists will accompany "A" Echelons

4. (a) Distances will be maintained on the march as follows:-

   50 yards between Regiments.
   20 yards between Squadrons and similar units.

   (b) Each unit will be responsible for maintaining touch with the unit in rear of it.

5. "C" Battery R.H.A. is marching to RENANCOURT area today under separate orders, and will come under the order of 6th Cavalry Brigade on arrival in that area.

6. "B" Echelon, Heavy Section 6th C.F.A., and Dismounted Parties will march to HANGEST tomorrow, in accordance with March Table "B" attached. instructions to be issued later.

7. Brigade Report Centre will close at LE MESGE at 10.30 p.m. August 6th, and re-open at RENANCOURT on arrival.

8. ACKNOWLEDGE.

D. Wallace

Captain,
Issued at 12.45 p.m.   Brigade Major 6th Cavalry Brigade.

Copies to No.1. 3rd D.Gds.   Copy No.8. 6th Signal Tp.
          2. Royals.   9. Camp Commdt.
          3. 10th Hussars.   10. Supply Officer
          4. 'C' Battery.   11. Lt.H.H.NEWMAN
          5. 6th M.G.Sqn.   12. Staff Capt.
          6. 6th C.F.A.   13. 3rd Cav.Div.
          7. 13th M.V.S.

M A R C H   T A B L E   "A"   —   NIGHT 6th/7th AUGUST.

Issued with 6th Cavalry Brigade Order No. 12.

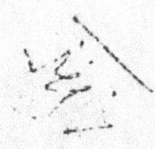

Serial No.	Units in Order of March.	From	Starting Point Place.	Time	Route.	Remarks.
1	Bde.H.Q.& Sigs	LE MESGE	Road junction I.24.a.4.1.	11.00 p.m.	CAVILLON	
2	Royals.	RIENCOURT	"	11.01 p.m.	FOURDRINOY	
3	10th Hussars	RIENCOURT	"	11.11 p.m.	X roads J.23.a.	
4	6th M.G.Sqdn.	LE MESGE	Road junction I.10.b.4.2.	10.50 p.m.	FERRIERES	Follow X.R.H.from I.24.a.4.1 at 11.21 p.m.
5	3rd D.Gds.	LE MESGE	"	10.57 p.m.	Road junction Q.9.d.2.9.	
6	6th C.F.A.	LE MESGE	"	11.07 p.m.	PONT de METZ.	Not to cross R.LANDON till 3rd D.Gds. are clear.
7	13th M.V.S.	LE MESGE	"	11.10 p.m.		Not to pass present Bde.H.Q. till 6th C.F.A. are clear.

SECRET.

6th CAVALRY BRIGADE ORDER No.14.

Copy No. 17

References 1/40,000 Sheets 62D and 66E.   6th August, 1918.

1. (a) The Fourth Army will attack the enemy's positions between MORLANCOURT and the AMIENS – ROYE Road (inclusive) on a date to be notified later. The 1st French Army will co-operate with an attack on the enemy's positions between the AMIENS – ROYE Road (exclusive) and the AVRE Valley.

    (b) Objectives and boundaries have been pointed out at Brigade Conference, and are marked on maps issued down to Squadron Leaders.

    (c) The 3rd Cavalry Division will work under Canadian Corps until the whole of the RED Line on Canadian Corps front has been reached by the Infantry, when it will revert to the Cavalry Corps.

2. The task of the 3rd Cavalry Division with 1 Bn. Whippet Tanks is to follow up the advance of the 1st and 3rd Canadian Divisions, and of the 1st Cavalry Division with 1 Bn. Whippet Tanks to follow up the 2nd Canadian Division to the RED Line, where the Cavalry will pass through the Infantry and proceed to capture and hold the BLUE Dotted Line, northwards from ROYE Road to Railway, at the same time exploiting their success East of the BLUE Dotted Line and South and South East of the ROYE Road.

3. In consequence, the 3rd Cavalry Division will be ready to move on ZERO day, from the Assembly area about N.32 and T.2 (shewn on map issued) along the Cavalry Track.
    Order of March:-

    Canadian Cavalry Brigade.
    1 Brigade of 1st Cavalry Division.
    7th Cavalry Brigade.
    6th Cavalry Brigade.
    Field Squadron (after completion of special mission).
    Batteries R.H.A. and R.C.H.A.Bde. will accompany Brigades.
    Two Companies of Whippet Tanks, 16 in each Company, will move with Canadian Cavalry Brigade and one Company with 6th Cavalry Brigade in support.

4. The Canadian Cavalry Brigade will keep in close touch with the Infantry Advance of 1st and 3rd Canadian Divisions by means of patrols and will also detail patrols to reconnoitre crossings over the River LUCE from DEMUIN to CAIX, both inclusive, reporting on their suitability for Tanks and Cavalry.

5. On crossing the River LUCE the Division will move forward on a 2 Brigade frontage, Canadian Cavalry Brigade on the right (South) and 7th Cavalry Brigade on the left (North).
    Objective will be BLUE Dotted Line from ROYE – AMIENS Road to E.13.c.7.0.
    First Bound A line running from D.29.central to E.7.central.
    Dividing Line between Brigades: K.3.a.1.4 – E.26.central – E.19.central – D.11 central.
    The Canadian Cavalry Brigade will gain touch with Canadian Motor Machine Gun Brigade along the ROYE Road and the 7th Cavalry Brigade with 1st Cavalry Division on their left.
    The 6th Cavalry Brigade and 16 Tanks will be in Divisional support.

6. If the crossings over the River LUCE are impracticable for Tanks, the Canadian Cavalry Brigade and 7th Cavalry Brigade with the Battalion of Tanks will move North of River LUCE via CAIX.

Role for Canadian Cavalry Brigade and Tanks will be to mop up enemy in the quadrilateral CAIX - CAYEUX - BEAUCOURT - LE QUESNEL prior to seizing objective.

Role of 7th Cavalry Brigade will be to support Canadian Cavalry Brigade if required and to form a flank to the East on the objective, until the Canadian Cavalry Brigade will seize have completed the mopping up, when Canadian Cavalry Brigade will seize their objective.

6th Cavalry Brigade will be in Divisional Support.

7. The 6th Cavalry Brigade will follow the 7th Cavalry Brigade from the Assembly area in the following order of March:-
"A" Coy. No.3 Light Tank Bn.
Royals.
"C" Battery R.H.A.
6th M.G.Sqn.
10th Hussars.
3rd D.Gds.

8. Fighting Troops Limbers and Maltese Carts will march in rear of 6th M.Gun Sqn.

9. A.1 Echelon will be Divisionalised on arrival in Assembly area, and will follow 3rd Field Squadron when the Division advances.

10. A.2 Echelon will remain in PONT de METZ area when the Brigade moves up to the Assembly positions.

It will be brought up under Divisional arrangements to an Assembly position North of BOVES at Z plus 4 hrs

11. 6th C.F.A. and 13th M.V.S. will act under orders of A.D.M.S. and A.D.V.S. respectively.

12. Liaison Officers, Gallopers, and detachments will be found as in Appendix "A".

13. Brigade Report Centre will be at the Head of the leading Regiment, unless otherwise ordered.

14. ACKNOWLEDGE.

D. Wallace
Captain,
Brigade Major 6th Cavalry Brigade.

Issued at 7 p.m.

Copies No.1 3rd D.Gds.
2. Royals.
3. 10th Hussars.
4. 'C' Battery.
5. 6th M.G.Sqn.
6. 6th C.F.A.
7. 13th M.V.S.

Copy No. 8. Camp Commdt.
9. 6th Signal Troop.
10. Supply Officer.
11. Lt.H.H.NEWMAN.
12. Staff Captain.
13. "A"Coy.3rd Lt.Tank Bn.
14. 3rd Cav.Div.

APPENDIX "A".
****
(Issued with 6th Cavalry Brigade Order No 14)

DETAIL OF DETACHED PARTIES.

Serial No.	Duty.	Detail of Party.				To report at		Remarks.
		Regt.	Officers.	N.C.Os.	Men.	Place	Time	
1.	Liaison 1st Canadian Division.	3rd D.Gs.	Major GIBBS	-	5	To be notified later.		
2.	Liaison 1st Cavalry Division.	10th Hrs.	Major GOSLING		9			
3.	Liaison, 3rd Cavalry Division.	Royals.	Lt. HARRISON	1*	9	H.Q. 3rd Cav. Div. T.3.b.2.4.	Zero hour.	* Sergt.
4.	Gallopers 6th Cavalry Brigade.	3rd D.Gs. Royals 10th Hrs.	2/Lt. FORD Lt. COURAGE 2/Lt. B.A. WILSON		1 1 1	H.Q. 6th Cavalry Bde.	Zero hour.	
5.	Liaison 7th Cavalry Brigade.	Royals.	Lt. WEATHERSTONE		5	H.Q. 6th Cavalry Bde.	Zero hour.	
6.	Liaison Canadian Cavalry Bde.	3rd D.Gds	Lt. W.B. STARKEY		5	Remain with Regt. till called for.		
7.	Provost Duty.	10th Hrs.		1*	3	A.P.M. 3rd Cav. Div. T.3.b.2.4.	On arrival in Assembly area	* Sergt.
8.	Tank Liaison	3rd D.Gds			2	H.Q. 3rd Cav. Div. T.3.b.2.4.	Zero hour.	Each man leading 1 spare horse, suitable for Tank Liaison Officer.

NOTES: All the above - will report fully rationed.
All Officers must have 1/40,000 and 1,000 maps, notebooks, Message Pads, & envelopes.
Numbers of men detailed include 1 servant as horseholder.

S E C R E T.
****

Copy No. 14

6th CAVALRY BRIGADE ORDER No.16.

Ref.Map AMIENS 1/100,000   15th August, 1918.

1. The Brigade will march tonight to the LE MESGE area, in accordance with Table overleaf.

2. Units will occupy billets and bivouacs as on August 4th.
    'C' Battery R.H.A. will billet in LE MESGE.

3. 10th Hussars will detail one Advanced Squadron to picquet the road.
    This Squadron will not leave bivouac before 7.45 p.m.
    Picquet to remain out till "B" Echelon has passed.

4. The Brigade will march closed up as far as ESTREES-SUR-NOYE.
    Fourth Army distances will be maintained from ESTREES-SUR-NOYE onwards.
    On reaching that place, each unit will halt and get it's distance without further orders.

5. 6th C.F.A. will detail one horsed Ambulance to march in rear of each Regiment.

6. 'A' Echelon will march in rear of units.

7. 'B' Echelon will be brigaded, under Lt.H.H.NEWMAN, 10th Hussars, as far as the Western exit of CAVILLON.
    From this point units will be responsible for guiding their own wagons to billets.

8. Brigade Report Centre will close at FOUENCAMPS at 8 p.m. and open at LE MESGE on arrival.

9. ACKNOWLEDGE.

D. Wallace
Captain,
Brigade Major 6th Cavalry Brigade.

Issued at 5 p.m.

Distribution: Normal.
    Copy No.19 Lt.H.H.NEWMAN, 10th Hussars.

MARCH TABLE - NIGHT 15/16th AUGUST.

Issued with 6th Cavalry Brigade Order No. 16. dated 15/8/18.

Serial No.	Units in order of march.	Starting Point.	Time.	ROUTE.	Destination.	Remarks.
1	Cyclists.	Road and track junction 1000x North of D in DOMMARTIN.	8.00 pm.	DOMMARTIN - road junct.800x SSE. of COTTENCHY Church - GUYENCOURT - ESTREES-sur-NOYE - RUMIGNY - VERS - CLAIRY SAULCHOIX - PISSY - FLUY - BRIQUEMESNIL - CAVILLON.	Units' areas.	Under an officer to be detailed by 3rd D. Gds.
2	Bde.H.Q. Signals.		8.20 pm.		LE MESGE.	
3	10th Hrs.		8.20 pm.		RIENCOURT.	
4	Royals.		8.30 pm.		SOUES.	
5	6 M.G.Sqdn.		8.40 pm.		RIENCOURT.	
6	3 Dgns.		8.45 pm.		LE MESGE.	
7	C Bty.		8.55 pm.		LE MESGE.	
8	6th C.F.A.		9.00 pm.		RIENCOURT.	
9	13th M.V.S.		9.05 pm.		LE MESGE.	
10	B Echelon.		9.10 pm.		Units' areas.	Under Lt. NEWMAN, X.R.H. No wagons to be on main FOUENCAMPS - DOMMARTIN road until all Fighting troops of the Bde. have cleared FOUENCAMPS.

"A" Form
MESSAGES AND SIGNALS.

Army Form C. 2121
(In pads of 100).

TO	3	Cav	Div

Sender's Number	Day of Month	In reply to Number	AAA
M39	16.		

Cancel 0017 of today

From: Cav Div

SECRET
****

Copy No. 14

6th CAVALRY BRIGADE ORDER No.17

Map 1/100,000 AMIENS & LENS.   16th August, 1918

1. The Brigade will march tonight to the area St.LEGER-LES-DOMART - BERTEAUCOURT-LES-DAMES

2. Starting Point: N. exit of SOUES.

3. Times to pass Starting Point :-

Royals.	8.00 p.m.
Bde.H.Q.)	
6th Signal Tp.)	8.20 p.m.
'O' Battery	8.25 p.m
3rd D.Gds.	8.40 p.m.
10th Hussars	9.00 p.m.
6th M.G.Sqn.	9.20 p.m.
6th C.F.A.	9.35 p.m.
13th M.V.S.	9.40 p.m.
"B" Echelon	10.00 p.m.

4. Route :- HANGEST - BOURDON - FLIXECOURT - S.E. end of St.OUEN

5. Distances :-   As in Fourth Army Orders.

6. Picquoting of road in HANGEST - BOURDON and FLIXECOURT will be done by Brigade M.M.P.

7. Cyclists will march independently by units, but must be under a senior N.C.O., and not leave SOUES before 8 p.m.

8. "A" Echelons will march in rear of units.

9. "B" Echelons will be brigaded, under Lieut.H.H.NEWMAN, 10th Hussars and will keep clear of main RIENCOURT - SOUES Road till all fighting troops have passed.

   Units guides to meet at Y Roads 1100 yards North of N in St.OUEN

10. Brigade Report Centre will close at LE MESGE at 7.45 p.m. and open in new area at same hour.
    Exact location will be notified later.

11. ~~ACKNOWLEDGE~~.

D.R.Wallace
Captain,
Brigade Major 6th Cavalry Brigade.

Issued at 12.15 p.m.
Distribution: Normal
   Copy No.19   Lt.H.H.NEWMAN, 10th Hussars.

Army Form C. 2118.

Sheet 2.

WAR DIARY
or
INTELLIGENCE SUMMARY.

(Erase heading not required.)

6th Cavalry Brigade.

5/8/18 = 12/8/18.

Instructions regarding War Diaries and Intelligence Summaries are contained in F.S. Regs., Part II. and the Staff Manual respectively. Title pages will be prepared in manuscript.

Place	Date	Hour	Summary of Events and Information	Remarks and references to Appendices
	8th			
	(about)	4 pm	Royals and 10th Hussars however had been unable to advance beyond the Wood in E.15 owing to high ground East of LE QUESNEL being strongly held by M.G. Royal were holding a series of posts from E.15.b.9.0. to E.21.b.9.0. with 1 Squadron and Machine Guns holding Southern edge of WOOD in E.15. Patrols tried to push forward and 10th Hussars were ordered to work round the left flank of Royals through E.22.b. and E.23.c.	
Bosin		5.30 pm	Orders were received from 3rd Cavalry Divn. that the Brigade was to remain in the line it then held, and the following order was issued :- BM.10 8th AAA 2 Cav.Div. have been ordered to advance in direction of ROYE leaving 3 Cav.Div. to hold AMIENS OUTER DEFENCES AAA 6 Cav.Bde. have been allotted Sector K.3.a.1.4. to E.16.d.8.6 both inclusive AAA 10 Hussars will hold Right Sub-sector and Royals Left Sub-Sector AAA Point of junction E.21.d.7.7. inclusive to Royals AAA 1 Section 6 M.G.Sqn. is allotted to each of above Regiments AAA Remainder of 6 M.G.Sqn. will be disposed under orders of O.C. to hold the line held by the Brigade AAA 'C' Battery will cover the exits of BEAUFORT and the Wood West of it AAA 3 D.G will be in Bde.Reserve West of the Wood in E.15. AAA 10 Hussars will get touch with 7th Cav.Bde. and Royals with 1 Cav.Div. AAA Units will report what portions of their line are occupied by Infantry but will not vacate them without further orders AAA Brigade H.Q. will be established about E.15.c.2.6.at 6.15 p.m. AAA added.all units 6 Cav.Bde.reptd.7 Cav.Bde Right Bde.1 Cav.Div. 3rd Cav.Div. 6 Cav.Bde. E.10.b.1.9 5.45 p.m." Brig.General A.G.SEYMOUR was obliged by illness to hand over his command to Lt.Col. F.H.D.C.WHITMORE,Commanding 10th Hussars ; Captain GORDON CANNING assumed Command of 10th Hussars.	
		6 pm.	Following message sent to 3 Cav.Div. AAA BM.11. AAA 8th "Situation on Right flank of Bde. 5.50 p.m. AAA 12 Canadian Inf.Bde. in touch with Royals AAA Line prolonged by 8 Hussars North of CAIX - ROSIERES Road AAA 4 D.G. and 1 Canadian Battn. in Reserve in E.9.b. AAA 6 p.m. 6 Cav.Bde.	
End D67		6.30 pm	B.H.Q. moved to E.14.d.8.7.	
		6.40 pm	Royals reported enemy dribbling in small parties into Wood in E.23.c. 'C' and 'K' batteries fired on this Wood	

Army Form C. 2118.

SHEET 3.

WAR DIARY
or
INTELLIGENCE SUMMARY.
(Erase heading not required.)

6th Cavalry Brigade.   5/8/18 to 12/8/18.

Instructions regarding War Diaries and Intelligence Summaries are contained in F. S. Regs., Part II. and the Staff Manual respectively. Title pages will be prepared in manuscript.

Place	Date	Hour	Summary of Events and Information	Remarks and references to Appendices
E.14.d.8.7.	8th 8.7.	7 pm	Following message sent to 3 Cav.Div. BM.13. 8.W AAA " Situation Left flank AAA 10 Hussars report Canadian Infantry hold line E.21.b.3.6. to E.26.d.3.7. unable advance to BLUE Line owing to M.G.fire from high ground between LE QUESNEL and BEAUFORT AAA 10 Hussars are stiffening up this line. 6 Cav.Bde. 7 pm. ".	

		8.25 pm	Following from 7 Cav.Bde.
			         G.G.10. 8. AAA
			"S.O.S. has gone up from S.E. corner of Wood AAA Please be ready to reinforce dismounted E.15.d. AAA Enemy massing S.E. of Wood.
			                  7 Cav.Bde. 8.20 p.m."
			
			In consequence, Royals were ordered to be prepared to reinforce with 2 Squadrons which were already dismounted	

		9. pm.	Led horses were moved on to slope West of the Valley in E.15. owing to the great congestion there, and following message sent to 3 Cav.Div.
			          BM.19. 8 AAA
			"Situation 9 pm AAA Royals Squadron in S.E. corner of Wood in E.15. were fairly heavily shelled about 8.30 p.m. AAA Infantry have sent up S.O.S. in E.22.B.AAA Certain amount M.G.fire from direction BEAUFORT AAA A counter-attack from BEAUFORT down valley N.W. seems likely AAA
			            6 Cav.Bde. 9.10 p.m."	

		10.45 pm	Galloper from 3 Cav.Div. arrived with request for details of dispositions, and following was despatched B.M.20 8 GC.16. "The state of the defences of 3rd Cavalry Divn Sector are approximately as followsAAA E.26.central E.20.d.9.0. E.21.central E.22.a.5.5. E.16.d.7.7. AAA A few forward positions are in front of the line from E.26.central to E.21.central AAA Many machine guns and Hotchkiss are employed in this Section of the line commanding the high ground East of LE QUESNEL and BEAUFORT AAA Distribution of Troops as follows AAA	

Army Form C. 2118.

SHEET 4.

WAR DIARY
or
INTELLIGENCE SUMMARY.
(Erase heading not required.)

6th Cavalry Brigade.
5/8/18 - 12/8/18.

Instructions regarding War Diaries and Intelligence Summaries are contained in F. S. Regs., Part II. and the Staff Manual respectively. Title pages will be prepared in manuscript.

Place	Date	Hour	Summary of Events and Information	Remarks and references to Appendices
E.14.d.8.7.8th	8th		7 D.G. on right flank guarding flank Inniskillings E.27.a.# 17 Lrs. and 10 Hrs. South edge of Wood E.21.a.and b. Royals from that point to E.16.b.7.7. AAA 12 and 11 Canadian Bdes. are holding a line in conjunction with 3 Cav.Div. AAA Intermittent M.G.fire continues from LE QUESNEL and BEAUFORT AAA A large concentration of enemy troops at and about BEAUFORT AAA Preparations for enemy counter-attack in morning as followsAAA All troops in line in Battle positions at 4 a.m. AAA 3 D.G. intact in hand E.15.AAA Led horses 6 Cav.Bde. 1 man to 4 E.14.central Led horses 7 Cav.Bde. in valley E.15. AAA 'C' and 'K' Battys. in action E.15.b. and E.14.d.respectively AAA 11 Canadian Bde. on our right and Scottish Canadian Battn. on the left AAA Ammn. O.K. AAA Watercarts badly wanted AAA By request of Col.PATERSON I have taken over command of Divl.Sector for the night. 6 Cav.Bde. 11.25 p.m. "	
			The Counter-attack did not materialise, and the situation remained quiet throughout the night.	
	9th	4.50 am	Message received from 78 Canadian Battn.that 11 Canadian Bde. had been ordered to advance to the BLUE Dotted Line.	
		7.45 am.	Orders received for the Divn. to concentrate on the River between CAIX and CAYEUX.	
		8.15 am.	Brigade ordered to arrange relief with 12 Canadian Bde. and withdraw to W.26.c. BM.25. # 9 AAA " Royals and 10 Hrs. will withdraw from positions now held as soon as relieved by InfantryAAA The Bde. will concentrate in area CAYEUX - CAIX and water on South side of River AAA 1 Officer and 2 O.R. per unit will meet Staff Captain at 9.30 a.m. at Y Rds in E.2.d. AAA 3 D.G. and 'C' Battery will march independently so as to arrive at E.2.d. at 9.45 and 10 a.m respectively AAA Royals 10 Hrs. and 6 M.G.S. independently as soon as relieved AAA Guides will meet all units in E.2.d. AAA OsC.Royals 10 Hrs. and 6 M.G.S. to report at B.H.Q. forthwith to arrange details of relief AAA B.H.Q. will march to new area as soon as relief is complete AAA Ack AAA 6 Cav.Bde. 8.40 a.m.	
		9.15 am	O.C.85 Canadian Battn. asked that Royals should remain in support of his Battn. until he was satisfied with the progress of our attack which was due to start at 10 a.m. 6 M.G.Sqn. were also left in position.	

Army Form C. 2118.

SHEET 5.

WAR DIARY
or
INTELLIGENCE SUMMARY.
(Erase heading not required.)

6th Cavalry Brigade.
5/8/18 - 12/8/18.

Instructions regarding War Diaries and Intelligence Summaries are contained in F.S. Regs., Part II. and the Staff Manual respectively. Title pages will be prepared in manuscript.

Place	Date	Hour	Summary of Events and Information	Remarks and references to Appendices
W.26.c.	9th	12noon.	Brigade less Royals and 6 M.G.S. concentrated W.26.c. and off-saddled.	
		1.30 pm.	Royals and 6 M.G.S. rejoined.	
		3 p.m.	Bde. ordered to saddle up and G.O.C. to go to Divl.H.Q.	
		8.30 p.m.	Orders for Bde. to off-saddle and be ready to move at 5 a.m. tomorrow	
	10th	3.40 am	G.C.22 received from 3 Cav.Div. and following issued: BM.48. 10th. AAA "6th Cav.Bde. is to take over patrols now found by 2 Cav.Div. on front BOUCHOIR - ROUVROY both inclusive AAA 3 D.G. will take over Right Sector and Royals left Sector AAA These Regts. will each send 1 Sqn forward at 5 a.m. AAA Rest of Bde.will move 5.30 amAAA C.Os and all units and Leading Squadron Leaders of 3 D.G. and Royals meet Brigadier 4.45 am at present H.Q., Royals AAA 6th Cav.Bde. 4.10 a.m."	
		5 am.	'C' Sqn. 3 D.G. (Capt.VINCENT) and 'A' Sqn.Royals (Capt.MILES) marched to 2 Cav.Div.H.Q in E.30.a. and took over patrols from 5 Cav.Bde and 3 Cav.Bde.respectively.	
E.30.c.		6.45 am	Advanced B.H.Q. established at E.30.a.	
		8.20 am	Remainder of Bde.concentrated in E.23. AAA BM.51. 10 AAA "Dispositions AAA Sqn. 3 D.G. at FOLIES with patrols at L.1.c.5.5.and K.18.c.4.5. AAA Infantry in considerable numbers are in front of patrol AAA Sqn.Royals,dismounted,in support of 5 Canadian Inf.Battn.holding L.8.c.9.5. - L.8.c.4.2. with led horses behind ROUVROY Cemetery AAA Bde. alongside us here report that Infantry are attacking through them at 8 a.m. AAA Bde.Report Centre established here AAA E.30.a.1.9. 8.25 am.	
E.30.a.1.9		8.30 am	Following orders issued to Advanced Sqd.s AAA BM.52. 10. AAA "In event of Infantry advance patrols will be sent to keep closest possible touch with	

Army Form C. 2118.

SHEET 6.

WAR DIARY
or
INTELLIGENCE SUMMARY.

(Erase heading not required.)

6th Cavalry Brigade.
5/8/18 - 12/8/18.

Place	Date	Hour	Summary of Events and Information	Remarks and references to Appendices.
E.30.a.1.9.	10th		"The situation and Sqns. will be reported by their own Regts. if necessary AAA Dividing line AAA 3 D.G. BOUCHOIR ↑ LA CAMBUSE inclusive GOYENCOURT exclusive GRUNY inclusive to FOLIES PARVILLERS and CREMERY all inclusive, Royals thence to ROUVROY inclusive.FOUQUESCOURT exclusive FRANSART and HATTENCOURT both exclusive AAA. Situation reports to be sent to 6 Cav.Bde.direct every hour AAA B.H.Q. remaining at old 2 Cav.Div.H.Q. at E.30 a.1.9. 6 Cav Bde. E.30.a.1.9. 8.30 a.m.	
		10.30 a.m	Reports received that Infy.attack was making progress. Verbal orders issued to O&C 3 D.G. and Royals to move up in support of their advanced Sqn. and to remainder of Bde. to move forward. BM.53. 10th. AAA "Royals will move forward forthwith to neighbourhood of BEAUFORT and 3 D.G. to about BOUCHOIR AAA 'C' Battery 6 M.G.S. less sub-sections attached to Regts. and 10 Hrs. to about 2nd L of LE QUESNEL AAA B.H.Q. will close here at 11.15 a.m. and open about 800 North of FOLIES Church AAA. 6th Cav.Bde. E.20.a.1.9. 10.45 a.m	
K.11.c.8.5.		11.30 am	G.O.C. 32nd Div. and G.O.C. 97th Inf.Bde. interviewed. Both gave very good reports of Infantry advance, which were sent on to 3rd Cavalry Divn. This information subsequently proved to be very misleading.	
K.12.c.5.0.		11.56 am	Brigade Report Centre moved forward to K.12.c.5.0. Message received from Advanced Sqn.3 D.G. V.4. 10th AAA Enemy holding line running N. and S. in front of PARVILLERS and DAMERY AAA Line reported to be strongly wired AAA FOLIES 11.40 a.m.	
		11.57 am	Message received from 3 D.G.. 10th AAA A.215/1 " Just heard that PARVILLERS has fallen and sending leading Sqn. on to LE QUESNOY and going on myself with it to reconnoitre" 11.50 am. X Rds.just E. of FOLIES Church	
		11.58 am	Royals reported that G.O.C. 97 Inf.Bde.stated his Bde.had reached line FRANSART - LA CHAVETTE and enemy were on the run.	

SHEET 7.

WAR DIARY
or
INTELLIGENCE SUMMARY.

(Erase heading not required.)

Army Form C. 2118.

6th Cavalry Brigade.
5/8/18 - 12/8/18.

Place	Date	Hour	Summary of Events and Information	Remarks and references to Appendices
K.12.c.5.0.	10th	1 pm	1 Section 'C' Battery sent to join 3 D.G. 2 Officers patrols 10 Hrs. sent to report on suitability of ground on our front for movement of large bodies of Cavalry.	
		1.10 pm	Message from 3rd Cav.Div. that 16 Whippet Tanks were being sent to join the Bde. Message from Royals that PARVILLERS still held by enemy, and leading Squadron unable to advance.	
		1.30 pm	3rd D.G. reported that PARVILLERS was strongly held by cross fire from M.G. and our Infantry on a line 500X N.W. of it. Whippet Tanks arrived.	
		1.45 pm	Message to 3 D.G. and Royals BM.59. 10th AAA 14 Whippet Tanks will start about 2 p.m. from N.exit of WARVILLERS and advance on PARVILLERS AAA When near that place they will divide and go round either side AAA 3 D.G. and Royals will keep close touch with Royals and exploit any success. 1.45 p.m. 6 Cav.Bde.	
		1.50 pm	Royals reported that it was out of the question for Sqns. to advance at present. Country East of ROUVROY much wired and entrenched. 2 Officers patrols sent towards LA CHAVETTE and South of ROUVROY - ROYE Road.	
		2.20 pm	10th Hussars Officers patrols returned with report on ground BM.60. 10th AAA (to 3 Cav.Div) " 2 Officers patrols were sent out from here to report on ground on Bde.front especially towards PARVILLERS AAA They report that there is an old trench system about the line ROUVROY - LE QUESNOY and that the movement of large bodies of Cavalry at any pace would be quite impossible AAA Both Advanced Regts.have made similar reports and state that any further advance on present front must be made dismounted K.12.c.5.0. 6 Cav.Bde. 2.35 p.m. Tank Commander said ground would be impossible for Whippets. Plan given in B.M.59 cancelled. Arranged for Tanks to advance up ROUVROY - PARVILLERS and LE QUESNOY - PARVILLERS Roads supported by Royals and 3 D.G.	
		2.35 pm	Message from 3 Cav.Div. that Canadian Cav.Bde. had been ordered to pass through and seize	

Army Form C. 2118.

SHEET 8.

WAR DIARY
or
INTELLIGENCE SUMMARY.
(Erase heading not required.)

6th Cavalry Brigade.
5/8/18 – 12/8/18.

Place	Date	Hour	Summary of Events and Information	Remarks and references to Appendices
K.12.c.5.0.	10th.		high ground N. and E. of ROYE and 6th Cav.Bde were to support them.	
		2.45 pm	G.OsO. 3 Cav.Div. and Canadian Cav.Bde. came up to Bde.Report Centre.	
		2.55 pm.	Following message from 3 D.G.(Col.ROME) R.1. 10th AAA "My patrol along ROYE – AMIENS Road reports at 1.45 p.m. 1/ Enemy still holds ANDECHY – 2/ Our troops in LA CAMBUSE and W.edge of DAMERY. I am sending a Sqn. down the AMIENS – Roye Road, with orders to assist if possible in the attack on DAMERY. FOLIES 2.45 p.m."	
		3 p.m.	Report timed 1.58 p.m. from Lt.DIGBY,Royals, who had gone to Infantry front line that left flank of 32nd Div. was out of touch with Canadians and attack on PARVILLERS held up by M.Gs and snipers.	
		3.30 pm. 4.10 pm	3 D.G. confirmed that enemy still held PARVILLERS. Necessity of supporting Canadians on right flank and unsuitability of ground caused Tank attack to be abandoned. Tanks attacking from ROUVROY had already started but Lt.BIRCH 1 R.D. went forward and got them back. Royals withdrawn to K.12.a. so as to be ready to move south.	
		5.43 p.m.	Message from 3 Cav.Div. GC.38 10th AAA "Canadian Cav.Bde. have galloped Hill 100 with 1 Regt. and are now there AAA You must support them closely and keep in touch with them AAA 5.43 p.m." Ordered 10th Hussars to advance to support Fort a Garry Horse, under orders of Canadian Cavalry Bde. Royals to move to FOLIES.	
		6.15 pm.	Bde.H.Q. moved to L.25.b.5.0. S.W. of LE QUESNOY. Royals closed up on 10th Hussars in K.36.b. Battery and M.G.S. to L.19.a.	

Army Form C. 2118.

SHEET 9

WAR DIARY
or
INTELLIGENCE SUMMARY.

6th Cavalry Bde.
5/8/18 - 12/8/18.

(Erase heading not required.)

Instructions regarding War Diaries and Intelligence Summaries are contained in F. S. Regs., Part II, and the Staff Manual respectively. Title pages will be prepared in manuscript.

Place	Date	Hour	Summary of Events and Information	Remarks and references to Appendices
L.25.b.5.0.	10th		Message received from Liaison Officer that Fort Garry Horse had been unable to capture Hill 100. LA CAMBUSE and DAMERY were still held by the enemy.	
		7.40 pm	Situation as follows: 10th Hussars Royals 'C' Battery and M.G.Sqn. as at 6.15 p.m. 3 D.G. 2 Sqns at LE QUESNOY, 1 at FOLIES.	
		8 p.m.	Bde.H.Q. was heavily shelled, with loss of 2 O.R.(wounded) and 7 chargers.	
		8.30 pm	Bde.H.Q. moved back to K.17.c.5.6	
		9.30 pm	Bde.concentrated West of FOLIES (approx. in squares K.16 a. b. and d.) for the night.	
	11th	12.40 am	Orders issued to units to be ready to move at 1 hours notice from 5 am. The Brigade remained in bivouac throughout the day.	
		5.30 pm	Brigade moved Westwards keeping South of ROYE - AMIENS Road and arrived in BOVES - FOUENCAMPS area shortly before midnight.	

Captain,
Brigade Major 6th Cavalry Brigade.

Army Form C. 2118.

Sheet No. 1

WAR DIARY

INTELLIGENCE SUMMARY.

(Erase heading not required.)

6th Cavalry Brigade.
September, 1918.

Place	Date	Hour	Summary of Events and Information	Remarks and references to Appendices
NUNCQ	1st		Brigade remained on 6 hours notice.	
	2nd	5 am.	Orders received to be on 4 hours notice.	
		10.30am.	Telephone message received that Brigade less "B" Echelon would be ready to move at 1 hour's notice.	
		4.30 pm.	Notice extended to 3 hours.	
		7.0 pm.	Notice extended to 6 hours.	
	3rd	10.30pm.	Brigade ordered to be on 2 hours notice from 5 a.m. the following morning.	
		10.45pm.	Brigade ordered to be ready to move at 5 a.m.	
		10.55pm.	Above order cancelled. Brigade on 6 hours notice.	
	4th		Message received that 10th Hussars would rejoin the Brigade on the 5th.	
	5th	Noon.	10th Hussars rejoined and were billeted in SIBIVILLE.	
LE PLACITON	6th	9.30 am.	Brigade marched to WILLEMAN - WAIL - VIEIL HESDIN - ST. GEORGES - LE PARCQ area. Brigade Headquarters established at LE PLACITON (VIEIL HESDIN). Brigade was put on 24 hours notice and became G.H.Q. Reserve. G.O.C. and Brigade Major carried out Staff Ride with G.O.C. 3rd Cavalry Division over the ROUGEFAY area.	
	15th.		Os.C. Regiments carried out Staff Ride with G.O.C. Both these Staff Rides dealt with initial stages of the coming cavalry manoeuvres.	
	16th.		Brigade moved into the HESDIN - GRIGNY - MARCONNE area, preparatory to taking part in the cavalry manoeuvres the following day. Brigade Headquarters in HESDIN.	
HESDIN	17th		Brigade moved out of HESDIN at 4.45 a.m. and concentrated in forward assembly area N.W. of OEUF by 7.30 a.m. The General Idea of the manoeuvres was that the 1st Cavalry Division was to seize the crossings over R. AUTHIE and hold the high ground to the North of it. The 3rd Cavalry Division was then to go through the 1st Cavalry Division and seize and hold the line BEAUMETZ - BERNAVILLE. The Brigade remained in Concentration Area till 10.30 am. and then moving South with a short halt near CONCHY-sur-CANCHE, came in touch with the enemy/S.E. of MAIZICOURT. (a Brigade of 66th Div.) Cease fire sounded at about 3.30 p.m. The G.O.C. attended a Conference at AUXI-le-CHATEAU. The Brigade rendezvoused round BEALCOURT and then moved into the AUTHEUX - BOISBERGUES - GEZAINCOURT area for the night.	
LE PLACITON.	18th		Brigade moved back for one night to former area round VIEIL HESDIN and WAIL.	

Army Form C. 2118.

Sheet No. 2.
WAR DIARY
INTELLIGENCE SUMMARY

6th Cavalry Brigade.
September 1918.

Instructions regarding War Diaries and Intelligence Summaries are contained in F.S. Regs., Part II. and the Staff Manual respectively. Title pages will be prepared in manuscript.

(Erase heading not required.)

Place	Date	Hour	Summary of Events and Information	Remarks and references to Appendices
REBREUVE	19th		Brigade moved into new area as under:— Bde.H.Q., 6th C.F.A., 13th M.V.S. REBREUVE. 3rd Dragoon Guards. Gnd.BOURET and Pit.BOURET. Royals. FREVENT. 10th Hussars. LIGNY-sur-CANCHE. 'C' Battery R.H.A. FORTEL. 6th M.G.Sqdn. NUNCQ.	
	24th		Brigade carried out a Communication Scheme.	
	25th		Lieut. G.H.L.F. PITT RIVERS (Royal Dragoons) joined the Brigade temporarily as A.D.C., vice Captain HOWARD.	
BUS-les-ARTOIS		9 p.m.	The Brigade moved via LUCHEUX and PAS to BUS-les-ARTOIS – LOUVENCOURT – COIGNEUX – COUIN – ST.LEGER-les-AUTHIE area.	
	26th	8.15pm.	Brigade moved via ALBERT into bivouac at MEAULTE. Brigade H.Q. was in the village and all units in the vicinity, the Royals being at BECORDE L BECOURT.	
MEAULTE	27th	7.30pm.	Brigade marched to bivouacs in area about 1 mile N.E. of HEM. Most of the men were in old dug-outs.	
HEM	28th		Brigade remained at HEM.	
	29th	noon	Brigade received orders to be ready to move at 3 hours notice.	
		1 pm.	Telephone message received to be ready to move at 2.30 p.m.	
		2.45 pm.	Brigade moved via PERONNE – DOINGT – POEUILLY in to area round VERMAND – BIHÉCOURT. Brigade Hd.Qrs. established in huts at N.E. corner of VERMAND. Regiments in bivouac between VERMAND and BIHECOURT.	
VERMAND	30th	11.30pm.	Orders received for Brigade to be in readiness to move at 10 a.m. following morning.	
		5 am.	Orders received for Brigade to remain on 3 hours notice from 7 a.m.	

B. Wallace
Captain,
Brigade Major 6th Cavalry Brigade.

SHEET. 1.

Army Form C. 2118.

WAR DIARY
or
INTELLIGENCE SUMMARY

(Erase heading not required.)

6th CAVALRY BRIGADE.

XXXXX OCTOBER XXXXX 1918.

Instructions regarding War Diaries and Intelligence Summaries are contained in F. S. Regs., Part II. and the Staff Manual respectively. Title pages will be prepared in manuscript.

Place	Date	Hour	Summary of Events and Information	Remarks and references to Appendices
VERMAND.	1st.	07.00	Bde. on 1½ hours' notice.	
		23.40	Head of Bde. ordered to be at X-roads North of PONTRU.	
	2nd.	08.30	Divnl. Conference at X-roads North of PONTRU.	
		09.00	Brigade moved straight on to Assembly Area S.W. of BELLENGLISE. Brigade was detailed as leading Brigade.	
		10.00	Cavalry plan cancelled. Division ordered back across country to last night's areas.	
		12.30	Brigade back in BIHECOURT - VERMAND area. Proper track up to Assembly Area made and marked during evening by Field Troop R.E., attached to Brigade.	
		19.00	Brigade ordered to be saddled up 08.30.	
	3rd.	08.30	Brigade saddled up ready to move from VERMAND - BIHECOURT area.	
		10.00	G.441 received, ordered Brigade to Assembly Position S.W. of BELLENGLISE.	
		10.30	Brigade started from BIHECOURT, reaching Assembly area by 11.15.	
S.W. of BELLENGLISE.		12.30	Brigade ordered to be ready to move at once to carry out role given in event of 3rd Cavalry Division going before 1st Cavalry Division.	
		12.40	Brigade Intelligence officer, Observation Section and leading troop 3rd Dragoon Guards sent to JONCOURT.	
		13.30	G.C.506 received, "1st Cav.Divn. have been ordered forward to get in touch with situation between MONTBREHAIN and BEAUREVOIR; 3rd Cav.Divn. to be ready to support them."	
		13.40	Brigade Intelligence officer reported he was going on to RAMICOURT to observe.	
		13.45	G.O.C. ordered to Divisional H.Q.	
		14.25	Brigade ordered to go forward and seize high ground N.E. of BRANCOURT-LE-GRAND.	
		14.40	B.97 received from Intelligence officer : "Boches counter-attacking from MONTBREHAIN AAA We hold RAMICOURT but not MONTBREHAIN."	
		15.00	G.O.C. Division came up and said that as a result of Intell: officer's last message, Brigade was only to move up and remain in observation with bulk of Brigade in MAGNY-LA-FOSSE valley.	
		15.30	B.98 received from Intellig: officer that Boches were hesitating and ground S.E. of RAMICOURT open and suitable for Cavalry. In consequence, Divnl. Commander, (who was at Brigade H.Q.) ordered Brigade to carry out original role of seizing high ground N.E. of BRANCOURT-LE-GRAND if possible.	
		15.45	Head of Brigade (3rd D.Gds), crossed Canal at B ELLENGLISE.	
		16.15		
S.W. of JONCOURT.		16.20	Advanced Squadron reached high ground S. of JONCOURT. (SEE SHEET 2.)	

BWallace
Captain,
6th Cavalry Brigade.

Brigade Major
Brigade.

SHEET. 2.
Army Form C. 2118.

WAR DIARY
or
~~INTELLIGENCE SUMMARY~~
(Erase heading not required.)

6th CAVALRY BRIGADE.
OCTOBER 1918.

Place	Date	Hour	Summary of Events and Information	Remarks and references to Appendices
S.W. of JONCOURT. (cont.)	3rd.	16.20	B.99 received from Intellig.Officer that Boches seemed to be retiring S.E. of MONTBREHAIN.	
		16.40	3rd D.Gds. reached RAMIECOURT-PRESSELLES road and Bde.H.Q. was established at H.15.B.174 with rest of Brigade in valley S.W. of JONCOURT.	
		16.50	G.O.C., B.M. and Intellig:Officer made a reconnaissance from hill in H.15.B. and went on to H.Q., 3rd D. Gds. at H.17.b.6.2.	
		17.16	3rd D. Gds. reported enemy in strength on hill in I.19.b. and high ground S.E. of MONTBREHAIN.	
		17.30	Brigade ordered to move up the valley N.W. of PRESSELLES.	
		17.35	3rd D.Gds. heavily shelled just W. of RAMIECOURT-PRESSELLES road.	
		17.40	G.O.C. decided that the Brigade was not strong enough to attack the high ground S.E. of MONTBREHAIN.	
H.17.b.6.2		17.55	B.M.67 sent to 3rd Cavalry Division giving the situation. During this time, 1 sub-section 6th Machine Gun Sqdn. and 1 section 'C' Battery, RHA., had engaged the enemy who could be seen moving about South and South-East of MONTBREHAIN.	
		18.30	G.O.C. and B.M. left H.Q. 3rd D.Gds. to return to Brigade H.Q.	
		18.40	GG.512 received from 3rd Cav.Divn. Lt.Col. WHITMORE according started to move the Brigade (less 3rd D.Gds.) back to PONTRUET area.	
		19.00	G.O.C. received GG.512 from Rear H.Q., and orders were issued to 3rd D. Gds. to withdraw leaving 1 Squadron at H.19.b. for the night, to watch IX Corps front next day.	
		20.00	Staff Officer 46th Division, asked G.O.C. to halt the Brigade as the enemy were reported to have broken through our line. G.O.C. and 3rd D. Gds.(all left East of BELLENGLISE) were accordingly halted off the road. G.O.C. and B.M. remained at H.Q., 46th Division.	
		20.45	Message sent to 3rd D. Gds.Advanced Sqdn. to act under orders of 46th Division tomorrow, and come and see G.O.C. as soon as possible.	
		21.00	Other Reserves having been placed at disposal of 46th Division and situation reported ~~XXXXX~~ quiet, Royals and 3rd D. Gds. were ordered to rejoin Brigade N. of PONTRUET.	
		22.00	Bde.H.Q. established at road junct. M.3.b.5.4 (North of PONTRUET).	
		22.15	Brigadier went to Advanced Divnl. H.Q. at TUMULUS and saw Divnl. Commander.	
		23.30	Brigade reported all in bivouac. Orders issued to be ready to saddle up at once from 05.45 onwards.	

B.Warre
Captain,
Brigade Major 6th Cavalry Brigade.

SHEET. 3.
Army Form C. 2118.

WAR DIARY
OF
~~INTELLIGENCE SUMMARY~~

(Erase heading not required.)

6th CAVALRY BRIGADE
OCTOBER 1918.

Instructions regarding War Diaries and Intelligence Summaries are contained in F.S. Regs., Part II. and the Staff Manual respectively. Title pages will be prepared in manuscript.

Place	Date	Hour	Summary of Events and Information	Remarks and references to Appendices
	4th.	08.15	Advanced Squadron, 3rd D. Gds. reported DOON HILL and high ground S.E. of MONTBREHAIN held by enemy Machine guns; patrols unable to get on, and situation at present impossible for mounted advance.	
		12.00	Brigade spread out in bivouac area and dug in for the night.	
		14.00	Orders issued for relief of 'A' Squadron, 3rd D.Gds., by 1 Squadron of Royals at 16.00	
		21.30	Orders received for Brigade to withdraw to TREFCON area tomorrow.	
	5th.	09.45	Brigade marched from X-roads BELLENGLISE – VERMAND – VILLERET – PONTRU in 2 columns. Mounted troops across country and wheels by road.	
TREFCON.		12.00	Brigade in TREFCON. B.M. carried out reconnaissance of assembly areas and routes through wire between BEAUREVOIR and PRESSELLES. Brigade on 4 hours' notice.	
	6th.	15.00	Conference at Divnl. H.Q. when G.O.C. explained plan for next operation.	
		19.00	Orders for concentration of Brigade on Z day received.	
	7th.	12.00	C.O.' Conference: orders and instructions issued.	
		13.45	Message received – Z Day October 8th.	
		14.00	'A' Echelon, Cavalry F.Ambulance and Mobile Veterinary Section left Brigade area and came under Divnl. control. One Officer per Regiment reconnoitred assembly area with B.M.	
		18.00	Divnl. Conference: minor alterations in plans explained.	
	8th.	03.45	Brigade started from cross roads N. of C in TREFCON (Ref. 1/100,000 ST.QUENTIN).	
		08.00	Brigade assembled in G.30.c. and d. and G.36.a. and b. (Ref. Sheet 62B). Report centre G.30.b.5.9.	
		08.05	GO.C. and Brigade Major to Divnl. H.Q. H.19.b.	
		08.40	Escort Squadron ordered to join H.Q. Cavalry Corps at ESTREES.	
		09.55	Brigade ordered to move to valley in H.7.	
		11.05	Brigade H.Q. established at H.1.b.3.2. Brigade in valley H.7.	
		11.10	Order sent from Adv.H.Q. at B.22.d. for Brigade to move up to B.28.a. and b.	
		12.20	Brigade H.Q. established at B.22.c.1.0. Brigade in valley B.28.a. and b.	
		12.35	Bde.H.Q. moved to B.22.d. joining Adv.B.H.Q. at Div nl. Report Centre.	
		17.15	Brigade ordered to withdraw and bivouac in G.30.c. and d. and G.36.a. and b.	
		19.00	Report centre established in dug-out G.35.b.2.2.	

Sheet 4.

Army Form C. 2118.

WAR DIARY
INTELLIGENCE SUMMARY.
(Erase heading not required.)

6th Cavalry Brigade.
October, 1918.

Instructions regarding War Diaries and Intelligence Summaries are contained in F.S. Regs., Part II. and the Staff Manual respectively. Title pages will be prepared in manuscript.

Place	Date	Hour	Summary of Events and Information	Remarks and references to Appendices
Sheet 62B G.35.b.2.2. H.19.b.	9th	01.50	Brigade ordered to be concentrated in B.12.a. and b. by 07.00.	
		04.00	G.O.C. and B.M. attended Conference at Div.H.Q., and received 3 C.D. O.O. 70, in which the Brigade was ordered to advance in echelon on right of 7th Cavalry Brigade, with objective spurs overlooking valley between LE CATEAU and ST.BENIN.	
C.12.d.1.1.		07.00	Brigade concentrated in C.18b. 1 Field Troop joined Brigade.	
		08.35	B.M.12 (Operation Order) issued to all units. Brigade ordered up to C.2.b. at a trot, as our infantry were reported to be 1½ miles in front of MARETZ, and touch had been lost with 7th Cavalry Brigade, who were advance guard to Divn.	
C.2.cent.		09.00	G.O.C. saw C.O's, and ordered Royals to act as advance guard to Brigade, and move at once parallel to and Sotuh of the main LE CATEAU Road with objectives as given in B.M.12; 10th Hussars to follow Royals, detailing 1 Sqdn. as right flank guard.	
		10.05	Patrols reported BUTRY FARM held by enemy, and our infantry attacking it.	
S. of MARETZ		10.30	Advanced Sqdn. reported our infantry held up by M.G. fire from railway P.28.c. and P.34.a.	
		11.00	10th Hussars ordered to send Sqdn. to work round East of Railway in V.9. This order was subsequently cancelled, on receipt of information that our infantry in V.4. were going to attack.	
Sheet 57C. V.1.b.		11.10	Main body of Brigade ordered to V.1.b.	
		12.00	Royals were now about P.32.c., with advanced Sqdn. at P.33.b. Patrols in touch with infantry who were now on high ground at P.38.d. and meeting strong M.G. opposition from HONNECHY.	
		12.05	The Brigade less Royals and B.H.Q. was withdrawn behind the MARETZ - BUSIGNY road, owing to heavy shelling of the ground N.E. of it.	
		12.15	Conference of two leading Brigadiers and Divnl. Commander at V.1.b.1.8., at which it was decided that if HONNECHY was taken by our infantry, or an opportunity occurred for an advance, 6th and Can. Cav. Bdes. would seize the high ground from P.23.a. to P.16.cent., and then push on and seize the high ground from Q.13.d. to P.5.d.; 6th Cavalry Brigade to move S. of HONNECHY, and Can. Cav. Bde N. of MAUROIS.	
		13.00	B.M.19 issued ordering Royals to advance if opportunity occurred.	
		13.15	Report from Royals from Brigade O.P. at P.34.c.0.8. shewed that the ground would only permit of a rapid advance on HONNECHY from two directions, the road from MARETZ or the road from BUSIGNY.	

D. Wallace
Captain,
Brigade Major, 6th Cavalry Brigade.

Army Form C. 2118.

Sheet 5.

WAR DIARY
INTELLIGENCE SUMMARY.
(Erase heading not required.)

6th Cavalry Brigade.
October, 1918.

Place	Date	Hour	Summary of Events and Information	Remarks and references to Appendices
Sheet 57B. V.1.b.	9th	13.25	G.O.C. decided to send 3rd D.Gds., with two armoured cars, to seize the high ground at P.23.a. from the direction of BUSIGNY. This attack was to take place at 14.00 and Royals were ordered to advance simultaneously on their left.	
		13.45	Inniskillings were placed at disposal of G.O.C. 6th Cav.Bde., and were ordered to advance in echelon to right rear of 3rd D.Gds., and seize spur in P.35.	
		14.10	3rd D.Gds. advanced from N. of BUSIGNY, under heavy enfilade M.G. fire from ESCAUFOURT and B. PROYART. Royals advanced simultaneously through P.28., P.22. and N. of MAUROIS. The advance was made under considerable shell fire, and very heavy M.G. fire from a large number of E.A.	
P.28.cent. HONNECHY		14.30	Report received that Can.Cav.Bde. had captured MAUROIS, and handed it over to infantry.	
		14.40	3rd D.Gds. captured HONNECHY and high ground P.23.c. Advanced B.H.Q. moved to HONNECHY.	
		15.25	G.O.C. decided to send 10th Hussars on to spur in Q .13.c and d. and Inniskillings S. of river towards ST.BENIN.	
		15.45	Message from Can. Cav. Bde., timed 15.05 that enemy held REUMONT.	
		16.00	'C' Battery ordered up to HONNECHY. HONNECHY and the ground round it was heavily shelled ever since it was captured, and 3rd D.Gds. suffered heavy casualties from this, and from M.G. fire during their advance. Inniskillings reported that one Sqdn. was at P.35.a. and other two coming up. G.H.10 received from 3rd Cav. Div., ordering Brigade to push on at once as enemy had been seen retiring through LE CATEAU. At this time the only troops in hand were 1 Sqdn. 10th Hussars, holding E. edge of HONNECHY dismounted (who had been put in to save 3rd D.Gds. more horse casualties) and half the M.G. Sqdn who was in line with them. Remainder of 10th Hussars were not yet up, Royals were between MAUROIS and REUMONT and 3rd D.Gds. very scattered owing to patrols and casualties.	
		16.30	This was reported to 3rd Cav.Div. with a recommendation that the two fresh regiments of 7th Cav.Bde. should be sent forward.	
		16.50	3rd D.Gds. reported RE UMONT now clear (the message from Royals saying that they had captured it at 18.10 was not received at B.H.Q. till 17.18), and Royals were reported to be assembled SW of it.	

D.W. ____
Captain,
Brigade Major, 6th Cavalry Brigade.

Army Form C. 2118.

Sheet 6.

WAR DIARY
INTELLIGENCE SUMMARY.
(Erase heading not required.)

6th Cavalry Brigade.
October, 1918.

Place	Date	Hour	Summary of Events and Information	Remarks and references to Appendices
P.28.cent. HONNECHY.	9th	17.00	O.s.C. 10th Hussars and Royals were given verbal orders to push on at once.	
		17.05	G.O.C. ordered Inniskillings to move West of St.BENIN to high ground S. of LE CATEAU and interrupt Railway about Q.5.b.; if unable to advance past ESCAUFORT, to move through HONNECHY, MAUROIS, and REUMONT, and join 7th Cavalry Brigade.	
P.18.c.		17.18.	Brigade H.Q. established in P.18.c. Message received from Inniskillings timed 16.30 that 2 Squadrons had been diverted N. of HONNECHY to join 7th Cavalry Brigade; the other one would remain in P.35.a. to cover right flank of 6th Cavalry Brigade. Message received from Royals timed 16.10 reporting capture of REUMONT, and that Canadian Cavalry Brigade did not appear to have made progress beyond Squares P.10. and 16.	
		17.30	Brigade now ready to move on to final objective, and Royals were just starting, when fresh orders were received from 3rd Cavalry Division that 7th Cavalry Brigade had been ordered to take final objective. 6th Cavalry Brigade was assembled in P.17.d. ready to support 7th Cavalry Brigade closely.	
		17.50.	A line of posts and M.Gs. was established from HONNECHY to REUMONT, both inclusive. Heavy M.G. fire continued from E. of REUMONT and there was considerable shelling with H.E. and BLUE Cross. A low flying E.A. succeeded in dropping 2 bombs on a Squadron of 10th Hussars, wounding 4 officers and a number of men, and killing a lot of horses.	
P.17.c.7.8.		17.55	Brigade H.Q. established in P.17.c.7.8. and Brigade scattered about in P.17.c. and d.	
		18.15.	XVIII Cyclists arrived at Brigade H.Q. and O.C. reported that he had been ordered to take over the line from 6th Cavalry Brigade. This was started at once.	
		19.05	On relief Royals remained were in support, with 7th Dragoon Guards. 3rd D.Gds. and 10th Hussars were in Reserve. Quiet night.	
	10th	02.50	Orders received for Brigade to be in P.5.c. by 06.00. Brigade moved at 05.00 to P.5.c. and were concentrated there at 06.00. Report Centre at P.5.central.	
P.5.cent.		06.30	Orders received to get in touch with 7th Cavalry Brigade at RAMBOURLIEUX Fme. and be ready to support them in seizing the river crossings between MONTAY and NEUVILLY.	
		08.00	Brigade ordered to move to valley E. of TROISVILLES to begin closer support.	

B.Mourmen Captain,
B.M.6 Cav: Bde:

Army Form C. 2118.

Sheet 7.

WAR DIARY
or
INTELLIGENCE SUMMARY.

(Erase heading not required.)

6th Cavalry Brigade.
October, 1918

Instructions regarding War Diaries and Intelligence Summaries are contained in F.S. Regs., Part II. and the Staff Manual respectively. Title pages will be prepared in manuscript.

Place	Date	Hour	Summary of Events and Information	Remarks and references to Appendices
J.30.c.Cent.	10th.	0850.	Brigade H.Q. established J.30.c. central. Message received that 7th Cavalry Brigade had met with strong opposition and had been ordered to withdraw troops between LE CATEAU and NEUVILLY out of observation.	
		12.45.	Brigade ordered to move back to P.5.c.9.5. to make room for 7th Cavalry Brigade who were obliged to withdraw further owing to heavy shell fire. 'C' Battery came under orders of 'C.R.H.A.'.	
P.5.c.9.5.		13.30.	Brigade H.Q. established P.5.c.9.5.	
		14.15	Brigade ordered to withdraw across country to MONTIGNY and bivouac in O.12.b. and d.	
		14.40	Brigade moved back North of BERTRY.	
		16.30.	Bivouaced in O.12.b. and O.6.d.	
O.6.c.7.3.			Brigade H.Q. O.6.c.7.3.	
			'C' Battery rejoined in the evening, after firing barrage for Infantry attack at 17000 17.00	
		20.35.	Orders received to be saddled up and ready to move at 08.30 on 11th.	
	11th.	08.30	Brigade saddled up ready to move.	
		09.35	Orders received to off-saddle and be on one hours notice.	
		11.55	Orders received to move to ELINCOURT at 13.30.	
		13.30	Brigade marched across country to ELINCOURT. 'C' Battery R.H.A. and transport moved by road.	
ELINCOURT			Good billets and cover for all men and horses. Ede. on 5½ hours notice.	
	12th.	19.00	Orders received to move West at 07.00 on 13th.	
	13th.	07.00	Brigade started from Road junction 1 mile N.N.W. of SERAIN Church, and marched across country to BANTEUX. 'C' Battery R.F.A. and transport moved by road.	
BANTEUX	14th	00.50	Orders received to march to the MANANCOURT area.	
		07.15	Brigade marched across country round GONNELIEU and GOUZEAUCOURT, and then via FINS and EQUANCOURT to billets as follows:-	
			B.H.Q., 6th C.F.A. and 13th M.V.S. HENNOIS WOOD.	
			3rd D.Gds. and 10th Hussars. MANANCOURT.	
			Royals, 'C' Battery and 6th M.G.Sqdn. ETRICOURT. "E" Echelon rejoined the Brigade.	
HENNOIS WOOD.	15th		135 mounted men arrived as reinforcements.	
	17th		42 mounted men arrived as reinforcements.	
	18th		Re-fitting of Brigade complete	
			Ground reconnoitred and arrangements made for Brigade Tactical Exercise on 19th.	

B.C.Mauree Captain,
Brigade Major, 6th Cavalry Brigade.

Sheet 8.

Army Form C. 2118.

WAR DIARY
~~INTELLIGENCE SUMMARY~~

(Erase heading not required.)

Instructions regarding War Diaries and Intelligence Summaries are contained in F. S. Regs., Part II. and the Staff Manual respectively. Title pages will be prepared in manuscript.

6th CAVALRY BRIGADE

October, 1918.

Place	Date	Hour	Summary of Events and Information	Remarks and references to Appendices
HENNOIS WOOD.	20th		Captain E.A. FIELDEN, M.C., 10th Hussars, Brigade Major 6th Cavalry Brigade, rejoined from Staff School, CAMBRIDGE.	
	22nd.		Brigade Tactical Exercise.	
	23rd		6th M.G.Sqn. and 'C' Battery R.H.A. moved to billeting area EQUANCOURT.	
	28th		Brigade Tactical Exercise.	
	30th		Brigadier inspected "A" Squadron 10th Hussars.	
	31st		Brigadier inspected "B" Squadron 3rd Dragoon Guards.	

E A Fielden Captain,
Brigade Major 6th Cavalry Brigade.

6th CAVALRY BRIGADE.

NARRATIVE OF OPERATIONS, October 9th, 1918.

Note. This narrative only gives the situation as known to Brigade H.Q. from the information available at the time decisions were made.

01:50.   G.O.C. and B.M. ordered to attend Conference at Divl H.Q.

04:00.   Brigade ordered to be concentrated in B.12.a. and b.(Sheet 62B)

04:00.   3rd C.D. order No. 70 received at Conference. Brigade ordered to advance in Echelon on right of 7th Cav. Bde. with objective spurs overlooking valley between LE CATEAU and ST BENIN.

07:00.   Bds. concentrated in C.18.b. with H.Q. at C.12.d.1.1.

1 Field Troop joined Brigade.

B.M. 12 (Operation Order) issued to all units.

07:10.   G.c.31 received (continuation of O.O.70 in event of success), and issued verbally to C.O's.

08:20.   G.O.C. and Brigade Major ordered to meet Divisional Commander C.2. cent.

08:35.   Brigade ordered up to C.2.b. at a trot, as our Infantry were reported to be 1½ miles in front of MARETZ, and touch had been lost with 7th Cavalry Brigade, who were advanced guard to Division.

09:00.   Brigadier saw Commanding Officers at C.2.cent, and ordered Royals to act as advanced guard to Brigade, and move at once parallel to and S. of the Main LE CATEAU Road with Objectives as given in B.M.12; 10th Hussars to follow Royals, detailing one Squadron as right flank guard.

Liasson Officer was despatched to keep touch with Canadian Cavalry Brigade, who were advancing on our left.

09:50.   Royals were seen to have crossed the MARETZ-BUSIGNY Road.

10:05.   Patrols reported BUTRY Farm held by enemy, and our Infantry attacking it.

10:30.	Advanced Squadron reported our Infantry held up by Machine Gun fire from Railway P.28.c and P.34.a.
	Squadron sent to high ground in V.3.cent., to turn the position from the South.
	There was, however, too much wire just east of the Railway for a mounted advance to be feasible.
11:00.	10th Hussars were ordered to send a Squadron to work round E. of Railway in V.9.
	This order was subsequently cancelled, on receipt of information that our Infantry in V.4. were going to attack.
11:10.	Main body of Brigade ordered to V.1.b.
12:00.	Royals were now about P.32.c. with advanced Squadron at P.33.b.
	Patrols in touch with Infantry, who were now on high ground at P.28.d. and meeting strong machine Gun opposition from HONNECHY.
13:05.	The Brigade, less Royals and Brigade H.Q was withdrawn behind the MARETZ-BUSIGNY Road, owing to heavy shelling of the ground N.E. of it.
	Brigade Intelligence Officer reported that his O.P. was established at Railway Junction P.34.c.0.8. at 11:40 and our Infantry were along stream in V.4.
12:15.	Brigadier met G.O's.C. 3rd Cavalry Division and Canadian Cavalry Brigade at V.1.b.1.8.
	It was decided that if HONNECHY was taken by our Infantry, or an opportunity occurred for an advance, 6th and Canadian Cavalry Brigades were to seize the high ground P.23.a.-P.16.cent and then push on and seize the high ground Q.13.d.-P.5.d.; 6th Cavalry Brigade to move S. of HONNECHY and Canadian Cavalry Brigade N. of MAUROIS.
13:00	B.M. 19 issued ordering Royals to advance if opportunity occurred.
	During the Conference at 12:15 reports were ~~issue~~ received from Brigade I.O. and Royals Advanced Squadron, to the effect that the enemy was holding the high ground P.34.a. and P.35.b.

strongly, and that situation in BUSIGNY and LA SABLIERE WOOD was not yet cleared up.

13:15. Reports from Royals and Brigade O.P. showed that the ground would only permit of a <u>rapid</u> advance on HONNECHY from two directions, the road from MARETZ or the road from BUSIGNY.

Royals and Brigade O.P. reported that Infantry were going to have 5 minutes bombardment at 13:55, and then attempt to advance on HONNECHY and South of it.

G.C.39 received from 3rd Cavalry Division that armoured cars reported that they had been through HONNECHY and MAUROIS.

In view of other information in possession, this was considered very unlikely, and subsequently proved to be quite untrue.

13:25. G.O.C. decided to send 3rd Dragoon Guards with 2 armoured cars to seize the high ground at P.23.a. from the direction of BUSIGNY.

This attack to take place at 14:00, and Royals were ordered to advance simultaneously on their left.

13:45. Inniskillings were placed at disposal of G.O.C. 6th Cavalry Brigade and were ordered to advance in echelon to right rear of 3rd Dragoon Guards and seize spur in P.35. (B.M.21.)

13:55. Barrage arranged by Infantry did not come down, as they had seen signs of enemy retirement and cancelled it.

14:10. 3rd Dragoon Guards advanced from North of BUSIGNY, under heavy enfilade M.G. fire from ESCAUFORT and B. PROYART.

Royals advanced simultaneously through P.28. P.22 and North of MAUROIS.

This advance was made under considerable shell fire, and very heavy M.G. fire from a large number of E.A.

14:30. Report received that Canadian Cavalry Brigade had captured MAUROIS, and handed it over to Infantry, and were pushing on to N.E. of REUMONT.

14:40. 3rd Dragoon Guards captured HONNECHY, and high ground P.23.c. Brigade H.Q. established P.28.cent. Advanced H.Q.

moving to HONNECHY.

15:25. G.O.C. decided to send 10th Hussars on to spur in Q.13.c and d. and Inniskillings South of River towards St. BENIN.

15:40. B.M. 26 despatched to Inniskillings by Liaison Officer giving orders accordingly.

15:45. Canadian Cavalry Brigade B.X.28 timed 15:05, received saying that enemy held REUMONT.

16:00. "C" Battery ordered to HONNECHY.

HONNECHY and the ground round it was heavily shelled ever since it was captured, and 3rd Dragoon Guards had suffered heavy casualties from this and from Machine Gun fire during their advance.

16:22. The situation, as known at Brigade H.Q. was that enemy held REUMONT and a line running down the St SOUPLET Road.

This was reported to Divisional H.Q. (B.M.280 and tanks were asked for to clear REUMONT.

16:30. Inniskillings reported (16:05) that one Squadron was at P.35.a. and other two coming up.

16:30. G.H.10 received from 3rd Cavalry Division ordering Brigade to push on at once as enemy had been seen retiring through LE CATEAU.

At this time the only troops in hand were one Squadron 10th Hussars holding E. edge of HONNECHY dismounted (which had been put in to save 3rd Dragoon Guards more horse casualties) and half the machine gun squadron who were in with them.

Royals were between MAUROIS and REUMONT, and 3rd Dragoon Guards very scattered owing to patrols and casualties.

16:40. G.O.C. informed Division of this and recommended that the two fresh Regiments of 7th Cavalry Brigade should be sent forward.

16:50. 3rd Dragoon Guards reported REUMONT now clear, and Royals were reported to be assembled S.W. of it.

10th Hussars were also in hand, and G.O.C. therefore decided to push on at once.

17:00. O.Cs. 10th Hussars and Royals given verbal orders, and 3rd

Cavalry Division informed of this decision (B.M.30).

17:05.   B.M.31 despatched to Inniskillings, ordering them to move West of St BENIN to high ground South of LE CATEAU and interrupt Railway about Q.5.b.; if unable to advance past ESCAUFORT, to move through HONNECHY, MAUROIS, and REUMONT and join 7th Cavalry Brigade.

17:18.   Brigade H.Q. established in P.18.c.

Message from Inniskillings, timed 16:30, that two Sqdns had been diverted N. of HONNECHY to join 7th Cavalry Bdge.; the other one would remain in P.35.a. to cover right flank of 6th Cavalry Brigade.

Message from Royals, timed 16:10, received, reporting capture of REUMONT, and that Canadian Cavalry Brigade did not appear to have made progress beyond squares P.10 and 16.

17:30.   The Brigade was now ready to move on final objectives, and Royals were just starting, when G.C.46 was received from 3rd Cavalry Division that 7th Cavalry Brigade had been ordered to take final objective.

Division were therefore informed, both by visual and galloper, that the Brigade was assembled in P.17.d. and ready to support 7th Cavalry Brigade closely.

17:50.   A line of posts and machine guns was established from HONNECHY to REUMONT, both inclusive.

Heavy Machine Gun fire continued from East of REUMONT and there was considerable shelling with H.E. and Blue Cross.

A low flying enemy aeroplane succeeded in dropping two bombs on Squadron of 10th Hussars, wounding 4 Officers and a number of men, and killing a lot of horses.

17:55.   Brigade H.Q. established P.17.c.7.8. and Brigade scattered about in P.17.c. and d.

18:15.   XVIII Corps Cyclists arrived at Brigade H.Q. and O.C. reported that he had been ordered to take over the line from 6th Cavalry Brigade. This was started at once.

19:05.   Following order was issued:-

B.M.35.   9   AAA

"XVIII Corps Cyclists are taking over our line AAA As soon as relieved units will water and off-saddle AAA B Squadron 7th D.G. will be in support to the left Sector, i.e. up to BOIS FME, inclusive AAA Royals will be in support to the remainder of the line i.e. up to HONNECHY AAA 3 D.G. and X.R.H. will be in reserve AAA Brigade H.Q. at P.17.c.7.8.

                              6 Cav. Bde.   19:05

19:15. Brigadier rode to Divisional H.Q. to report on days operations.

23:00. Warning order received to be ready to move at 06:00 hours on 10th.

Quiet night.

                (sgd) D.E.WALLACE, Captain.
                Brigade Major 6th Cavalry Brigade.

11th October 1918.

WAR DIARY
INTELLIGENCE SUMMARY

(Erase heading not required.)

Army Form C. 2118

6th Cavalry Brigade.

November, 1918.

Place	Date	Hour	Summary of Events and Information	Remarks and references to Appendices
HENNOIS Wood.	1st. 2nd.		Brigade billeted about MANANCOURT, ETRICOURT, EQUANCOURT. Brigade H.Q. at HENNOIS Wood. Brigade and Regimental Training.	
	3rd. 4th. 5th.		Orders received for Brigade to be ready to move on 4th inst. and training to be suspended. Brigade to be at same notice to move as on 5th as on 4th inst. Brigade placed at 2½ hours notice and Echelons packed.	
MARQUION 6th. ESQUERCHIN.7th. PERONNE 8th. 9th			Brigade marched to MARQUION and SAINS-lez-MARQUION, via TRESCAULT and HAVRINCOURT. Brigade marched to ESQUERCHIN, via EPINOY - AUBENCHEUL-AU-BAC - BUGNICOURT and DOUAI. Brigade marched to FRETIN, PERONNE, LOUVIL, via DOUAI - RACHE - MOLPAS - TEMPLEUX. "K" Battery R.H.A. attached to 6th Cavalry Brigade (in consequence of 7th Cavalry Brigade being detached from 3rd Cavalry Division under Second Army).	
RUMES & RAMECROIX	10th		Brigade marched to BACHY area, arriving about 10.00 hours. On arrival at BACHY orders received for Brigade to move to RUMES where Brigade halted till 15.00 hours, when march was continued to VAUX-lez-TOURNAI and GAURAIN - RAMECROIX area.	
	11th.		Conference of Brigadiers and Brigade Majors at Divisional H.Q. at ANTOING at 06.00 hours. Brigade concentrated with head at 11th mile stone on TOURNAI - LEUZE Road at 08.15 hours. Brigade moved forward at 08.30 hours as Advanced Guard to 3rd Cavalry Division, with objective ENGHIEN - STEENKERQUE. Royal Dragoons were detailed as Advanced Guard to 6th Cavalry Brigade, with first objective the line ATH - CHIEVRES. 10th Hussars ordered to send 2 officer Patrols to ENGHIEN and STEENKERQUE. Patrol directed on ENGHIEN in contact with enemy about noon North of SILLY. On arrival of Head of main body at LEUZE about 10.00 hours verbal orders received from Cavalry Corps that hostilities would cease at 11.00 hours and that all troops were to stand fast in positions reached at that hour. Orders to this effect issued to Advanced Guard and sent to patrols of 10th Hussars. An impromptu ceremony was arranged and carried out at 11.00 hours in the Square at LEUZE to celebrate the Armistice and cessation of hostilities. The ceremony was attended by representatives of units of the Brigade, an Infantry Battalion, and the Civilian population. Message received at 14.00 hours from Cavalry Corps (dropped by aeroplane) in accordance with which the Brigade moved and occupied billets as for night 10th/11th.	

Ta Fielden
Captain.

Army Form C. 2118

WAR DIARY
INTELLIGENCE SUMMARY
(Erase heading not required.)

6th Cavalry Brigade.
November, 1918.

Instructions regarding War Diaries and Intelligence Summaries are contained in F.S. Regs., Part II. and the Staff Manual respectively. Title Pages will be prepared in manuscript.

Place	Date	Hour	Summary of Events and Information	Remarks and references to Appendices
PONTENCHE	12th.		Brigade moved to area BERTINCROIX – PONTENCHE – WILLAUPUIS – BAUGNIES – WASMES. Brigade H.Q. on main road opposite PONTENCHE Chateau. Conference at Divisional Headquarters at 17.00 Hours.	
	13th 16th 16th.		Brigade remained in above area.	
37 mile stone on ATH-ENGHIEN Road.	17th.		1 Troop 3rd Dragoon Guards joined Headquarters 3rd Cavalry Division as Escort to the Divisional Commander. "K" Battery R.H.A. rejoined 7th Cavalry Brigade. 6th Cavalry Brigade commenced advance Eastwards in accordance with terms of Armistice. Brigade moved to line DENDEWINDEKE – HORRUES Road and established line of Outposts. Billeting area GRATTY MARCQ CULOT DU BOIS THORICOURT FOULENS. 1 Troop 3rd Field Squadron R.E. attached to 6th Cavalry Brigade. 1 Squadron 10th Hussars joined H.Q. Cavalry Corps as Escort to Corps Commander.	
SAINTES	18th		Brigade advanced to line R. SENNETTE, establishing Line of Outposts. Billets HENNUYERES STEHOUX TURBISE GENETTE QUENAST SAINTES.	
	19th		Captain D.E.WALLACE, M.C. to England on leave. Captain C.WYNN-JONES 17th Lancers joined as Acting Staff Captain.	
	20th.		1 Troop Royals ordered to HAL at request of Burgomeister to keep order in consequence of a disturbance amongst the inhabitants.	
OTTIGNIES.	21st.		Brigade advanced to line GEMBLOUS – WAVRE Road, establishing line of Outposts and taking over dumps of material left by Germans. Billeting area OTTIGNIES – MONT ST. GUIBERT COURT ST. ETIENNE LIMAL CEROUX MOUSTY.	
EGHEZEE	22nd.		Brigade advanced to line East of HEMPTINNE, establishing line of outposts. Billeting area EGHEZEE HANRET AISCHE-en-REFAIL NOVILLE-sur-MEHAIGNE – GRAND ROSIERE LONGCHAMPS.	
UPIGNY	24th.		Brigade moved to area UPIGNY LIERNU ST. GERMAIN DHUY WARISOULX VEDRIN. 1 Squadron Royals marched to NAMUR to take over Guards there. 1st Cavalry Division moved East to GERMANY with Second Army. 3rd Cavalry Division remaining in present area.	
	25-30th.		Brigade remained in above area.	

Th Fielden
Captain,
Brigade Major 6th Cavalry Brigade.

Army Form C. 2118.

WAR DIARY
~~INTELLIGENCE SUMMARY~~

(Erase heading not required.)

6th CAVALRY BRIGADE.

December 1918.

Instructions regarding War Diaries and Intelligence Summaries are contained in F.S. Regs., Part II. and the Staff Manual respectively. Title pages will be prepared in manuscript.

Place	Date	Hour	Summary of Events and Information	Remarks, and references to Appendices
UPIGNY.	1st) 10th)		Brigade in billets North of NAMUR, about VEDRIN, WARISOULX, ST.GERMAINE, DHUY, LEUZE, with Bde.H.Q. at UPIGNY. Brigade finding guards over German ceded material at NAMUR, EGHEZEE and DAUSSOULX.	
VINALMONT.	9th. 10th		Divisional Education Conference at PERWEZ. Brigade marched to area MOHA - ANTHIET - HUCCOIGNE - VINALMONT. Captain C.J.WYNNE-JONES proceeded on leave and Lieut. J.B.BICKERSTETH, M.C., assumed duties of Acting Staff Captain.	
CHATEAU DE WARFUSEE.	12th.		Brigade marched to permanent winter area, ST.GEORGES - SERAING LE CHATEAU - JEHAY BODEGNEE - AMAY - ENGIS - AWIRS - Bde.H.Q. at Chateau de WARFUSEE near STOCKAY.	
	16th.		Brigadier-General, E. PATERSON, D.S.O., proceeded to 3rd Cavalry Division H.Q. to command 3rd Cavalry Division temporarily during absence on leave of Maj.Gen. A.E.W.HARMAN, D.S.O.. Lieut.Colonel F.H.D.C.WHITMORE, C.M.G., D.S.O., took over temporary command of 6th Cav. Bde.	
	20th.		Education Conference at Bde. H.Q.	
	28th.		Brigadier-General E. PATERSON, D.S.O., rejoined to command 6th Cavalry Brigade.	

Ed Fiennes
Captain,
Brigade Major 6th Cavalry Brigade.

Army Form C. 2118.

WAR DIARY
or
INTELLIGENCE SUMMARY

(Erase heading not required.)

6TH CAVALRY BRIGADE.

JANUARY 1919.   SHEET. 1.

Ref: Map.1/100,000 LIEGE.

Place	Date	Hour	Summary of Events and Information	Remarks and references to Appendices
STOCKAY.	1st 31st.		Brigade remained in billets as during latter part of December 1918.	
	3rd.		Brigadier-General E.PATERSON, D.S.O. proceeded with Lieut.H.C.SOUNDY, MC. on month's leave to United Kingdom. Command of Brigade assumed by Lieut.Col.C.L.ROME, D.S.O., 3rd D.Guards.	
	13th.		Committee assembled at Divisional H.Q. to consider scale of equipment necessary for Cavalry. Lieut-Col. C.L.ROME, DS.O. represented 6th Cavalry Brigade.	
	19th.		Captain C.J.WYNNE-JONES, 17th Lancers, joined for duty from leave to United Kingdom. Lieut.Col.F.W.WORMALD, DS.O. assumed command of 6th Cavalry Brigade vice Brig.Gen.E.PATERSON, D.S.O. on leave.	
	21st.		Classification of horses commenced by Remount Board, and completed on 25th.	
			Lieut. A.F.W.GOSSAGE, M.C., 17th Lancers, arrived to act temporarily as Staff Captain vice Captain D.E.WALLACE, MC. 2nd Life Guards.	
	24th.		Lieut.Col. F.H.D.C.WHITMORE, C.M.G., D.S.O., 10th Hussars, assumed command of Brigade, vice Brig.Gen. E.PATERSON, D.S.O., on leave.	
	25th.		Captain E.A.FIELDEN, MC., 10th R.Hussars, Brigade Major, 6th Cavalry Brigade, proceeded on leave to United Kingdom. Captain C.J. WYNNE-JONES, 17th Lancers, acting as Brigade Major.	
			GENERAL: During the month, demobilization proceeded at the average rate of 2 Officers and 40 Other Ranks per diem. German material both ceded and abandoned in the area, was evacuated by all units to Railhead, the Brigade area now being reported clear of same.	

for Brigade Major 6th Cavalry Brigade.

Army Form C. 2118

WAR DIARY
or
INTELLIGENCE SUMMARY.
(Erase heading not required.)

Place	Date	Hour	Summary of Events and Information	Remarks and references to Appendices
STOCKAY.	February.			
	14th.		Throughout February the Brigade remained in the same Billeting Area as January. 'C' Squadron 10th. Hussars remained at SPA as escort to Corps Commander. Brig.-Gen. E. Peterson, D.S.O. with Lt, H.C.Soundy M.C. returned from leave, and Lt-Col. F.H.D.C. Whitmore again resumed command of the 10th. Hussars.	
	15th.		Sale of 'Z' horses began.	
	17th.		First Sale of 'Z' Horses of 6th. Cav. Bde. at LIEGE took place.	
	18th.		Capt, E.A.Fielden, M.C. returned from Leave and Lt, A.F.W.Gossage (17th. Lancers) rejoined his regiment.	
	24th.		Capt, C.J.Wynne-Jones (17th. Lancers) rejoined his Regiment and Lt, J.B.Bickersteth, M.C. again became A/Staff. Captain.	
	27th.		Sale of 6th. Cav. Bde 'Z' Horses at Huy took place.	
			During this period the horses of the 6th.-Cav. Bde. which had been classified during January as "C" "Z" and "Y" were disposed of. "C" and "Y" being sent to England, "Z" being sold at LIEGE and HUY. Only "X" Horses i.e. those for the Army of Occupation and SS and R.P. Horses (i.e. Officers Chargers) remained. Demobilization of releasable Officers and Men continued during the earlier part of the month but after February 21st. only Pivotal Officers and Men were allowed to go, as the minimium number of men necessary to look after the horses still remaining with Units have been reached. During the latter part of the month the 3rd. Dragoon Guards were engaged in reducing their strength to Cadre "A" preparatory to returning to England early in March.	
	11/3/19			

M. Ackworth
Captain.
A/Staff Captain 6th. Cavalry Brigade.

www.ingramcontent.com/pod-product-compliance
Lightning Source LLC
Chambersburg PA
CBHW080806010526
44113CB00013B/2336